DAILY LIFE IN

Elizabethan England

DAILY LIFE IN
Elizabethan England

JEFFREY L. SINGMAN

The Greenwood Press "Daily Life Through History" Series

GREENWOOD PRESS
Westport, Connecticut • London

Library of Congress Cataloging-in-Publication Data

Singman, Jeffrey L.
   Daily life in Elizabethan England / Jeffrey L. Singman.
      p.   cm.—(Greenwood Press "Daily life through history"
   series, ISSN 1080–4749)
   Discography: p.
   Videography: p.
   Includes bibliographical references (p.   ) and index.
   ISBN 0–313–29335–X (alk. paper)
   1. England—Social life and customs—16th century.   2. Great
Britain—History—Elizabeth, 1558-1603.   I. Title.   II. Series.
DA320.S56   1995
942.05′5—dc20   95-3807

British Library Cataloguing in Publication Data is available.

Library of Congress Catalog Card Number: 95–3807
ISBN: 0–313–29335–X
ISSN: 1080–4749

First published in 1995

Greenwood Press, 88 Post Road West, Westport, CT 06881
An imprint of Greenwood Publishing Group, Inc.

Printed in the United States of America

The paper used in this book complies with the
Permanent Paper Standard issued by the National
Information Standards Organization (Z39.48–1984).

10 9 8 7 6 5 4 3

Contents

Acknowledgments

The author wishes to thank the Centre for Renaissance and Reformation Studies at the University of Toronto for permission to reproduce various illustrations in this volume, and for their help in obtaining them.

Special credit is due to David Hoornstra for several of the illustrations in this book.

Special credit is also due to Victoria Hadfield for her work on the illustrations in this volume, some of which are her own.

Thanks also to David Kuijt for providing the rules for Primero.

Daily Life in Elizabethan England is in part a revision of *The Elizabethan Handbook*, a manual for Elizabethan living history produced by the University Medieval and Renaissance Association (now the Tabard Inn Society) at the University of Toronto for its "Fencing, Dancing, and Bearbaiting" event in June 1991, and subsequently revised and expanded for private publication by the present author. Although relatively little of the original text survives, some credit is due to the people who originally produced it, or who had a hand in later revisions, including Susan Carroll-Clark, Maren Drees, Victoria Hadfield, Lesley Howard, Shona Humphrey, A. J. S. Nusbacher, Tricia Postle, and Tara Jenkins.

Illustrations from Herbert Norris, *Costume and Fashion*, appear by permission of Viking Books.

Introduction

The reign of Elizabeth is for many of us one of the most appealing periods in the history of English-speaking peoples. Our images of the Elizabethan age, whether derived from the stage, screen, or books, have an enduring romantic appeal: the daring impudence of the sea-dogs, the dashing valor of Sir Philip Sidney at Zutphen or the Earl of Essex at the gates of Cadiz, the elegant clash of steel as the masters of the rapier display their skill. In addition to its imaginative appeal, the period is one of considerable historical importance. In political terms, Elizabeth's reign saw the definitive emergence of England as a significant naval power, as well as the growth of England's commercial and colonial activities: the British Empire, which so shaped the world in which we live, had its roots in the reign of Elizabeth. In the cultural sphere, England's achievements were no less significant, most notably in the person of William Shakespeare.

Elizabethan daily life has received a good deal of attention during the past two hundred years. Yet although many books have been written on the subject, this volume is very different in one fundamental respect, which has influenced its shape in many ways.

This is the first book on Elizabethan England to arise out of the living history movement. In its broadest sense, living history might be described as the material re-creation of elements of the past. In this sense it includes a wide variety of activities. People who play historical music (especially on reproduction instruments) or who engage in historical crafts are practicing a form of living history.

In its fullest sense, living history involves the attempt to re-create an entire historical setting. Perhaps the best example is the historical site of

Plimoth Plantation in Massachusetts, where the visitor will find not only reconstructed houses of the pilgrim settlers of 1627, but a staff of highly trained interpreters who represent the individual men and women who were at the settlement in that year, even down to the dialect of English likely to have been spoken by the persons they are portraying.

This book began its life as *The Elizabethan Handbook*, a brief guide written by the University Medieval and Renaissance Association of Toronto (an amateur living history group based at the Unversity of Toronto), to accompany its "Fencing, Dancing, and Bearbaiting" Elizabethan living history event in 1991. It was later published in expanded and revised form by Vox Clamantis Monographs in 1993, as part of a series of manuals geared for living history use. Very little of the original text still remains, but the underlying connection with living history is very much present.

The living history background of this book gives it two particular advantages over previous works. The first is its hands-on approach. In addition to telling the reader what sort of foods people ate, what sort of clothes they wore, and what sort of games they played, this book includes actual recipes, patterns, and rules, based on sources from the period. We ourselves have had great fun reproducing such aspects of the past, and hope that readers will enjoy them too.

The second important advantage is the perspective that living history affords. The people who contributed to this book have not simply read about the Elizabethan period. We have also spent time living in thatched cottages, cooking over open hearths, and sleeping on straw mattresses. The simple act of doing these things cannot actually tell you how they were done, but there is no better way to focus your attention on the essential parts of historical daily life than by actually trying to live it. As a result, this book offers a uniquely clear, focused and detailed account of the Elizabethan world. Many fundamental topics that other books mention only briefly (if at all) are given full attention here.

This book is also distinguished by its attention to the daily life of ordinary people. Books about Elizabethan England often tend to focus on the world of the aristocracy, leaving the impression that every man in Elizabethan England wore an enormous starched ruff, every woman wore a rich brocade gown, and they all lived in huge brick mansions. Yet the lives of ordinary people can be just as interesting and informative. This book tries to give the other 98% of the population a degree of attention more in keeping with their numbers.

Another important feature of this book is that it attempts to incorporate a high quality of scholarly research in a form that is accessible to a broad readership. There tends to be a great divide between "scholarly" and "popular" accounts of the past. Scholarly accounts generally offer high-quality information based on primary sources (primary sources being sources of information contemporary with the period in question, as opposed to secondary sources, which are modern works that make use of primary sources, or tertiary sources, which are modern works that rely on secondary sources). The information in scholarly works is generally superior, since the authors are in closer contact with the original sources of information, but their language and content tend to be geared towards the specialist. On the other hand, popular works are written for a broader audience, but often rely on inferior secondary and even tertiary sources of information.

As far as has been possible with so vast a subject, this book relies directly on primary sources; in particular, it has made use of some original books and manuscripts that are especially rich sources of information but are not well known even in scholarly circles (the rules for games, for example, derive from a forgotten seventeenth-century treatise on the subject). This is particularly true in the hands-on sections of the book: the patterns, recipes, rules, and so on are all based as far as possible on primary sources. Where primary sources are impractical, the book strives to make use of the best and most recent secondary work on the period.

At the same time, we have attempted to present this information in a format that will be accessible and enjoyable for a wide audience. After all, the greatest value of the past lies in its interaction with the present. If history only touches the historians, it is truly a lifeless form of knowledge. Readers of this book may be surprised to find just how much of Elizabethan life is relevant to the present. The Elizabethans were dealing with many of the same issues that face us today: unemployment resulting from an economy in transition, conflicting views over the relationship between religion and the state, a technological revolution in the media of communication, bitter cultural strife, and a general sense that the established social order was at risk of disintegration. In the modern age, where we are increasingly worried about our ability to sustain our standard of living and about the impact of our activities on the environment, we can benefit by learning how people lived in a period when their material expectations were much lower and the degree of industrialization was still quite limited. This is not to suggest that we should idealize the Elizabethan age—it was also a period of hardship and intolerance; but we can acquire a much clearer perspective on the present by comparing it to the past.

DAILY LIFE IN

Elizabethan England

1

A Brief History of Tudor England

The Middle Ages are customarily taken to have ended when Richard III was defeated by Henry Tudor in the Battle of Bosworth in 1485. Henry's accession as Henry VII marked the end of the Wars of the Roses, which had dominated English politics for much of the fifteenth century, and was to herald the beginning of an unprecedented period of peace that lasted until the outbreak of civil war in 1642.

Henry VII devoted his reign to establishing the security of his throne, which he passed on to his son Henry VIII in 1509. Henry VIII is best known for having married six wives, but his marital affairs were of great political importance as well. His first wife, Catherine of Aragon, produced only a daughter, named Mary. Desperate for a male heir, Henry applied to the Pope to have his marriage annulled. For various reasons the request was refused, so Henry had his Parliament pass a body of legislation that withdrew England from the Catholic Church, placing the king at the head of the new Church of England.

As head of his own church, Henry now divorced Catherine and married Anne Boleyn. This marriage proved no more successful in Henry's eyes, as it produced only a daughter (little did he know that this daughter, as Elizabeth I, was to become one of England's most successful and best-loved monarchs). Henry had Anne Boleyn executed on charges of adultery. His third wife, Jane Seymour, died of natural causes, but not before bearing him a son, Edward. Of Henry's three subsequent wives, none bore any heirs.

Upon Henry's death in 1547 his son came to the throne as Edward VI. Edward was still underage and his reign was dominated by his guardians, who furthered the Protestant reformation of the English church that had begun with Henry's break with Rome. Edward died in 1553 before reaching the age of majority. The throne passed to his eldest half-sister, Mary. Being a devout Catholic, she brought England back into the Catholic Church. However, she died in 1558 after a brief and undistinguished reign. She had allied England with Spain by marrying the Spanish king, Philip II, who involved England in his war against France. The war went poorly and England lost Calais, the last remnant of its once huge French empire. Mary is most often remembered as Bloody Mary, in memory of her persecution of Protestants.

The throne now passed to Henry's second daughter, Elizabeth. According to the Catholic Church, Henry's divorce from Catherine of Aragon had been invalid, which meant that his marriage to Anne Boleyn was invalid too. Elizabeth's very legitimacy as Henry's daughter and heir relied on England's independence from the Catholic Church. Elizabeth had Parliament withdraw England from the Catholic Church once more and was established as head of the Church of England, as her father had been.

The new queen faced serious international challenges. Her country was still officially at war with France and Scotland. Elizabeth swiftly concluded a peace treaty, but Scotland remained under the authority of a French regent, Mary of Guise. Mary was mother of the actual queen, Mary Stuart (known today as Mary Queen of Scots), who was in France. However, Elizabeth was aided by the rise of Protestant feeling in Scotland. France was a Catholic country, and the Protestants in Scotland were inclined to draw Scotland out from under French domination and closer to England. In 1559 John Knox, the spiritual leader of this militant Scottish Protestantism, returned to Scotland from exile in Geneva, and the country rose against the regent. After some hesitation, Elizabeth sent military support. The French were expelled from the country, and the Protestant party took effective control.

France too had a growing Protestant movement, and a civil war between Protestants and Catholics erupted in 1562. Elizabeth sent troops to Normandy, with an eye to re-establishing the foothold on the Continent that her sister had lost, but the army was ravaged by illness and had to be withdrawn in 1563. Religious conflict between French Catholics and Protestants was to recur throughout most of the rest of Elizabeth's reign, substantially undermining French power in international affairs.

In the meantime, Scotland was under new stresses of its own. Mary Queen of Scots, who had been married to Francis II, King of France, returned to Scotland after his death in 1560. Her reign was tumultuous, and relations with her subjects were not helped by her firm Catholicism. After a series of misadventures, Mary's subjects rose against her, and she was ultimately forced to seek refuge in England in 1568.

The situation was extremely awkward for Elizabeth, who believed in the divine right of a ruler to occupy her throne but who was also dependent on the Protestant party in Scotland to keep England's northern border secure. To make matters worse, Mary had some claim to the English throne by right of her grandmother, a sister of Henry VIII. According to the Catholic Church, Elizabeth was illegitimate and Mary was the rightful queen. Mary remained in comfortable confinement in England during a series of fruitless negotiations to return her to the Scottish throne.

Unfortunately, Mary was not content to confine herself to Scottish politics. Many Catholics wanted to see her replace Elizabeth as Queen of England, and Mary was only too willing to entertain the idea. There were still quite a number of Catholics in northern England. In 1569 several of the northern earls led a rebellion against Elizabeth, thinking to place Mary on the throne. The rebels were swiftly suppressed, but the incident was a reminder of the threat posed by this Catholic claimant to the throne. The following year the Pope issued a Bull, or papal decree, excommunicating Elizabeth and declaring her deposed, a move that further aggravated religious tensions.

Mary became even more involved in English politics. In 1572 a plot was organized by Roberto Ridolfi, a Florentine banker, to have Mary wed the Duke of Norfolk, the foremost nobleman in England, with an eye to creating a powerful Catholic alliance to topple the Queen. The plot was discovered and Norfolk, already under suspicion for his involvement with the northern rebellion, was executed for treason. Many people urged Elizabeth to have Mary executed as well, but she was extremely reluctant to kill a queen, knowing the implications to herself.

In the meantime, relations with Spain were becoming progressively worse. At first Elizabeth had worked to preserve something of the alliance between England and Spain created by her sister's marriage to Philip II, but growing religious divisions in Europe made this increasingly difficult. In the Low Countries, an increasingly Protestant population was still under the rule of the Catholic Philip II. Rebellion erupted in 1567. At first Protestantism was widely spread throughout the area, but over time a successful Spanish counteroffensive succeeded in regaining the southern provinces (equivalent to modern-day Belgium), leaving only the Netherlands proper in a state of rebellion. Popular sentiment in England was strongly in support of the Protestant rebels, and many Englishmen volunteered to fight in the Netherlands against Spain over the years. Even the more conservative Elizabeth was not happy about the presence of a large Catholic force suppressing Protestantism practically on England's doorstep.

Spain's very size and power made it a threat, and the situation was made worse by Spain's vast and profitable empire in the New World.

Elizabeth was reluctant to undertake the risks and expense of war, so she turned to more subtle means of undermining Spanish power. In particular, she gave her support to the "sea-dogs," privateers who preyed on Spanish shipping. Perhaps the greatest was Francis Drake, who circled the globe in 1577-80, wreaking havoc on Spanish shipping and colonies and bringing back a phenomenal 4700% profit to those who had invested in the voyage. The Queen herself was the largest shareholder.

By 1584 the international situation was becoming extremely threatening. A Catholic fanatic had assassinated William of Orange, the leader of the Dutch Protestants, reminding Elizabeth how real and personal the dangers were. The Catholic faction that dominated France was negotiating an alliance with Spain, and Antwerp was on the verge of falling to a Spanish siege. Elizabeth concluded a treaty with the Dutch Protestants and sent an English army to aid them in their cause.

Under the circumstances, Mary Stuart was a grave liability. She continued to be at the center of plots against Elizabeth. In 1583 a Catholic agent named Francis Throckmorton was arrested and found to be carrying a list of leading Catholics and potential landing places for an invading army. Under torture, he revealed plans for a major Spanish invasion of England.

The Queen's advisors urged the death of Mary, but still Elizabeth refused. In 1586 a plot was uncovered in which another young Catholic gentleman named Anthony Babington had engaged with several accomplices to assassinate the Queen. Mary had given her explicit assent to the scheme. After a trial and lengthy delaying by Elizabeth, an order was sent in 1587 for Mary's execution; but afterwards Elizabeth denied that this had been her intent and made a show of punishing those involved.

All this while, Spain had been making preparations to remove Elizabeth by force. A massive fleet was assembled in various Spanish ports. The fleet was to sail to Flanders, rendezvous with the Spanish army stationed there, and make the short crossing to England. In the summer of 1588 the Invincible Armada set sail.

The expedition was a disastrous failure. The English ships, smaller, more agile, better crewed, and more heavily armed with cannon, harassed the Spanish fleet as it sailed up the English Channel. In the face of bad weather, the Spanish anchored at Calais; during the night the English set several of their own ships on fire and sent them in among the Spanish ships, forcing the Armada to disperse. The next day there was heavy fighting off the Flemish coast, as winds from the west forced the Spanish ships eastward, and several of them were lost to the coastal shoals. It proved impossible to rendezvous with the army, and the Armada was forced to sail all the way around the British Isles, battered by storms and decimated by malnutrition and disease, until about half the original fleet finally made it back to Spain in mid-September.

The Spanish made several more attempts to invade, but none proved successful. Though the war dragged on, England itself was at relative peace. Elizabeth's greatest problem was Ireland, where centuries of resistance to English domination were coming to a head. In 1579-83 there had been a protracted rebellion by one of the leading Irish lords in the southern part of the country. In 1580 the Spanish had sent a small and unsuccessful expedition to Kerry. In 1596 Hugh O'Neill, the Earl of Tyrone and perhaps the most powerful man in northern Ireland, began a major revolt against England, assisted by Spanish supplies. In 1599 Elizabeth sent Robert Devereux, the Earl of Essex, to suppress the revolt, but he proved thoroughly incompetent as a military commander. He was recalled, and promptly became embroiled in a plot to take over the government. The scheme failed miserably: Essex was imprisoned and, ultimately, executed.

Two years later, in 1603, Elizabeth herself died. Willful to the end, she refused to take to her bed: she passed away upright in her chair. She had never married, and she left no immediate heirs. The crown passed to James VI of Scotland, son of Mary Stuart. He came to the English throne as James I of England, ending the age of the Tudors and beginning that of the Stuarts.

A fight at sea. [Holinshed]

A CHRONOLOGY OF TUDOR ENGLAND

1485	Accession of Henry Tudor as Henry VII
1509	Accession of Henry VIII Birth of Mary Tudor (first child of Henry VIII, by Catherine of Aragon)
1530-39	Henry VIII breaks with the Catholic Church and dissolves the monasteries
1533	Birth of Elizabeth (second child of Henry VIII, by Anne Boleyn) Birth of Edward VI (third child of Henry VIII, by Jane Seymour)
1547	Accession of Edward VI
1553	Accession of Mary
1558	Accession of Elizabeth.
1559	Elizabeth withdraws England from the Catholic Church
1561	Return of Mary Stuart (Mary Queen of Scots) from France to Scotland
1562	First religious war between Catholics and Protestants in France
1563	Plague
1564	Birth of William Shakespeare
1567	Second religious war in France Rebellion against Spain in Flanders is ruthlessly suppressed by the Duke of Alva
1568	Mary Stuart flees to England
1569	Northern rebellion Third religious war in France
1570	Pope Pius V excommunicates Elizabeth
1572	Ridolfi plot against Elizabeth St. Bartholomew's Day massacre of Protestants in France
1577	Sir Francis Drake sets out on a voyage around the globe
1580	Jesuits first come to England
1583	Sir Humphrey Gilbert attempts to found an English colony in Newfoundland Throckmorton conspiracy to overthrow Elizabeth

1584	Shakespeare's first plays
	Sir Walter Raleigh attempts to found an English colony in Virginia
1585	Sack of Antwerp by Spanish troops
	English troops are sent to fight Spain in the Netherlands
1586	Babington conspiracy to overthrow Elizabeth.
	Poor harvests
1587	Execution of Mary Stuart
	Poor harvests
1588	Invincible Armada
	Poor harvests
1594-95	Poor harvests
1596	Poor harvests
	English expedition against Spanish port of Cadiz
	Irish rebellion under Hugh O'Neill
1597-98	Poor harvests
1599	Globe Theater opens
	Earl of Essex's expedition to Ireland
1600	Rebellion and execution of the Earl of Essex
1603	Plague
	Death of Elizabeth

2

The Elizabethan World

SOCIETY

The population of England was probably over 3 million when Elizabeth came to the throne in 1558, and it grew to **The Population** over 4 million by the time of her death in 1603. These figures represent roughly a tenth of the population of England today. This rapid growth meant that a large part of the population at any time were young people: it has been estimated that roughly a third were under the age of 15, a half under age 25. Population density was highest in the south and east, with the mountainous areas of the north and west more sparsely settled. The overwhelming majority lived in rural areas, although London was growing rapidly.

Not all of this population were ethnically or culturally English. Wales and western Cornwall were subject to the English crown, and were often counted as a part of England, yet they still spoke Welsh and Cornish—languages similar to each other but quite unintelligible to an Englishman. Ireland was also officially under English rule, although effective English control was limited to the eastern part of the country. The population of Ireland included Englishmen and English-speaking Irishmen in the east, with the remainder of the country inhabited by Gaelic-speaking Irishmen. Scotland was still an independent kingdom, although England and Scotland came to be under a single ruler when the Scottish king, James VI, inherited the English throne in 1603. Southern Scotland spoke its own dialect of English, whereas the northern and western parts of the country still spoke Scottish Gaelic, a close relative of Irish Gaelic.

Within England itself there was a significant population of foreign immigrants, typically Protestants who had fled the Continent because of wars or religious persecution. These immigrants came primarily from the Low Countries, Germany, and France, with a few from Spain and Italy. The proportion of foreigners was highest in London—perhaps close to 10% of the population. It was much lower in other areas, and there were few in the countryside. Finally, by this period the Romany, or gypsies, had come across the Channel to England. The gypsies were a culture largely to themselves; they had a language of their own and led wandering lives on the fringes of society. They did not generally assimilate to mainstream English society, although they had a significant impact on the culture of vagrancy and the underworld.[1]

The Social Hierarchy
Elizabethan society was in many ways still dominated by the feudal and manorial system inherited from the Middle Ages. During the Middle Ages, society and the economy had focused on people's relationship to land, a relationship of "holding" rather than owning. A landholder inherited the right to occupy and use a certain allotment of land—the landholding—under certain terms. Theoretically, all land actually belonged to the monarch, and was passed downwards in a hierarchical chain, each landholder providing service or payment to a landlord in exchange for the landholding. Landholdings were not owned outright, for they could not be freely bought or sold, and it was very difficult in the Middle Ages to acquire land by any means other than inheritance of a holding.

The upper ranks of society were supposed to pay for their land with military service. When their lord called upon them, they were expected to come to him fully equipped as mounted knights with a following of soldiers. This was the gentlemanly form of service, and those who owed military service were considered to be of gentle birth, as was everyone in their families. Gentle status went hand in hand with political influence, social privilege, and cultural prestige. A gentleman's landholding would be large—a hundred acres or so was the lower end of the scale.

Part of a gentleman's landholding was demesne land, that is, land that he himself administered, hiring workers to cultivate it. The rest was rented out as landholdings to tenants (a word that means "holders"). This rental was likewise determined by inheritance: a landlord's tenants inherited the right to their landholdings, and paid for them according to the custom associated with the holding, typically a combination of labor service and rents in kind. The labor service was usually an obligation to spend a certain amount of time doing work for the landlord. The rents in kind were produce from the land—especially grain and livestock. Tenants who paid in labor or material rents were considered commoners. In fact, the label "commoner" applied to everyone who did not belong to the gentle class (except the clergy, who in the Middle Ages were considered a class by themselves).

Royal officials in Ireland. [Scott]

This was the principle; it was of course much more complex in practice, and there had been some important changes since the height of medieval feudalism. By the end of the Middle Ages, labor rents and rents in kind had largely been replaced by money rents: people simply paid a certain amount of cash annually for their holding. When Henry VIII abolished the monasteries during the 1530s, a great deal of monastic land came onto the market; unlike traditional medieval holdings, this land could be freely bought or sold. Another major change was in the nature of gentlemen's landholdings. By the Elizabethan period, the armored knight and his followers were no longer very useful on the battlefield. Armies were now relying on professional soldiers instead, so the gentleman's responsibility for military service had become somewhat nominal.

However, the privileges of gentle birth persisted. The gentlemen of Elizabethan England still dominated government and society, and they were the effective owners of most of the land in the country. Whereas the medieval aristocrat had been defined by his military activities, the Elizabethans laid more emphasis on the other aspects of gentle birth. The classic Elizabethan definition of the gentleman is the formulation offered by Sir Thomas Smith in his treatise on English society, *De Republica Anglorum*:

> Who can live idly and without manual labor and will bear the port, charge, and countenance of a gentleman, he shall be called "master," for that is the title which men give to esquires and other gentlemen, and shall be taken for a gentleman.

As Smith suggests, the principal characteristic of the gentleman was that he could live handsomely without labor, which generally meant having enough land to live off the rents. Many people of gentlemanly birth held little or no land, but there were alternatives. Government service was considered an acceptable occupation for a gentleman, who might also supplement his income through commercial speculation. Military service, although no longer required, was still a gentlemanly occupation: the officers of Elizabeth's army and navy were invariably gentlemen. In addition, anyone with a university education or working in a profession (i.e., as a physician, lawyer, priest, etc.) was considered a gentleman.

The gentlemanly class was subdivided into its own hierarchy. At the top was the titled nobility, comprising around fifty noblemen and their families. Titles of nobility were inherited: the eldest son would receive the title of his father, and his siblings would be lords or gentlemen, ladies or gentlewomen, depending upon their father's actual rank. The Elizabethan titles of nobility were, in descending order, Duke, Marquis, Earl, Viscount, and Baron; the female equivalents were Duchess, Marchioness, Countess, Viscountess, and Baroness. Below these was the title of Knight, which was never inherited; it had to be received from the monarch or a designated military leader. Knighthood in the Middle Ages was supposed to be a military status, but by the Elizabethan period it had become a general mark of honor. There were probably about 300 to 500 knights in England at any given time.

At the bottom of the gentlemanly hierarchy were esquires (also called squires) and simple gentlemen. The distinction between the two was not always clear. In theory, an esquire was a gentleman who had knights in his ancestry, but he might also be a gentleman of especially prominent standing. Esquires and gentlemen together may have numbered some 16,000 at the end of Elizabeth's reign. Seventeenth-century estimates suggest that lords, knights, and esquires accounted for well under 1% of the population, and simple gentlemen for about 1%.

Special mention should be made of the clergy, who had once been considered a class of their own but were now more likely to be identified with the gentlemanly class. They were far fewer in number than they had been during the Middle Ages, especially since there were no longer any monks, friars, or nuns. However, they still enjoyed considerable prestige, and the church remained one of the best avenues by which a commoner might advance in society. Furthermore, the Catholic ban on clerical marriage had been lifted as part of the Protestant reformation, so it was now possible to be a clergyman and have a family as well. Among the clergy, archbishops and bishops were classed with the titled nobility and sat in the House of Lords. Below these were some 8,000 parish clergymen, as well as a smaller number of other church officials—notably deacons and archdeacons, who were responsible for church administration.[2]

Below the gentlemen in the manorial hierarchy were the landholding commoners. The most privileged, called **Rural** freeholders, held their lands in perpetuity: their holdings **Commoners** were passed on from generation to generation with no change in terms. The rent charged for freehold lands had generally been fixed in the Middle Ages, and inflation had rendered the real cost of these holdings minimal. A freeholder was therefore in a very strong financial position, and was almost the effective owner of his landholding. Freeholders may have numbered around 100,000 in all.

Less fortunate than the freeholders were the leaseholders. Their tenancies were for fixed periods, sometimes as much as a lifetime, sometimes as little as a year. When the tenancy ended, it was usually renewed, but the landlord was able to change the terms of the lease: he might charge a higher rent from the tenant or his heir, or even terminate the lease altogether. At the very bottom among landholders were the copyholders, also called customary tenants or tenants at will. Their holdings were simply by custom, and the rent could be altered or the tenancy terminated at any time.

This does not mean that all such tenants were in constant danger of homelessness or impoverishment. Not all landlords were inclined to raise rents or evict tenants. There was a genuine belief in tradition and social stability, and many landlords were reluctant to engage in behavior that would so obviously disrupt the social system. Still, in an age of rising prices and intense economic pressures, there were strong incentives for landlords to make the most of their lands at whatever social cost. Many contemporaries complained about landlords who were either "racking" (increasing) rents or evicting tenants so they could use their lands more efficiently or even convert arable lands into pasture.

A countryman. [Hindley]

The nature of a tenant's holding was theoretically independent of its size, although the larger holdings were more likely to be held by freeholders, smaller ones by leaseholders or copyholders. Freeholders whose lands yielded revenues of at least 40 shillings a year were considered yeomen, a very respectable title for a commoner, that not only implied a fairly high degree of economic prosperity but also entitled the holder to vote in Parliamentary elections. A seventeenth-century estimate suggests that yeomen constituted about 15% of the total population of England; a sixteenth-century estimate numbers greater yeomen at around 10,000. A large landholding for a commoner would be some 50 to 100 acres. Lesser landholders were known as husbandmen, a term that might also be applied generally to anyone who worked his own landholding. The smallest landholders were called cottagers: these held only the cottage they lived in and perhaps a few acres of land. Their holdings were too small to support them, so they had to supplement their income by hiring themselves out as laborers.

Townsfolk The rural hierarchy was the most prominent in the Elizabethan world-view, but there also existed a fully developed and independent social structure in the towns. Towns had been established during the Middle Ages to encourage commerce. They were independent of the feudal hierarchy, owing allegiance directly to the monarch, and they enjoyed extensive privileges of self-government. They were semi-democratic, being in the control of the citizens (sometimes called burgesses). Citizenship in a town was a privilege restricted to male householders who were not dependent on others for their wages, typically craftsmen and tradesmen who had their own shop. Citizens may have numbered as many as a quarter to a half of the adult male population in any given town; a seventeenth-century estimate suggests that citizens constituted roughly 5% of the overall population. As the towns were self-governing, they relied heavily on their own population for filling public offices: perhaps 1 freeman in 4 or 5 held office at any given time.

Whereas the rural hierarchy was centered on agriculture, the urban hierarchy was based on trades and crafts. Each craft and trade had a hierarchy of its own, based on the medieval "guild" system. For example, all grocers in a given town would belong to a corporate body, governed by the master grocers, who would regulate the manner in which the trade was plied. Elizabethans usually called these bodies "companies," although today they are often referred to as guilds. A boy would begin in his teenage years as an apprentice to a master. After seven years he might finish his apprenticeship and become a journeyman; this meant he was free to sell his services in the craft or trade. Those who had adequate means or connections could ultimately become masters themselves, which meant that they could set up a business of their own and take on their own journeymen and apprentices. The citizenry of a town consisted primarily of its master tradesmen and craftsmen.

Shepherds. [Ashdown]

At the base of both the rural and urban hierarchies were the laborers and servants. In the country, there was need of shepherds, milkmaids, harvesters, and other hired hands; the towns required porters, water carriers, and other **Laborers and Servants** unskilled workers. In the country, paid labor sometimes went to cottagers, but increasingly it fell to a growing class of mobile and rootless laborers who followed the market in search of employment. Unskilled laborers in the city and hired workers in the country made up the bulk of the population—agricultural laborers alone represented a quarter to a third of the rural population. In addition, there was a small but increasing demand for labor in a few industries, notably coal and iron production. Such people were always at risk of slipping into the ranks of the vagrants and chronically unemployed.

Table 2.1: The Social Hierarchy

Aristocracy	Clergy	Rural Landholders	Guildsmen	Others
Queen				
Duke (1, executed 1572)	Archbishop (2)			
Marquis (1-2)				
Earl (c20)	Bishop (22)		Mayor of London	
Viscount (2)				
Baron (c40)				
Knight (c300-500)	Archdeacon		City Alderman	
Esquire, Gentleman (c16,000)	Priest (c8000)		Merchant	University Graduate (including Physician, Lawyer, etc.)
	Deacon	Yeoman (c 500,000)	Craftsman, Tradesman	
		Husbandman	Journeyman	
		Cottager	Apprentice	Servant, Laborer
				Vagrant

A schematized table of the social hierarchy. Approximate numbers have been included where available to give a sense of proportions. Ranks at the same horizontal level were considered to be roughly equivalent to each other.

A distinctive feature of Elizabethan society was the very high proportion of the population who were employed in service. Both rural and urban families hired servants: a quarter of the population may have been servants at any given time, and a third or more of households may have had servants. The relationship of servants to their employers in many ways resembled that of children to their parents. They were not just paid employees, but subordinate members of their employer's household who actually lived with the family. Servants might be in a better position than laborers, since service was often a temporary stage on the road to a better social position. For young people, service could be a means of accumulating money, making useful contacts, and acquiring polish in the ways of polite society. Even aristocratic youths might spend some time as pages, gentlemen-ushers, or ladies-in-waiting in a prestigious household. Between the ages of 20 and 24, some 80% of men and 50% of women were servants; two-thirds of boys and three-quarters of girls went away from home in service from just before puberty until marriage, or a period of about 10 years.

At the very base of the social hierarchy was a substantial
and growing number of unemployed poor. The number of poor   **The Poor**
people unable to sustain themselves may have been 10% in the
country and 20% in towns. The poor particularly included children,
widows, abandoned wives, the elderly, and the infirm; but their ranks
were increased by growing numbers of unemployed but able-bodied men
displaced by economic transformations or returning home from service in
the army or navy. There was also a significant community of permanent
beggars and vagabonds, who may have numbered as many as 20,000. In
combination with the gypsies, they were beginning to create an
underworld culture of their own; in fact, the Elizabethans were both
fascinated and horrified with their world of lawlessness, much as people
today are intrigued by stories of the Mafia and of street gangs.

In response to growing concerns over the problems of poverty and
vagrancy, Elizabeth's government began to take active steps to suppress
vagrants while helping those who were genuinely unable to work. For
some time there had been local provisions to deal with poverty, but under
Elizabeth a body of legislation known as the Poor Laws established a
national system for assisting the poor, acknowledging for the first time the
existence of involuntary unemployment. The Poor Laws sought to solve
the problem of poverty at the level of the parish. Parishioners were to pay
money to a parish fund, which would be used to support those unable to
support themselves. The able-bodied unemployed were to be given work,
whereas those able-bodied people who shirked labor might be whipped or
imprisoned. Vagrants from outside the parish were to be sent back to their
own places of origin. The Poor Laws were a serious attempt to address a
growing problem, but their effectiveness was limited. Poverty was an
enormous national problem, and it was linked to an ever-increasing
degree of geographic mobility. Under these circumstances, a parish-by-
parish solution could only have a limited effect, and it was often difficult
to ensure that parishes would enforce the laws effectively, especially given
the expense of implementing them.

In addition to social class, the status of every Elizabethan
was governed by whether they were male or female. In fact,   **Women**
gender was an even more determining factor: social class can be
vague and flexible, but gender is obvious and permanent.

According to a proverb that was current in Elizabeth's day, England
was "the Hell of Horses, the Purgatory of Servants, and the Paradise of
Women." The phrase is highly revealing. On the one hand, it confirms the
observations of contemporary visitors from the Continent who remarked
that English women were particularly free and had substantial control
over their own households. At the same time, it reminds us that women,
like horses and servants, were expected to be in a position of

subordination. The Elizabethan political theorist Sir Thomas Smith, in his *De Republica Anglorum*, offered this view of a woman's role in society:

> Women . . . nature hath made to keep home and to nourish their family and children, and not to meddle with matters abroad, nor to bear office in a city or commonwealth no more than children or infants.

Whereas a male child might have some expectation of moving to a position of relative social and economic independence at some point in his life, a girl would exchange subordination to her father for subordination to an employer or husband. Only in widowhood was a woman legally recognized as an independent individual. A widow took over as head of her husband's household; if he left her sufficient means to live on, she might do quite well, perhaps taking over his trade, and she would be free to remarry or not as she chose.

Yet the theory was rather harsher than the practice. Women played a very important role in the Elizabethan economy, a fact which must have enhanced their real status. They sometimes even served as churchwardens or manorial officials.[3] Even if husbands believed that God had placed them in authority over their wives, their power could not be exercised through sheer force, as recognized in Nicholas Breton's advice on how a husband should treat a wife:

> Cherish all good humors in her: let her lack no silk, crewel, thread, nor flax, to work on at her pleasure, force her to nothing, rather prettily chide her from her labor, but in any wise commend what she doeth: if she be learned and studious, persuade her to translation, it will keep her from idleness, and it is a cunning kind task: if she be unlearned, commend her to housewifery, and make much of her carefulness, and bid her servants take example at their mistress. . . . At table be merry to her, abroad be kind to her, always be loving to her, and never be bitter to her, for patient Griselda is dead long ago, and women are flesh and blood.[4]

The Household   Elizabethan England was truly a family-oriented society: the family constituted the basic unit not only of the society but of the economy as well. A household consisted not only of the nuclear family of father, mother, and children, but might also include employees, notably servants and apprentices. The mean household size was about 4 to 5, but it varied with social class. According to one seventeenth-century estimate, a typical lord's household would include some 40 people, a knight's 13, a squire's or gentleman's 10, a merchant's 6 to 8, a freeholder's 5 to 7, a tradesman's, craftsman's, or cottager's 3 to 4. It was unusual for relatives beyond the nuclear family to live within the household—one region that has been studied in detail shows this happening in only 6% of households, with only 2% including more than one married couple in the same household. This was less true in upper-class households, which were more likely to house additional relatives. Due to the high rate of mortality, single-parent families and stepparents were fairly common. In one village in 1599, a quarter of the children living at home had lost one parent.

It was through the family that the individual was connected to society: everyone was expected to be either a head of household or subject to one. Society was considered to consist not of individuals but of households, and in counting population it was customary only to reckon householders; wife, children, servants, and apprentices were subordinate to the householder. The family was also the typical unit of production—the family business was the rule rather than the exception.

In principle, Elizabethan society was a rigid and orderly hierarchy. Social and economic advancement of the individual were not priorities. People were expected to live within the social class of their parents, a man **Social Stability and Ambition** following his father's vocation or one comparable to it, a woman marrying a man of her father's status. Each person was supposed to fit into a stable social network, remaining in place to preserve the balance of the whole. For most people in Elizabethan England, this principle probably held true.

An apprentice. [Norris]

In practice things were not always so straightforward. Sometimes it was difficult to be entirely certain of a person's social status. Actual titles were easy to verify, as in the case of a nobleman, a knight, or a master craftsman. However, the distinction between an esquire and a gentleman, or between a gentleman and a yeoman, was not always so clear. A prosperous yeoman might hold as much land as a minor gentleman; by subletting it to tenants of his own, he could live off the rents and slip into the gentlemanly class. Successful burgesses often used their profits to purchase land and make themselves gentlemen. A woman might marry a man of significantly higher social station. William Shakespeare is one good example of Elizabethan social mobility: born the son of a glover in Stratford-upon-Avon, he returned from his successful theatrical career in London to live as a gentleman, the proud possessor of a coat-of-arms and the largest house in town. Conversely, a gentleman who acquired excessive debts might slide down the social scale, and we have already seen that landholders and laborers could sometimes find themselves without a livelihood.[5]

GOVERNMENT AND THE LAW

The government of England centered on the figure of the monarch, who relied heavily on her Privy Council for the day-to-day running of the country. The monarch, and the Council acting in the monarch's name, had some power to issue decrees enforceable at law, but the exact extent of these powers was ill-defined. This constitutional ambiguity led to bloody results in the 1640s when King Charles and his Parliament came to civil war over the issue of the King's authority.

The most comprehensively powerful organ of government was the monarch sitting in Parliament: a bill passed by Parliament and assented to by the monarch was the highest legal authority in the land. Parliament was divided into two houses: the House of Lords, consisting of approximately 65 lay peers, 22 bishops, and the country's 2 archbishops (Canterbury and York); and the House of Commons, consisting of 2 representatives chosen from each of England's 39 shires, 2 from each of about 65 English cities and towns (with some exceptions, including London, which sent 4), as well as a single representative from each of 12 Welsh shires and 1 each from 12 Welsh towns, for a total of about 450 representatives. The exact means by which the representatives were chosen depended on the shire or town, but in the shires any holder of lands worth 40 shillings a year was entitled to vote.

In general, the institutions of Elizabethan government seem haphazard by modern standards. The basic unit of governmental organization in both town and country was the parish. Each parish had its own officials, such as a constable who was responsible for basic law enforcement, ale-conners who ensured that the laws regulating the quality of ale were observed, and churchwardens who were responsible for the state of the parish church. In towns there were also scavengers who oversaw public sanitation.

The actual bureaucracy was small and woefully underfunded. This meant that the governmental apparatus required extensive participation by the citizenry. Great lords might serve in the Privy Council or in major offices of the state, army, or navy; local gentlemen were vital in administrating the individual shires; and even ordinary craftsmen, yeomen, and husbandmen might be called upon to serve in minor local offices of the village, town, or parish. At the same time, this kind of unpaid work was a cause of governmental corruption; men who had to spend considerable time and money on an unsalaried government office would frequently find other ways to make the post profitable.

The mechanisms for legal enforcement were quite complex. There were several legal institutions for trying a criminal case. It might be tried in one of several royal courts; it might fall under the jurisdiction of ecclesiastical courts; a minor matter might be handled summarily by a gentleman commissioned as a justice of the peace. Professional law enforcement did not exist—there was no actual police force, which meant that the various tasks associated with police work had to be done by other sorts of officers or not at all. At the local level, two important institutions were the town watch, responsible for patrolling the streets of the town at night, and the constable, the closest thing to a local policeman, although this was always a temporary and part-time office.

Administering the law. [Furnivall (1879)]

Capital offenses were treason, murder, and felony, of which the last included manslaughter, rape, sodomy, arson, witchcraft, burglary, robbery, and grand larceny (stealing of goods worth at least 12 pence). All these offenses carried a mandatory death sentence, for which reason juries were sometimes reluctant to convict. A man convicted of a capital crime might be pardoned by the crown, or in the case of a felony might pray "benefit of clergy." In the Middle Ages the clergy had been exempted from secular punishment for felony, an exemption that extended to any man who could prove he was literate. The custom was still in use in the late sixteenth century, but in slightly altered form: benefit of clergy could only be exercised once, at which time the convict would be branded on the thumb to mark that he had exercised this privilege. Benefit of clergy was not available to those convicted of the most serious felonies, such as burglary and robbery. In some instances, serious crimes might be punished by branding or loss of a body part such as a hand or ear.

In addition, there were diverse lesser crimes of the sort which that now be called misdemeanors. Punishments for such crimes might include fines, whipping, or imprisonment. In some cases the punishment might be confinement in the stocks or the pillory. The pillory was more unpleasant, as it confined both the head and hands, leaving the convict vulnerable to the abuse of passers-by. The stocks confined only the legs, and most of the time only one leg was confined.

Ecclesiastical courts might impose public penance, which would involve some form of public ritual in which the wrongdoer would publicly acknowledge his or her offense. It was difficult for the church courts to enforce their punishments against the truly recalcitrant. The ultimate sanction was excommunication, or exclusion from church services. This punishment theoretically excluded the wrongdoer from society, but in practice many people defied such sanctions—in fact, as many as 5% of the population may have lived excommunicate.[6]

RELIGION

To be a part of Elizabethan society was considered the same as being part of the church, and everyone in Elizabethan England was expected to receive basic religious instruction. By law, every parish minister was required to provide religious instruction on alternate Sundays and on all holy days; all children over age 6 were required to attend. In particular, every child was expected to memorize the Ten Commandments, the Articles of Belief (also called the Creed—the basic statement of Christian belief), and the Lord's Prayer. They were also to memorize the catechism, a series of questions and answers regarding Christian belief. Parents who failed to send their children to receive this instruction might be prosecuted in the church courts, and children who could not recite the catechism might be required to do penance.

Religion played a very different role in people's lives than it does today. There was no question of the separation of church and state. Only one church was legally permitted, the Church of England. To be a citizen of England was to be a part of its church, and the parish was the basic unit of political as well as religious organization. People were required to attend the church of the parish where they lived. Religion was not merely a personal matter, but a contentious social issue. Few people actually believed in freedom of worship: instead, they argued over what form the country's official religion should take.

During the Middle Ages, the countries of western Europe had been officially part of the Catholic Church. In the 1530s, soon after the first Protestant reformations on the Continent, Henry VIII of England found himself at odds with the Pope: he wanted a divorce from his first wife Catherine of Aragon, who had born him a daughter but no sons. The Pope refused, and Henry withdrew England from the Catholic Church, placing the English church under the authority of the king.

A sermon outside St. Paul's Cathedral in London. [*Shakespeare's England*]

Henry himself had no desire to make any significant changes in church teachings, but there was growing pressure in the country to follow the lead of the Continental Protestants such as Martin Luther; English Protestants were later heavily influenced by Jean Calvin, a French Protestant who established a rigidly Protestant state in Geneva. The differences between the ideas of Catholicism and those of Protestantism were complex, but many of them related to the contrast between concrete and intellectual approaches to religion. Catholicism tended to adhere to the concrete aspects of religion, such as religious ceremony, veneration of saints, and charitable deeds; the Catholic Church taught that such things had the power to bring people closer to God. Protestants generally rejected this idea and stressed a more abstract kind of religion: a person would not go to heaven by doing good deeds but by having faith in God, and the word of the Bible was to be taken as more important than traditional ceremonies. As one seventeenth-century author put it, "Calvin's religion was too lean, and the Catholic religion too fat, because the one had many ceremonies, the other none."

The English church moved only very slightly toward Protestantism in Henry's lifetime. During the brief reign of Henry's young son Edward VI, the government came to be dominated by more eager reformers and became a fully Protestant church. In 1553 Edward died, and his half-sister Mary came to the throne. Mary was the daughter of Henry VIII by his first wife, Catherine of Aragon. Mary was opposed to the changes that had begun with her father's divorce, and she brought England back into the Catholic Church. Her reign is remembered for the execution of some 300 Protestants, which is why she is known by the nickname Bloody Mary.

Mary died three years later, leaving her half-sister Elizabeth to inherit the throne. Elizabeth was the daughter of Henry VIII and his second wife, Anne Boleyn. She was not an ardent Protestant, but she was of Protestant leanings. Even more important, her claim to the throne depended on the independence of the English church. The Pope had never recognized Henry's divorce, so in Catholic eyes Elizabeth was the illegitimate child of an adulterous union and could not be queen. Elizabeth duly withdrew England from the Catholic Church once more.

The Elizabethan church was Protestant in its teachings but still retained conservative features inherited from Catholicism. For example, the number of saints' days was severely reduced, but they were not entirely eliminated; the garments worn by Elizabethan ministers were simpler than those of Catholic priests, but still more elaborate than the severe gowns of the Protestants of Geneva. The decoration of the church was more austere than in Catholic churches. However, an important feature that the church inherited from Catholicism was its administration by bishops and archbishops, who were ultimately subject to the Queen.

On the whole, Elizabeth was primarily concerned with her role as a queen: religion was important to her, as it concerned the social well-being of the nation, but she took a much more pragmatic and tolerant approach to religious matters than was common in Europe at the time. Her laws on religion insisted on outward conformity and obedience but did not meddle too deeply in people's actual beliefs. People were required, under pain of a fine, to attend church each Sunday. Public officials, teachers, and other persons of authority were required to take the Oath of Supremacy, which stated that the swearer upheld the official religion of England and the Queen as the supreme governor of the Church. Beyond this, there was comparatively little persecution of people for their religious beliefs, especially in comparison to the religious wars that were rocking the Continent at this time.

In fact, there were still quite a number of Catholics in England. They may have constituted some 5% of the population, and were especially numerous in the north. Elizabeth was inclined to let English Catholics believe as they pleased. To some degree, her policy of tolerance diminished from the late 1560s onwards, as international tensions between Protestants and Catholics increased. In 1568, Mary Stuart, the Queen of Scotland (known today as Mary Queen of Scots), fled her rebellious kingdom to become a prisoner in England. As the principal Catholic claimant to the English throne, Mary became a focus for Catholic plots. In 1569 there was an unsuccessful rebellion in the north, especially supported by Catholics. In 1570 the Pope issued a decree officially deposing Elizabeth from the crown. At this point it became very difficult to maintain loyalty both to the Catholic Church and to the Queen, and it was in this year that the Queen first began to execute Catholics for acts in support of the Pope and his policies. Tensions rose even further in the 1580s when the Pope sent Jesuit missionaries into England, with the intent of ministering to English Catholics and winning converts. The Jesuits were regarded as the worst sort of spies, and if caught they were subject to a protracted and agonizing execution.

Catholicism was not the only sort of church separatism. Many English Protestants felt that the Church of England had not gone far enough along the path of reform; they wanted a more fully Protestant church like those in Scotland, the Netherlands, and Geneva. They objected to even the minor degree of ritual retained in the church. The continuing existence of bishops was a matter of especially heated controversy: many people wanted a "presbyterian" church government, run by assemblies of clergy and godly laymen, an idea that Elizabeth considered a threat to her royal authority. These extreme reformers came to be known as Precisians or Puritans.

Initially the reformers focused their efforts on reshaping the Church of England, but eventually some came to feel that if they wanted a truly pure church, they would have to form one of their own. Notable among these were the Brownists, forerunners of the Congregationalists, who formed small independent congregations for common worship. In the eyes of the government, such separatism was treasonous; it was ruthlessly suppressed, although it was later to play a major role in the founding of the early colonies in America.

By law, everyone was required to attend the morning service at their local parish church every Sunday. During the course of an Elizabethan church service, the parishioners would sing psalms and the priest would offer two biblical readings, one each from the Old and New Testaments, followed by the ceremony of communion and a sermon. The sermon was a major vehicle for public propaganda in both religious and political matters, and the priest was not allowed to preach a sermon of his own devising unless he had been specifically licensed to do so. Instead, the government published books of approved sermons that stressed religious conformity and political obedience, as well as the teachings of Christian doctrine.

Communion, the ceremony in which the parishioners received the sacred bread and wine, had always been a particularly important ritual in the Christian church. The Protestant Church of England taught that communion was a ceremony of commemoration, rather than the mystical transformation of bread and wine into the body and blood of Christ, as in the Catholic Church. In contrast with modern religious customs, people did not normally take communion every time they went to church, and the ceremony might even be omitted; it was only required on certain major holidays.

Most churches had been built in the Middle Ages, but the Protestant reformation brought about many important changes in the interior arrangement of the church. The Catholic crucifix above the altar was replaced by the royal coat-of-arms, and as stained-glass windows decayed they were replaced with plain ones. In Catholicism, the church was arranged so that the religious ceremonies, particularly that of communion, took place in a special holy space: the altar was located at the far east end, away from the parishioners, and was separated from them by a screen. The Protestants considered this arrangement superstitious; in an Elizabethan church the elaborate altar was exchanged for a simple communion table, which was placed in the center of the church right in front of the congregation, without any separation. Pews were in use by this time, but the church was equally likely to be outfitted with stools for the parishioners. Seating in church was sometimes a contentious issue, since a seat in front was considered a mark of high social rank. In some traditional communities, seats were assigned to particular landholdings, but in many places this system had broken down, and there was a great deal of jockeying for the most prestigious positions.

Religious observance did not stop at the church door. Elizabethan people lived in a society steeped in religion, so it was naturally a major part of their ordinary life. It was common for people to pray every morning and evening, and to say grace before and after meals. As literacy spread, more and more people were able to read the Bible; naturally, the next step was to discuss it and how it should be applied to the world around them. Even those who could not read were familiar with the contents of the Bible, since they heard readings from it every week in church. Another important book was John Foxe's *Book of Martyrs*, which told of the faithfulness of English Christians throughout history, with special emphasis on Protestants who had died under the persecutions of Bloody Mary. In a world where church and state were indivisibly linked, Protestantism was seen by many as a form of patriotism.

Yet in spite of earnest efforts at public religious education, atheism and irreligion were still present; doubtless, many people maintained religious uniformity only because of the severe sanctions against nonconformity. Contemporaries complained that it was "A matter very common to dispute whether there be a God or not." Some citizens were known to profane religious sacraments: on one occasion a goose and gander were married; on another a horse's head was baptized; on yet another an entire dead horse was brought to receive communion.

Side by side with the official teachings of the church was a continuing belief in magic. Many people still believed in supernatural creatures, particularly fairies; they used magical charms and recipes, and consulted people believed to have supernatural skills or powers, especially in matters such as illness, childbirth, loss of property, or love-longing. Witchcraft was accepted as real not only by simple folk but by the church and government—it was a crime punishable by death. Witchcraft accusations peaked in 1580s and 1590s, although they were never as numerous as they tend to be in the modern popular imagination. On the whole, superstition was more firmly entrenched in the country than in the city.[7]

THE ECONOMY

Work in Elizabethan England was more personal in nature than it is today. There was less distinction between people's work and their personal lives, or between work spaces and personal spaces. In many cases employees were fed by their employer, and in some instances they lived in their employer's house. Offices, commercial buildings, and factories were still far in the future. Work and business tended to be conducted in or around the home: merchants, craftsmen, and shopkeepers all worked in their houses; in the country, women labored at home while the men were out in the fields.

England in the late sixteenth century was still overwhelmingly rural, so for most people, work meant farm work. The production of food was a vital necessity, and very **Agriculture** labor-intensive since hardly any machinery was involved. This meant that a substantial proportion of the population was engaged in the growing of staple foods, especially grains. Yet contrary to what is sometimes imagined, the Elizabethan rural economy was already market-oriented. Each household might produce some goods for its own use, notably foodstuffs, but it was not self-sufficient: people supported themselves by producing surpluses of agricultural goods for sale, rather than subsisting on their own produce.

Land productivity was improved by crop rotation, typically the "three-field" system. Over the centuries it had been discovered that constant farming of land exhausts its ability to produce crops. However, certain kinds of crops were found to help refortify the land for producing wheat. In the three-field system, the fields were divided into three parts. The agricultural year would begin in late September or October, when one part would be sown with a winter crop of rye and wheat (it was a winter crop because it was sown in the winter—all the crops were harvested in August-September). The second part would be sown with a "spring crop" of peas, beans, oats and barley in February-March. The remaining land would lie "fallow," or unused, and would be plowed and fertilized during the spring and summer to help restore its strength. The next year the fields were rotated: the fallow fields would be planted with the winter crop, the winter fields would be planted in the spring, and the spring fields would lie fallow.

There were two general forms of crop-raising in Elizabethan England: "champion" (or "open field") and "woodland" agriculture. In general, champion agriculture was most common in the central part of the country, woodland around the edges.

In champion areas all the fields around the village were open, without any hedges or divisions, and they belonged to the village as a whole. Each year the active fields were divided into a multitude of long, thin, half-acre strips. Each villager received a number of scattered strips according to the size of his landholding—the scattering of the strips ensured that no villager would receive all the inferior land. In champion lands, the villagers traditionally had the right to pasture their livestock on the village's pastures, on the fields and hay-meadows after they were harvested, and on the fallows (where the manure helped refertilize the ground). There were also common rights over wastelands: forested areas were useful places for feeding pigs (they love acorns) and gathering firewood, and marshy lands could be used for pasturing livestock and gathering reeds. In a champion village, administration of agricultural matters would be subject to a court held by the landlord, or to a village meeting.

The mode of life in woodland areas was more individualistic and more efficient. There were no common lands, and each landholding was separate from the others. Since there were no commons there was not the same need for the community to cooperate, and manorial courts and village meetings were not a part of woodland life. Woodland areas were not actually wooded: the borders of each holding were marked by tall hedges, which gave such regions a more wooded look.

During this period, landowners receiving fixed rents saw their real incomes decline, as the value of the rents was consumed by inflation. The inflation also hurt smaller landholders: only those with larger holdings produced enough surplus for their increased incomes to stay ahead of rising costs. This meant that smaller holdings were becoming less viable.

For many landowners and landholders, an obvious response to rising costs was to focus on raising sheep, which is much less labor-intensive than crop-raising. Many landowners were finding means of ending tenancies and were enclosing open fields and commons for pasture. Contemporaries complained vociferously about this process of enclosure, which left increasing numbers of people without land or employment. They may have exaggerated the extent of the problem, but it was certainly a factor in the growing social displacement of the age.

Wool was England's principal source of wealth, its principal product, and its principal export. There were some 10-11 million **Wool** sheep in the country in 1558, or nearly 4 times the human population! Sheep-raising provided little agricultural employment, but it did support a great deal of manufacturing work.

Once the sheep were shorn and the wool had been washed, it had to be carded. This involved stroking the wool between a pair of special brushes so that all the strands were running parallel, free of knots and tangles.

The carded wool was then spun into thread. Spinning involved drawing out wool from the carded mass and spinning it so that it was tightly twisted. Wool fibers are covered with microscopic scales; when twisted in this way, the scaly strands cling to each other, making it possible for them to form thread. Woolen thread could be spun with a drop spindle, essentially a disk with a stick passing through the center. The spindle was suspended from the wool fibers and set spinning, which caused the fibers to twist into thread. Alternatively, wool might be spun with a hand-cranked spinning wheel—the treadle wheel was used only for spinning flax into linen thread.

Carding and spinning could easily be done at home, and many if not most women practiced them daily as a means of supplementing the family income. Carding was also an easy job for children.

After spinning, the thread was woven into cloth on a horizontal loom. The cloth then had to be "fulled," or washed, to shrink and felt it. This made the fibers join more tightly with each other, so that the fabric was both stronger and more dense, and therefore better at keeping out the English cold and rain. In fact, Elizabethan wools were so heavily felted that it was unnecessary even to hem them—they did not normally unravel. Sometimes the wool would be left its natural color, but often it would be dyed. This might happen as the very last stage, but sometimes it was done before the wool was even spun—hence the expression "dyed in the wool."

In towns, the economy was dominated by crafts and trades. There was very little actual industry at this time: **Crafts and** finished products were largely provided by craftsmen and **Trades** tradesmen out of small specialty shops. Among the most common craftsmen and tradesmen were shoemakers, glovers, tailors, tanners, bakers, weavers, butchers, smiths, carpenters, and joiners. The independent craftsman combined the functions of employer, workman, merchant, and shopkeeper: he did his own work, and he marketed and sold his products from his own workshop. The craftsman or tradesman's shop was usually the front ground-floor room of his home; he would live upstairs with his family, servants, and apprentices, and might hire additional workers, called journeymen, who would assist him during the day but live elsewhere.

A sailor. He is holding a cross-staff (a navigational instrument) and compass; he wears a cassock, with a bosun's whistle suspended around his neck; a knife hangs from his belt. [Norris]

Crafts and trades were entered through the system of apprenticeship. An apprentice might have some hope of real economic and social advancement. He would live in the home of his master, receiving bed, board, and even some pocket money in exchange for his labor in the master's shop. The apprentice thereby would learn a marketable skill; in some cases instruction in reading, writing, and perhaps arithmetic would also be provided. Apprentices were supposed to be under their master's strict supervision, although in practice it seems that many found opportunity to roam with their fellow apprentices. Apprenticeship lasted for seven years.

Another important form of work was service. Servants were very common in Elizabethan England; they were particularly likely to be young people who would eventually leave service for a more advantageous position. Less fortunate were the unskilled laborers and agricultural workers, who were likely to be locked in the same economic status for their entire lives. Fewer in number but nonetheless significant were the sailors and soldiers who helped build England's incipient commercial and colonial empire. They were widely glorified for their exploits and achievements, yet they were also mistrusted by the population at large, as they integrated poorly into the fabric of civilian life.[8]

Women at Work Although the economy was organized around men, women played a crucial role in the economic life of the country. In fact, both husband and wife were expected to work, although she was normally engaged in labor that could be done at home. One of her primary responsibilities was tending the family livestock. People often owned cattle—perhaps three-quarters of agricultural laborers had at least one cow, and even townsfolk would keep one on the town fields. Other common domestic animals were pigs, goats, sheep, chicken, ducks, geese, and pigeons. The woman's responsibility for the animals meant that she was also in charge of making cheese and butter, as well as collecting eggs from the poultry.

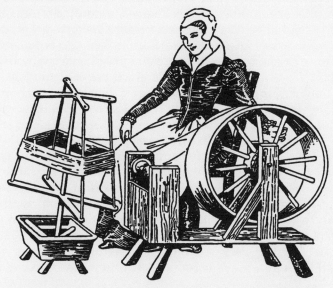

Spinning. Note the hand-rotated spinning wheel. [Norris]

The woman also had the care of the garden, a common feature of both rural and urban households. In harvest and haymaking time, a country woman might assist in the fields, since the pressures of time required as many hands as possible. She would also be involved in winnowing the grain after it was harvested. In addition, the woman was responsible for such domestic tasks as cooking, brewing, mending, and cleaning, and she often had some basic medical skills as well. Already in this period, women were often involved in elementary teaching. Women engaged in various home industries, especially the spinning of wool thread. Knitting was another means by which a woman might earn extra money. As men had to work in the fields, the task of traveling to the market to buy and sell goods often fell to the woman. In towns, women engaged in a wide variety of work: they were especially likely to be employed as seamstresses, laundresses, and street vendors. The wife of a craftsman or tradesman often helped her husband in his work; and if he died, she might carry on the business herself. There were even a few instances of women plying crafts or trades in their own right in the city, but these were quite rare.

It is difficult to compare Elizabethan money with modern money, since the economy was very different from ours. Labor was relatively cheap—principally because it was widely accepted that commoners should expect a low **Elizabethan Money** standard of living. Manufactured goods, on the other hand, were comparatively expensive. There was almost no mechanization, so the vastly increased hours of labor more than negated the lower rate of pay. Moreover, prices could fluctuate enormously according to time and place. Prices today tend to be fairly constant because we have a well-developed system of transportation and storage. Elizabethans did not have the same opportunities to shop around, nor could they stock up on perishable goods when they were cheap and plentiful. Prices were therefore very sensitive to the supply and demand at a particular time and place. Naturally, wages and prices were higher in London than in the country.

Overall, the sixteenth century was a period of unprecedented inflation; prices rose during Elizabeth's reign by about 100-150%. This was good news for some, and bad for others. Substantial landholders whose production was considerably larger than their expenditures profited: higher prices meant they could sell their surplus for more money. Small landholders, producing little or no surplus, were more at risk, since their income barely kept pace with their expenditures. Above all, wage-earners suffered from inflation, as the real value of their wages was eaten up by rising costs. By the early seventeenth century, the real wages of agricultural laborers were only half of what they had been two centuries before.

Elizabethan money consisted of silver and gold coins; even the smallest, the halfpenny, was worth more than most coins today. There was a serious need for smaller denominations, but the halfpenny was already so tiny (about half an inch across) that a smaller coin would have been unusable. The problem was not solved until Elizabeth's successor, James I, introduced brass coinage in the early seventeenth century. The typical Elizabethan coin bore the image of the Queen on one side and the royal coat-of-arms and a cross on the other. Its actual value was linked to the value of the gold or silver in it and was therefore susceptible to fluctuations in the prices of gold and silver, as well as to changes in the purity of the coins.

Some denominations were only "moneys of account," used only for reckoning, and did not actually exist as currency. Such were the mark and the pound, large denominations that served to simplify the task of dealing with large sums of money. Small-denomination moneys of account such as the groat and farthing had once existed as coinage, and continued to be a part of the vocabulary of money. There was no paper money, although it was sometimes possible to deposit money with a banker or merchant in exchange for a letter of credit.

Table 2.2 offers some idea of the value of Elizabethan money. The table includes equivalents in 1995 US dollars, but these should be taken as rough magnitudes, not values. An Elizabethan halfpenny did not actually have the same purchasing power as a modern dollar, but it was more similar to a dollar than to a cent or to ten dollars. The table also gives the Elizabethan abbreviations for various denominations—note that the normal abbreviation for a pound was "li." (as opposed to the modern symbol "£"), which went after the number instead of before it.

A more realistic idea of the value of these moneys can be obtained by comparing them with wages and incomes. Wages might be paid by the day, week, or year; the longer the term, the more likely that the wages included food and drink as well. In some cases (especially for apprentices) lodging was also part of the deal. Wages were regulated by law, although the theory was not always put into practice. The wages and incomes listed in Table 2.3 are only samples: actual wages and incomes varied according to time, place, and individual circumstances.[9]

The actual value of incomes can best be judged by comparing them to the prices of goods (see Table 2.4). Purchasing was much less straightforward than it is today. Measurements were not always uniform throughout the country, and a variety of systems were in use: for example, woolen cloth was purchased by the yard, but linen by the ell (45″). Prices were also subject to negotiation: haggling was the rule rather than the exception, except in the case of basic staples such as bread and ale, which were closely regulated. The system of taxation was also fairly complex, although sales taxes were generally low and applied to relatively few items.[10]

Elizabethan coins (actual size): halfpenny, penny, sixpence, shilling, and gold crown. [Ruding]

Goods might be bought at fairs or markets, from a maker, or from a middleman. Townsfolk had the best access, since strolling vendors, street stalls, markets, craftsmen, and tradesmen could provide them with everything they might need. Country folk relied more heavily on weekly markets and annual fairs—there was usually a market within 12 miles.

They also made use of pedlars, who roamed the countryside to bring goods to small localities. However, by now even small towns had retailers: a small-town draper, for example, might carry not only mercery (clothing articles such as cloth, lace, pins, thread, ribbons, and buttons) but also groceries (including dried fruits, sugar, spices, and soap) and stationery.

Used goods played a much larger role in the economy than is the case today. Crafted items such as furniture were quite expensive; clothing was especially costly, since so much labor went into producing the cloth. For this reason, many people bought such products second-hand from some sort of dealer, who might refurbish the goods to improve their resale value. The cost of materials likewise encouraged recycling, which was also a significant element in the economy: building materials, cloth, leather, and metal were all subject to reuse, and the paper industry relied wholly on recycled rags.

A tinker mends a pot. [Furnivall (1879)]

Table 2.2: Approximate Values of Elizabethan Money

	Denomination	Value	Purchase Value	Equivalent
Silver Coins	halfpenny (ob.)	1/2 of a penny	1 quart of ale	$1
	penny (d.)		1 loaf of bread	$2
	twopenny (half-groat)	2d.		$4
	shilling (s.)	12d.	1 day's earnings for a craftsman	$25
Gold Coins	half-crown	2s. 6d.	1 day's earnings for a gentleman	$60
	quarter angel	2s. 6d.		$60
	angelet	5s.		$100
	crown	5s.	1 week's earnings for a craftsman	$100
	angel	10s.	1 lb. of spices	$250
	sovereign (new standard)	20s. (1 li.)		$500
	sovereign (old standard)	30s.		$750
	Dutch florin	2s.		$50
	French crown	6s. 4d.		$150
	Spanish ducat	6s. 8d.		$150
Moneys of Account	farthing (q.)	1/4 of a penny		$.50
	three-farthings	$3/4$d.		$1.50
	three-halfpenny	$1^1/_2$d.	1 lb. of cheese	$3
	threepenny	3d.	1 lb. of butter	$6
	groat	4d.	1 day's food	$8
	mark (marc.)	13s. 4d. (2/3 of 1 li.)		$350
	pound (li.)	20s.	1 carthorse	$500

Table 2.3: Sample Wages and Incomes

Shepherd's Boy	2 1/2d./day with food
Shepherd	6d./week with food
Unskilled Rural Laborer	2-3d./day with food
Plowman	1s./week with food
Skilled Rural Laborer	6d./day
Laborer	9d./day 26s. 6d./year with food and drink
Craftsman	12d./day, 7d. with food and drink £4-10/year with food and drink
Yeoman	£2-6/year or more
Minor Parson	£10-30/year
Esquire	£500-1000/year
Knight	£1000-2000/year
Nobleman	£2500/year
30-acre landholding	£14, or a surplus of £3-5 after paying for foodstuffs
Soldier	5d./day
Sergeant, Drummer	$8^1/_2$d./day
Ensign	1s./day
Lieutenant	2s./day
Captain	4s./day

Table 2.4: Sample Prices of Goods and Services

Meal at an inn	4-6d.	Gentleman's meal in his room at an inn	2s.
Bed in an inn	1d.	Lodging a horse	12-18d.
Food for one day	4d.	Loaf of bread	1d.
Butter (1 lb.)	3d.	Cheese (1 lb.)	$1^1/_2$ d.
Eggs (3)	1d.	Fresh salmon	13s. 4d.
Beef (1 lb.)	3d.	Cherries (1 lb.)	3d.
Sugar (1 lb.)	20s.	Cloves (1 lb.)	11s.
Pepper (1 lb.)	4s.	Wine (1 qt.)	1s.
Ale (1 qt.)	$^1/_2$d.	Tobacco	3s./ounce
Officer's canvas doublet	14s. 5d.	Officer's cassock	27s. 7d.
Shoes	1s.	White silk hose	25s.
Candles (48)	3s. 3d.	Soap (1 lb.)	4d.
Knives (2)	8d.	Bed	4s.
Spectacles (2 pr.)	6d.	Scissors	6d.
Bible	£2	Broadside ballad	1d.
Small book	6d.-2s.	Theater admission	1, 2, or 3d.
Tooth pulled	2s.	Portraits	62s. to £6
Horse	£1-2		
Hiring a horse	12d./day or $2^1/_2$d. /mile	Hiring a coach	10s./day

3

The Course of Life

Childbirth in the sixteenth century normally happened at
home. There were hospitals in Elizabethan England, but their **Birth and**
purpose was different from that of modern hospitals. The **Baptism**
Elizabethan hospital was primarily a charitable institution,
providing long-term care for the infirm or elderly rather than short-term
treatment of acute medical problems. Nor was a physician likely to be
involved in the birthing process. The delivery of babies was primarily the
domain of the midwife. Indeed, a number of women might be present—
childbirth was often a major social occasion for women. Yet the event was
not without risk to the mother. The rate of maternal mortality in childbirth
may have been in the region of 1%; even .8% is abnormally high in the
modern Third World.

Soon after birth, the baby would be taken to the parish church for
baptism, commonly called christening: this was supposed to happen on a
Sunday or holy day within a week or two of the birth. Christenings at
home or by anyone but a clergyman were against church law. The only
exception was if the child was in imminent danger of death, in which case
it was considered more important to ensure that the child did not die
unchristened. The ritual of baptism involved dipping the baby in a font of
holy water in the parish church. At the ceremony the child was sponsored
by three godparents, two of the same sex and one of the opposite. These
godparents were considered genuine relatives; children would ask their
godparents' blessing whenever meeting them, much as they did of their
parents every morning and evening. A christening was a major social
occasion, and might be followed by a feast. It was customary for people to
give presents for the newborn—"apostle spoons," having the image of one

of the twelve apostles at the end of the handle, were a common choice, as were other gifts of pewter and silver.[1]

An infant in swaddling clothes. [Clinch]

A few weeks later the mother would go to the church for the ceremony called churching. This had originated in the Middle Ages as a purifying ritual, but in Protestant England it was reinterpreted as an occasion for thanksgiving, both for the safe delivery of the child and for the mother's survival of the dangers of childbirth. Churchings were popular social occasions among women.[2]

At the core of the baptismal ceremony was the assigning of a name. The surname was inherited from the child's father. Given names in Elizabethan England were mostly drawn from traditional stock, but they were much more varied and original than had been the case in the Middle Ages. Perhaps the most common were French names imported during the Middle Ages. For boys, these included (in approximate descending order of popularity) William, Robert, Richard, Humphrey, Henry, Roger, Ralph, Fulk, Hugh, and Walter. Girls names included Alice, Joan, Jane, Isabel, Maud, Juliana, Eleanor, and Rose. Some French names had been imported more recently, such as Francis for boys, and Joyce, Florence, and Frances for girls.

Also popular were the names of saints. Among boys, some of the most common saints' names were (roughly in descending order of popularity) John, Thomas, James, and George. Less common were Peter, Anthony, Lawrence, Valentine, Nicholas, Christopher, Andrew, Giles, Maurice, Gervase, Bernard, Leonard, and Ambrose. Female saints' names included (again in descending order) Catherine, Elizabeth, Anne, Agnes, Margaret (with its variant, Margery), Lucy, Barbara, and Cecily. The name Mary was also used, although it was much less common than on the Continent. Because Protestantism discouraged the veneration of saints, these names had lost much of their religious significance and were more likely to be chosen simply on the basis of the parents' preference.

Another religious source of names was the Old Testament, from which came such boys' names as Adam, Daniel, David, Toby, Nathaniel, and Zachary. Obscure Old Testament names were especially popular among the more extreme Protestant reformers. For girls, Old Testament names were rarer, although one occasionally finds a Judith. The names Simon and Martha derived from the New Testament.

A few names derived from Greek or Latin, such as Julius, Alexander, Miles, and Adrian for boys, Dorothy and Mabel for girls. Some names were ultimately inherited from the Anglo-Saxons, such as Edward and

Edmund for boys, Edith, Winifred, and Audrey for girls. A few names were taken from legend. For boys these included Arthur, Tristram, Lancelot, Perceval, and Oliver. For girls the principal example is Helen or Ellen. Among Puritans there was a growing fashion for creative names with religious themes, such as "Flee-Sin" and "Safe-on-High." By and large, the upper classes and townspeople were most likely to be innovative in naming their children; country folk were likely to use more traditional names.

Then as now, people were often known by shortened forms of their names, many of which are still in use today. Edward might be known as Ned, John as Jack, David as Davy, Robert as Robin, Dorothy as Doll, Mary as Moll, Catherine as Kate or Kit.

Baptism was not only a religious ritual. In the sixteenth century, to belong to society and to belong to the church were considered one and the same, so that the ceremony of baptism also marked the child's entry into the social community. In fact, rather than having birth certificates, the child's name and date of birth would be recorded in a parish register as a part of the ceremony of baptism; this registry would serve as a legal verification of that person's age and origin for the rest of his or her life.

Childhood was a dangerous time in Elizabethan England. The infant mortality rate may have been about 135 in 1000, **Childhood** and in some places as high as 200 in 1000. By comparison, a child mortality rate of 125 in 1000 is exceptionally high in the modern Third World; the rate in the United States is around 10 in 1000. Between the ages of 1 and 4, the mortality rate was around 60 in 1000, and about 30 in 1000 between the ages of 5 and 9. This means that out of every 10 live births, only 7 or 8 children lived to 10 years of age. The high mortality rate was primarily due to disease. Young children have relatively weak immune systems, so the diseases that plagued sixteenth-century Europe took an especially high toll among children.[3]

It is sometimes supposed that because of the high mortality rate, parents were reluctant to invest emotion in their children, but evidence suggests that love was considered a normal and necessary part of the parent-child relationship. The sentiments expressed by Sir Henry Sidney in a letter to his son were not at all uncommon:

> I love thee, boy, well. I have no more, but God bless you, my sweet child, in this world forever, as I in this world find myself happy in my children. From Ludlow Castle this 28th of October, 1578. To my very loving son, Robert Sidney, give these. Your very loving father.

Parents were expected to be strict, but this was seen as a sign of love. Children who were not disciplined properly would not learn how to interact with the rest of society: in the words of one Elizabethan proverb, "Better unfed than untaught." Undoubtedly there were cruel parents who abused their power, but there is no evidence to indicate that abusiveness was any more common then than now.

For the first six years or so, the Elizabethan child would be at home and principally under female care. Most children were cared for by their own mothers, although privileged children might be in the keeping of a nurse. Young babies were kept in rocking cribs and dressed in baby caps and "swaddling," bands of linen wrapped around their bodies to keep them warm and im- mobile so their limbs would grow straight. Elizabethan babies in wealthy families were often given pieces of coral attached to silver handles with bells on them: the bells provided amuse- ment, and the child could suck or chew on the coral much as modern babies have pacifiers and teething rings. Babies were breast-fed, and might be nursed in this way for about two years; aristo- cratic children often received their milk from a wet-nurse. After coming out of swaddling

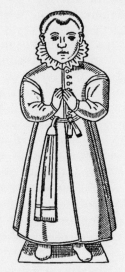

A boy wearing a gown. [Clinch]

clothes, both boys and girls were dressed in gowns and petticoats; only after age 6 or so were boys put into breeches. For Elizabethan children, like children today, the early years were primarily a time for exploration, play, and learning. During this time children would explore their world and begin to learn some of the basic tools of social interaction.

Elizabethan English

The first of these tools was the child's mother tongue. Elizabethan English was close enough to modern English that it would be comprehensible to us today. The main differences in pronunciation were in a few of the vowels: "weak," for example, rhymed with "break"; and "take" sounded something like modern English "tack." As in most modern North American accents, r's were always pronounced. Overall, Elizabethan English would most resemble a modern Irish or rural English accent; the pronunciation associated with Oxford and Cambridge, the BBC, and the royal family is a comparatively recent development. There was considerable difference in pronunciation from one place to another: the dialect of London was the most influential, but there was no official form of the language, and even a gentleman might still speak a local dialect.[4]

Etiquette

In learning the language, the child would also learn the appropriate modes of address, which were more complex than they are today. For example, the word "thou" existed as an alternative to "you." To us it sounds formal and archaic, but for the Elizabethans it was actually very informal, used to address a person's social inferiors and very close friends. You might call your son or daughter "thou," but you would never use it with strangers ("thee" stood in the same relationship to "thou" as "me" to "I"—"Thou art a fine fellow," but "I like thee well").

The child would also have to learn the titles appropriate to different kinds of people. As a rule, superiors were addressed by their title and surname, inferiors by their Christian name. If you were speaking to someone of high rank or if you wished to address someone formally, you might say "sir" or "madam"; you would certainly use these terms for anyone of the rank of knight or higher. As a title, "Sir" designated a knight (or sometimes a priest) and was used with the first name, as in "Sir John."

More general terms of respect were "master" and "mistress." These could be simply a polite form of address, but they were particularly used by servants speaking to their employers, or by anyone speaking to a gentleman or gentlewoman. They were also used as titles, "Master Johnson" being a name for a gentleman, "Master William" a polite way of referring to a commoner. Commoners might also be called "Goodman" or "Goodwife," especially if they were at the head of a yeomanly household. Ordinary people, especially one's inferiors, might be called "man," "fellow," or "woman." "Sirrah" was applied to inferiors, and was sometimes used as an insult. A close friend might be called "friend," "cousin," or "coz." Confidence tricksters often addressed their victims as if they were intimate friends, so that the term "to cozen" (i.e., "cousin") came to mean "to cheat."[5]

The child would have to learn the etiquette of actions as well as of words. Elizabethan manners were no less structured than our own, even if their provisions seem rather alien in some respects. The English commonly kissed each other as an ordinary form of greeting, although the practice declined in the first half of the seventeenth century. It was customary for men to remove their hats in the presence of superiors, but it was also customary to keep them on at the table. Children were expected to show great respect to their parents. Even a grown man would kneel to receive his father's blessing, and would stand mute and bareheaded before his parents.[6]

In spite of the vast social and economic differences in individual families, the lives of very young children were remarkably uniform in many respects. At about age 6 this changed, as the social differentiations of class and gender began to play a real role. Girls remained in the world of women, while boys began to enter the world of men; both began to be taught the skills appropriate to their rank in society.

Early Education

For boys of privileged families, this meant going to school. Only a small minority of Elizabethan children received formal schooling, although the number was growing. There was no national system of education, but a range of independent and semi-independent educational institutions. Those children fortunate enough to have a formal education most often began at a "petty school." Petty schools might be private enterprises or attached to a grammar school, but in many localities they were organized by the parish. The petty school typically taught the fundamentals of reading and writing, and perhaps "ciphering" (basic arithmetic with Arabic numerals). The content of petty school education was strongly religious: after being introduced to the alphabet on a "horn book" (a wooden tablet with the text pasted on it, covered with a thin layer of horn to protect the paper), the children would learn to read prayers and then move on to the catechism. Discipline was strict: schoolmasters had a free hand to use a birch rod to beat students for infraction of rules or for academic failures. Most of the students were boys, but girls occasionally attended the petty schools. Masters at these schools were a mixed lot. Some were men of only small learning; some were women, whose schools were sometimes known as "dame schools"; some were in fact well-educated men—about a third of licensed petty school teachers may have been university graduates.[7]

Schooling. [Furnivall 1879]

Basic literacy was expanding significantly during Elizabeth's reign, although it was still the exception rather than the rule. Some 20% of men and 5% of women may have been literate at the time of Elizabeth's accession; by 1600 literacy may have risen to 30% for men and 10% for women. Literacy was generally higher among the privileged classes and townsfolk—perhaps 60% of London's craftsmen and tradesmen were literate in the 1580s; and of a sample of London women in 1580, 16% could sign their names. Literacy was also more common among the more radical Protestants, and in the south and east. It tended to be lower among countryfolk and the poor, and in the north and west.[8]

The equipment used for writing at this time was typically a goose-quill pen, an inkhorn, and paper. The quill was shaved of **Writing** its feathers (contrary to our modern image), and a point or "nib" was cut into it. This was done with a small knife that folded into its own handle for safe transportation, to be brought out when the nib needed sharpening—the origin of the modern penknife. The pen and its accessories were kept in a leather case called a penner. People who had to do a lot of calculating, such as shopkeepers, often used a slate, which could be written on and wiped clear afterwards. Another form of temporary writing involved a wooden or metal stylus and a small thin board coated with wax, called a wax tablet. The writer would inscribe the letters into the wax with the stylus, which might have a rounded top end for rubbing out the letters afterwards. Such tablets were typically bound in pairs (or even in books) to protect their faces, and were known as a "pair of tables."[9]

Writing. [Holinshed]

There were two principal type of handwriting used by the Elizabethans, known as secretary and italic. The secretary hand had evolved in the late Middle Ages as a quick and workaday form of writing. In the Elizabethan period it retained its workaday character, and was often used for correspondence, accounts, and other practical uses, although to the modern eye it seems very difficult to read. The italic hand, essentially the same as the style known as italic today, is much more clear and elegant by modern standards; it was especially used by learned people in scholarly contexts.

The alphabet was essentially the same as we use today, with a few interesting exceptions. For a start, there were only 24 letters. The letters *i* and *j* were considered equivalent: *J* was often used as the capital form of *i*. The letters *u* and *v* were similarly equivalent, *u* commonly being used in the middle of a word and *v* at the beginning. So where we would write "I have an uncle," an Elizabethan might have written "J haue an vncle." Some Elizabethan letters have since dropped out of use. The normal form of *s* was the long form, resembling a modern *f*. The modern style of *s* was only used as a capital or at the end of a word. There was also a special character to represent *th*, which looked like a *y*, but actually came from an ancient runic letter called "thorn": when we see "Ye Olde Tea Shoppe," the "ye" should actually be pronounced "the." Roman numerals were more frequently used than today, although reckoning was usually done with the more convenient Arabic numerals.

There were no dictionaries, so Elizabethan spelling was largely a matter of custom, and often just a matter of writing the words by ear. Still, the normal spelling of words was for the most part very similar to the spelling known today. The most obvious difference is that the Elizabethans often added a final *e* in words where we do not: "school," for example, was likely to be written as "schoole."

In printed books there were two principal typefaces: blackletter and Roman. Blackletter type, like the secretary hand, was derived from medieval writing; it resembled what is sometimes called "Old English" type today. Roman type, like the italic hand, was associated with the revival of classical learning during the Renaissance, and eventually replaced the blackletter entirely: the standard type used today derives from Roman typeface. Italic type was also used, especially to set words apart from surrounding Roman text.

Grammar School After petty school, if the family was rich or if the boy showed enough promise to earn a scholarship, he might go to a grammar school. This stage of schooling would last some 5 to 10 years—typically to age 14 or so. The "grammar" taught at a grammar school was Latin language and literature. The school might also teach a bit of French or Greek, but the emphasis was on Latin, the traditional language of learning. A boy who learned Latin could not only absorb the wisdom of ancient authors but could also read the works of the finest contemporary scholars, for Latin was still the international language

The Secretary Alphabet

Lower Case Letters

a or *a* *b* *c* or *c* *d* *e* or *e* *f* *g*

f or *h* or *l* *i* *j* *k* or *k* *l* or *l* *m* *n*

o *p* *q* *r* *ſ* (used at the beginning and in the middle of a word) *s* (used only at the end of a word)

t *u* *v* *w* *x* *y* *z* or *z*

There are many variations among capitals. This is a sample capital alphabet:

A B C D E F G H

J (note that "I" and "J" are the same) K L M N O

P Q R S or ſ T

V ("U" and "V" are also the same) W X Y Z

A sample secretary hand [Hadfield].

The Lordes Praier

Our ffather which art in heauen; Hallowed be thy name. Thy kyngdom come. Thy will be done in earth, as it is in heauẽ. Geue vs this day our daily bread. And forgeue vs ours trespasses, as we forgeue them that trespasse against vs. And leade vs not into temptacion. But deliuer vs from euil. Amen.

The Lord's Prayer in secretary hand. The spelling and punctuation are typically Elizabethan; neither were standardized in this period. This would have been one of the first texts a child would learn to write [Hadfield].

of scholarship and science. Older students were expected to speak Latin at all times and were punished for speaking English. Grammar school teachers were usually university graduates. It was rare for a girl to be admitted to a grammar school, and such an arrangement would only last from the age of 7 to 9 or thereabouts. However, there were also some special boarding schools for girls.[10]

School hours were long. A typical school day would begin at 6 or 7, with a 15-minute break for breakfast at 9 or so. There would be another break for dinner at 11, with classes resuming at 1; then a 30-minute break at 3 or so, with classes ending at 5 or 5:30. Students generally had Thursday and Saturday afternoons off, as well as two-week holidays at Christmas and Easter. Some grammar schools boarded their students; others (particularly in the towns) were day schools from which the students would return home for their midday meal. Both petty and grammar schools were housed in single rooms. All the students at a particular level of schooling sat together on one bench, or "form"—to this day, the various grades in English schools are known as "forms."

In addition to these publicly available forms of schooling, wealthy families sometimes hired tutors for their children. A tutor might provide the child's entire education, especially for girls; in other cases, a tutor might cover subjects not included in the school curriculum. For example, if you wanted your child to learn modern languages, you might have to hire a tutor (except in larger towns, where there were often specialized schools for such purposes). This was a very important matter, for the child of a privileged family was expected to learn French, and perhaps Spanish or Italian as well—these were the primary languages of international culture and communication. Tutors were often hired to teach dancing and music; a boy might also be taught fencing, riding, swimming, or archery. A girl's education was likely to focus on such skills and graces as would make her a desirable match, notably modern languages, needlework, and music. Book learning was not generally a high priority for girls, although plenty of parents ensured that their daughters had a good education— Elizabeth herself was noted for her learning and was expert in both Greek and Latin.

In the Middle Ages, Latin and French had generally been the privileged languages in England. In the late sixteenth century they still carried a great deal of social prestige. Anyone of advanced learning would know Latin, and perhaps even a little Greek; those of social pretensions would learn French as a matter of course. Nonetheless, the English were showing deep pride and interest in their native tongue. This interest was not generally shared by other countries, however, and English in this period was not a significant international language.

After grammar school, a boy might pursue higher learning.
Universities   University education in the Middle Ages had been almost
exclusively the preserve of the clergy, but the sixteenth
century witnessed a rising tide of secular students. Sons of the aristocracy
came seeking the sophistication required of a Renaissance gentleman, and
bright young men of lesser status came to prepare themselves for an
intellectual career. There were only two universities in England, Oxford
and Cambridge, each subdivided into a number of semi-independent
colleges. The usual age of matriculation was 15 to 17 years; all students
were boys. The four-year course of study for a Bachelor of Arts included
two terms of grammar (i.e., Latin grammar), four terms of rhetoric, and
five terms of logic, or "dialectic," as well as three terms of arithmetic and
two of music. Candidates for the Master of Arts studied astronomy,
geometry, philosophy (including "natural philosophy," which we would
call science), and metaphysics; the degree required 3 or 4 years of study.
Doctorates, which took 7 to 12 years, were available in divinity, law, and
medicine. University teaching consisted primarily of lectures, and
examinations took the form of oral disputations.[11]

Elizabethan learning tended to be theoretical and old-
Science   fashioned. The Elizabethan age was in many ways a time of
broadening intellectual horizons, but Elizabethan science was
still dominated by medieval traditions. Early in the sixteenth century,
Copernicus had proposed the theory of a universe centered around the
sun rather than the earth; in the early seventeenth century, Galileo used a
telescope to discover that Jupiter had moons of its own. Yet the
predominant view of the universe remained that of the ancient astronomer
Ptolemy, who had envisioned the earth at the center of the orbiting
spheres of the heavens. The Elizabethans also adhered to the ancient belief
that all physical matter was made up of the Four Elements, each defined
by two properties: Fire (hot and dry), Air (hot and moist), Water (cold and
moist), and Earth (cold and dry). There were some noteworthy scientific
achievements during this period. In mathematics, for example, Robert
Recorde invented the sign =, and Thomas Hariot added the signs < and >.
However, the great scientific revolution was not to come until the
seventeenth century.[12]

In fact, a noteworthy feature of Elizabethan thought was that science
and magic were not very distinct from each other. Elizabethan scholars
adhered to the theory of "signatures and correspondences": it was
believed that different aspects of the physical world were in some way
related to each other and that these relationships were indicated by
physical resemblances. Such a theory was not fundamentally different
from the principle of sympathetic magic. Many learned people still
believed in alchemy, the mystical art of turning lead into gold. Indeed,
even a noteworthy scholar like the mathematician John Dee believed

deeply in the idea of magic, which he tried to pursue with scientific persistence and precision.

The only alternative institutions of advanced education were the Inns of Court and the Inns of Chancery. The Inns   **Studying the** were residential institutions in London where young men   **Law** could learn English law by attending lectures and observing actual legal and Parliamentary proceedings. The Inns of Court housed roughly 1000 students. Some of them were interested in legal careers, but most were acquiring a knowledge of the law and social graces and contacts which would prepare them for a position in elite society. The Inns of Chancery were for young students seeking a basic grounding in law; studies there might be followed by a stint at the Inns of Court.[13]

For those children not in school, age 6 was about the time for beginning the first steps towards work. Initially,   **Growing Up** children's work would be centered around the home and family. Young boys and girls performed light tasks about the house or helped out by minding younger brothers and sisters. In the country, children were expected to work in the fields at harvest time, when the demand for labor was at its highest, binding and stacking the grain after the harvesters had cut it down. At this age, girls began to learn the skills needed for running a household: spinning, dyeing, cooking, and basic medical skills. Boys in the country often helped with the lighter sorts of field work, such as chasing or shooting birds at sowing time to keep them from eating the seeds, or clearing stones from the fallow fields. Children also helped their mothers by carding wool to be spun into thread, and they might be taught to knit to bring extra revenue into the home.

As children grew in age and strength, they were given more and heavier work, and were increasingly likely to be sent to work outside the home, especially if they were boys whose families did not hold their own land. By the age of 12 or 14, a boy may not have been ready for the heaviest sorts of labor, but he was still expected to be fully integrated into the working economy: the Statute of Artificers declared that any boy aged 12 or older could be compelled to work.

During the teenage years, several points of passage marked a young man or woman's integration into the adult world. By age 14, those children not of the privileged classes or under apprenticeship were expected to be full working participants in the economy. Fourteen was also the youngest age at which children could go through the ceremony of confirmation, which allowed them to receive communion at church; however, the ceremony was often put off until age 16 or even 18. Boys were subject to military service at age 16. The official age of majority was 21. However, the most important turning point in the life of both men and women was marriage.[14]

Marriage and Sexuality
Marriage was the point at which an individual acquired full status in the society. For a man, to be married was to be a householder, and to be a householder was to be an independent person. Independent bachelors were extremely rare. Since marriage meant independence, it could not really take place until the couple were sufficiently established in the economy to support themselves. We tend to think of the Elizabethans marrying very young, an impression that has much to do with the 14-year-old Juliet of Shakespeare's play. In fact, the mean age of marriage was around 27 for men, 24 for women. The age was lower among the upper classes: 24 and 19 among the aristocracy, 27 and 22 among the gentry. Women in London also married a bit younger, the mean age being 22 to 24.

Betrothal was taken very seriously: it had to be conducted before witnesses, and it was considered a legally binding contract—those who reneged on a promise to marry could be prosecuted in the church courts. Often a symbolic exchange of gifts marked the occasion, or the man would give the woman a gift—rings were a common choice, but gloves and bracelets were sometimes chosen. Lovers often exchanged other love tokens during courtship; typical courting-gifts included handkerchiefs, gloves, garters, locks of hair, and sometimes a coin broken in half.

A family. [*Hymns Ancient and Modern*]

Parental permission to marry was required for anyone under age 21, and it was customary even for those who were of age. As part of the marriage arrangements, the bride's parents would bestow on her a dowry, an allotment of money or property of some sort that she would bring to the marriage.

Prior to the actual marriage, the "banns" were asked in the parish church on three successive Sundays. The banns were a form of marriage announcement; their main purpose was to provide an opportunity for people to reveal any impediments to the marriage. The marriage would be called off if the couple was closely related to each other or if there was a prior betrothal or marriage.

The wedding itself was celebrated in the church, and was marked by the man's placing a wedding ring on the woman's ring finger. It was also the practice for women to take their husbands' surname. The marriage was recorded in the parish register, which served the legal role of the modern marriage certificate. The married couple were legally required to live together. Separation was only permitted by court order, and only in such extreme circumstances as cruelty or adultery. In these cases the separated couple were to remain celibate, and the wife could receive alimony. Full divorce was very rare, but was possible if the couple proved to have been related to each other prior to marriage or if the man was found to be permanently impotent.[15]

Anyone who has read Shakespeare is aware of the Elizabethan penchant for bawdiness. The Elizabethans could be remarkably frank about sexuality—after all, their society allowed for comparatively little physical or social privacy, and therefore less isolation between people's sexual and public lives. However, it was important for women of any standing not to compromise their reputation for chastity. The standard for men was not quite as strict—to frequent brothels, for example, was considered immoral and disreputable but would not disqualify a man from a successful public life. Incontinence (fornication and adultery) were punishable by the church courts, or "bawdy courts" as they were popularly known. The church courts could also impose child support on a man who fathered an illegitimate child. Nevertheless, Elizabethan society was fairly permissive in the case of intercourse between a betrothed couple, which was illegal, but rarely punished.

The rapidly growing population and relatively high rates of mortality dictated that the population of Elizabethan England was rather young. Still, a 40-year old was not thought to be elderly. In fact, the forties and **Aging and Life Expectancy** fifties were considered the prime of a man's life. If any age marked the beginning of old age, it would be 60: laboring people were no longer required by law to work after that age, nor was one liable for military service. It has been estimated that nearly 10% of the population were age 60 or older. Nonetheless, the prevalence of disease and the primitive level of medicine meant that illness could easily end a life long before its prime. Life expectancy at birth was only about 48 years, although anyone who made it through the first 30 years was likely to live for another 30. Life expectancy varied from place to place—it was particularly low in the cities, where crowded conditions and poor sanitation increased the dangers of disease.[16]

The low life expectancy of Elizabethans was primarily the
Sickness and result of disease, aggravated by poor sanitary conditions.
Medicine Health conditions were worsened by the omnipresence of
vermin: rats were common, and lice a perennial source of
discomfort. Common diseases included smallpox, malaria, stones,
venereal diseases (especially syphilis), dysentery, influenza, and measles.
Typhus was a frequent problem in crowded living conditions; it was rife
in jails and among soldiers and sailors. Among sailors, scurvy was also
common. A less serious but very common ailment was toothache:
dentistry was even more primitive than medicine, and the means of tooth
care were very poor.[17]

Diseases often came and went in cycles. At the beginning of
Elizabeth's reign there was an epidemic of "New Ague," perhaps a form
of influenza, that lasted from 1557 to 1559. There was a particularly
serious outbreak of smallpox in 1562, which, surprisingly, struck the
upper classes hardest of all: Elizabeth herself almost died of the disease.

The most dreaded disease of all was the plague, or bubonic plague,
which had first come to Europe in the fourteenth century, and continued
to be a problem in England until the late seventeenth century (it is still
found in some parts of the world today). The plague is carried by the flea
Xenopsylla cheopis, which normally lives on rats. If plague-carrying fleas
transfer to a human host, there is a possibility they will communicate the
disease and cause an outbreak of bubonic plague, with a mortality rate of
about 50%. If the plague enters a person's pulmonary system, it can
become pneumonic plague, an even more virulent and deadly form of the
disease. Pneumonic plague can be transmitted directly from person to
person, and its mortality rate is near 100%.

During the sixteenth century, the plague was largely an urban
phenomenon and struck most severely in the summer. Epidemics
commonly came from the Netherlands to London, whence they might
spread to other towns, although occurences in any given town were often
independent of each other. London was visited by the plague in 1563,
1578-79, 1582, 1592-93, and 1603. The worst epidemics in London were
those of 1563 and 1603, which may have had mortality rates of almost 1 in
4; even worse was the outbreak in Norwich in 1578-79, which claimed
nearly 30% of the town's population. Children and the poor were
especially at risk.

The problem of disease was aggravated by the inability of medical
science to treat it or even understand it. The medical profession in
Elizabethan England was largely shaped by structures inherited from the
Middle Ages. At the top of the hierarchy of medical practitioners was the
physician, a university-trained theorist who specialized in diagnosis and
prescription of medicines. These medicines were provided by the
apothecary, who was considered a tradesman and therefore far below the

status of the physician, although he did belong to one of the most privileged and prestigious trades in England. Also ranking below the physician was the surgeon, who specialized in what we would call operations. Below the surgeon was the barber-surgeon, who performed similar procedures. Simple barbers also practiced basic forms of surgery, including teeth-cleaning and dentistry. In the latter part of Elizabeth's reign, there may have been one licensed medical practitioner for every 400 people in London. Outside of the formal medical hierarchy were the unlicensed practitioners, who typically practiced medicine only on a part-time basis. These included folk healers, midwives, and a fair number of outright quacks. Women often received some basic medical training as a part of their preparation for managing a household, and even an aristocratic lady might engage in charitable healing for her poorer neighbors.

If the structure of the medical profession was old-fashioned, its medical theories were even more so. By and large, there had been few major developments in medicine since the Middle Ages. Physiological theory was based on the ancient idea of the Four Humors, corresponding to the Four Elements: Melancholy (cold and dry, like Earth), Blood (hot and moist, like Air), Phlegm (cold and moist, like Water), and Choler (hot and dry, like Fire). Physicians often attributed illness to an imbalance of these humors and treated it by prescribing foods and medicines whose properties were thought to be opposite to those of the excessive humor. Surgical practitioners may have been somewhat more effective, as the mechanics of the body were better understood than its biology. Yet surgery was also fairly primitive—one of the commonest surgical procedures was bloodletting, whereby blood was removed from the patient either by an incision on a vein or by applying a leech (it was believed that this could help rid the patient of "bad blood" that might be causing illness).

As death approached, a person would be called upon to make a will, if this had not yet been done (estates under £5 did **Death and** not require a will). The will related principally to moveable **Burial** property, since most landholdings had to be passed on according to the custom of the holding. Among the upper classes and in open-field areas, land was passed on by primogeniture, the eldest son inheriting all of it; this would prevent the landholding from being broken up into pieces too small to support the landholder's needs. Woodland areas were more likely to follow "partible inheritance," whereby each of the sons was given a share of the land.

When a person was on the deathbed, the parish bell would toll. This was called the "passing bell," and was a signal for all hearers to pray for the dying person. After the death, there would be one short peal; from its sound the hearers could tell whether the deceased was male or female.

The deceased would be laid out at home; indeed, since hospitals were not used for acute medical treatment, death, like birth, typically happened at home. The corpse was then brought to the churchyard, where the priest met it at the gate to begin the religious ceremony of burial. Church bells would ring just before and after the burial ceremony. The privileged would be buried in coffins, often within the church under elaborate wood, brass, or stone markers bearing the effigies of the deceased. Ordinary folk were buried in the churchyard in a simple woolen shroud in unmarked graves. The funeral of an important person was often an occasion for almsgiving and a public feast. As baptism and marriage were recorded in the parish register, so too was burial, the ceremony of the third great passage of life.[18]

A deathbed scene. [Hindley]

4

Cycles of Time

THE DAY

For most Elizabethans the day began just before dawn, at cockcrow—or, strictly speaking, third cockcrow, since the cock would crow first at midnight and again about halfway to dawn. Artificial light was expensive and generally feeble, so it was vital to make the most of daylight. This meant, of course, that the daily schedule varied from season to season, dawn being at around 3:30 in the summer and 7 in the winter. According to law, from mid-September to mid-March laborers were supposed to begin work at dawn, and in other months at 5. Markets typically opened at dawn, and businesses at 7.

Portable clocks and watches were available to the Elizabethans, but they were expensive. Most people marked time by the hourly ringing of church and civic bells; there were also public sundials and clock towers. Time was invariably reckoned by the hour of the clock: normally only the hour, half-hour, quarter-hour, and sometimes the eighth-hour were counted, rather than the hour and minute—in fact, clocks and watches had no minute hands. In the country, people were more likely to reckon time by natural phenomena—dawn, sunrise, midday, sunset, dusk, midnight, and the crowing of the cock.

Mornings were always cold. Fire was the only source of heat, and household fires would have been banked from the previous night as a precaution against burning down the house. If there were servants in the house, they rose first and rekindled the fires before their employers left the warmth of their beds; the servants might even warm their employers' clothes. After rising, people would wash their face and hands. As there was no hot water available until someone heated it on the fire, most people had to wash with cold water (again, those who had servants could be spared this hardship). After washing, one could get dressed—since people often slept in their shirts, this might just mean pulling on the overgarments. It was customary to say prayers before beginning the day, and children were expected to ask their parents' blessing: they knelt before their parents, who placed a hand on their heads and invoked God's favor.

Some people ate breakfast right away, while others did a bit of work first—a typical time for breakfast was around 6:30. The law allowed a half-hour breakfast break for laboring people, and perhaps half an hour for a "drinking" later in the morning. Work was interrupted at midday for dinner, which took place around 11 or noon. By law, laborers were to be allowed an hour's break for this meal, probably their main meal of the day.

After dinner, people returned to work. In the heat of the summer afternoon, between mid-May and mid-August, country folk might nap for an hour or two; the law provided for a half-hour break for sleep for laborers at the same time of year. It also allowed a possible half-hour drinking in the afternoon. Work would continue until supper; according to law, laborers were to work until sundown in winter (around 5 PM on the shortest day), 7 or 8 o'clock in the summer. For commoners, supper was generally a light meal relative to dinner.

Bedtime was around 9 in the winter, 10 in the summer. As in the morning, people would say prayers and children would ask their parents' blessing before bed. Candles were extinguished at bedtime, although wealthy people sometimes left a single candle lit as a "watch light" (the hearth was a good place for this). Household fires were raked, or covered enough to keep them from burning themselves out, without allowing them to die entirely. As a result, nighttime

Time	Activity
4	Bed
-	Rise, Prayers, Wash
5	Work
-	
6	
-	Breakfast
7	
-	
8	
-	
9	Break
-	
10	
-	
11	
-	
Noon	Dinner
-	
1	
-	
2	
-	
3	
-	Break
4	
-	
5	
-	
6	
-	
7	
-	Supper
8	
-	Prayers
9	Bed

The shape of a working man's day as laid out in the Statute of Artificers. The shaded areas are times of work.

tended to be very cold and very dark—people often kept a chamber-pot next to the bed to minimize the discomfort of attending to nighttime needs! The wealthy often had special nightshirts, but commoners probably just slept in their underwear—shirts and breeches for men, smocks for women. A woman might wear a coif to keep her head warm, and a men might wear a nightcap.

Bedtime more or less corresponded to the hour of curfew, after which people were not supposed to be out on the streets. Both town and country streets tended to be very dark at night, although some towns had laws requiring householders to put lanterns outside their doors. It was assumed that nobody who was outside at night had any honest business, and towns had "watches," or patrols of civilian guards, who roamed the streets to keep an eye on matters and arrest anyone they found wandering after curfew.

A night-watchman, called a "bellman" from the bell he carries. [Hatcher]

The exact structure of the day depended on one's position in society. The orderly schedule described above presupposes a working person. People in the upper classes had more diverse schedules. Some were highly disciplined, and would follow a course of daily activity as demanding as that of a laborer. Others might rise later, spend several hours at dinner, begin their evening meal at 5 or 6, and perhaps carouse late into the night.[1]

THE WEEK

Elizabethans generally worked from Monday to Saturday, although many had Saturday afternoon off. Markets took place on regular days of the week—Wednesday and Saturday mornings were the commonest times. Wednesday, Friday, and Saturday were fasting days when no meat was to be eaten, except for fish. This requirement had been established for religious reasons by the medieval church, and was revived by Queen Elizabeth in order to foster the fishing fleet; it does not appear to have been meticulously obeyed, especially on Wednesdays and Saturdays.

Thursday afternoon was commonly a half-holiday for schoolchildren. Thursday and Sunday were the big nights for food—they were often occasions for roasts. Saturday afternoon was often a half-holiday for workers, and Saturday night was a favored time for carousing among common people since they did not have to work the next day. Saturday, coming at the end of the work week, was the typical day for washing and laundry; if possible, people would wear clean clothes on Sunday morning for church.

Sunday was the Sabbath. Everyone in England was required by law to attend church services in the morning, under stiff penalties. On every second Sunday afternoon the parish priest was required to offer religious instruction for the young people of the parish. After church, people were customarily allowed to indulge in games and pastimes; Sunday was the principal occasion for diversion and entertainment. However, many people of Puritanical leanings felt that such activities violated the holiness of the Sabbath, so there was often vocal opposition to such entertainments. Church services were also

A sermon in church. [Holinshed]

supposed to be held on Wednesdays and Fridays, although attendance was not compulsory.[2]

THE ELIZABETHAN YEAR

The basic reckoning of the passage of the year was similar to ours today, with a few important differences. To begin with, the number of the year did not change on New Year's Day. The English calendar had come down from the Romans, for whom January 1 was the first day of the year. Accordingly this was called New Year's Day and was observed as an official holiday as the Feast of the Circumcision of Christ. However, the number of the year did not actually change until March 25, the Feast of the Annunciation. England differed from the Continent in this respect. The day that a sixteenth-century Frenchman (and a modern person) would consider January 1, 1589 would be called January 1, 1588 in sixteenth-century England. Educated Englishmen sometimes dealt with this problem by writing the date as 1 January 1588/9. On March 25 the year would be written as 1589, and England would be in line with the rest of Europe until January 1 came around again.

To make things even more confusing, England was using a slightly different calendar from most of Western Europe (the exceptions being the other Protestant countries and certain Italian city-states). This was the Julian Calendar, so named because it had been introduced by Julius Caesar. This calendar had leap-years, which actually made the Julian year slightly longer than the actual solar year. The difference was slight, but over the centuries there had accumulated a 10-day discrepancy—so that, for example, the Spring Equinox, which should have fallen on March 21, fell on March 11. In 1582 Pope Gregory XIII established the Gregorian Calendar, which we still use today, by which three out of four years ending in -00 (e.g., 1900) are not leap-years. This calendar was much more accurate, but England was so fiercely anti-Catholic that it did not follow the Pope's lead until 1752. As a result, whenever you crossed the English Channel to France you jumped 10 days forward on the calendar, and you jumped 10 days backwards on your return![3]

The seasons as they were known to the Elizabethans were naturally more like those in England today rather than those familiar to North Americans. Spring was reckoned to begin in February, when the ground thawed and planting began; this season was often equated with Lent, the six weeks before Easter, when Christians traditionally abstained from eating meat. Summer began in May, when the Lenten fast and the heavy work of spring was over and the warm weather of summer began. Autumn came when the harvest began in August (the season was also called Harvest, but not usually Fall). Winter arrived in November when the grass died and animals had to be brought in from pasture.

In addition to the cycle of the seasons, the year was shaped by the festive and religious calendar of holy days, also called feasts. Every official holiday was ostensibly religious, with the exception of Accession Day (November 17), commemorating Elizabeth's accession to the throne. Nonetheless, holidays had their secular side as well: like modern-day Christmas and Easter, religious holidays had accumulated secular elements that sometimes swallowed up their religious component. By law, everyone was to attend church on holy days as well as Sundays, and to take communion three times a year, generally on Easter, Whitsun, and Christmas. People did not necessarily observe this law rigidly, but most probably took communion at least at Easter. The observance of any holy day began on the evening before, which was called the "eve" of the holy day—the principal surviving example is Christmas Eve. The eve of a major holy day was supposed to be observed by the same fast as on Fridays and in Lent.

The Protestant reformation in England had done away with many of the traditional saints' days and other religious holidays observed by the Catholic Church, and there continued to be pressures from Protestant reformers in the Church of England to take the process even further. Reformers especially objected to holiday names ending in -mas (like Christmas), because of the allusion to the Catholic ceremony of the Mass. However, these traditional celebrations were firmly established in the popular mind—especially among country folk, for whom such festivals gave shape both to the year and to their lives.

On the calendar following, the days listed in **boldface** were official holidays sanctioned by the Church of England (in some cases they fell on Sundays and would not have been working days anyway). The remainder of the holy days listed were included in the church calendar but were not observed as holidays. In addition to the feasts listed below, many parishes observed the feast day of the patron saint of the parish church: the celebration was known as the Wake Day or Dedication Day, and might be observed with the same sorts of activities as a village ale (see Whitsunday, under May). Finally, many towns had annual fairs appointed for a certain day of the year. Most fairs took place between May and November, although there were a few from December to April.[4]

JANUARY

In this month the ground was too frozen to be worked, so the husbandman would be busy with maintenance jobs around the holding, such as trimming woods and hedges, repairing fences, and clearing ditches.

1   **The Circumcision of Christ** (*New Year's Day*). New Year's Day came in the midst of the Christmas season, which ran from Christmas Eve to Twelfth Day, and was generally a time for merrymaking and sociability. People often observed the day with an exchange of gifts: favored choices included apples, eggs, nutmegs, gloves, pins, and oranges studded with cloves. They would also drink the Wassail, a spiced ale traditionally served in a brown bowl; there were traditional wassail songs as part of the ritual.

6   **Epiphany** (*Twelfth Day*). The Twelfth Day of Christmas (reckoned by counting Christmas itself as the first day) was the last day of the Christmas season. The evening before, called Twelfth Night, was traditionally the most riotous holiday of the year, an occasion for folk plays and merriment. One ritual was the serving of a spiced fruitcake with a dried bean and a dried pea inside. A man whose piece contained the bean would become the Lord of Misrule or King, and a woman who got the pea became the Queen; the two would preside together over the festivities. The Wassail Bowl was drunk as at New Year's.

—   *Plow Monday* (*Rock Monday*). This fell on the first Monday after Twelfth Night. On this day plows were blessed, and in parts of England the plowmen drew a plow from door to door soliciting gifts of money. The day also commemorated the work of women, under the name Rock Monday ("rock" is another word for a distaff).

8   *St. Lucian*

13   *St. Hilary*

18   *St. Prisca*

19   *St. Wolfstan*

20   *St. Fabian*

21   *St. Agnes.* According to tradition, a woman who went to bed without supper on the eve of St. Agnes would dream of her future husband.

22   *St. Vincent*

25   *The Conversion of St. Paul.* Elizabethan country folk believed that the weather on St. Paul's Day would reveal the future of the year: a fair day boded a fair year, a windy day presaged wars, and a cloudy day foretold plague.

FEBRUARY

This was considered the first month of spring. In February the snow would leave, the ground would thaw, and the husbandman could begin preparing the fields designated for the spring or Lenten crop. He would spread manure on the fields and plow them, and then begin to sow his peas, beans, and oats. Plowing was with horses usually, occasionally oxen in heavy soils.

2   Feast of the Purification of Mary (*Candlemas*). The name Candlemas derived from the tradition of bearing candles in a church procession on this day, although the custom was generally suppressed under the Protestant church.

3 *St. Blaise.* On this day the countrywomen traditionally went visiting each other, and burned any distaffs they found in use.

5 *St. Agatha*

14 *St. Valentine.* In Elizabethan times as today, this day was a celebration of love. Men and women drew one another's names by lot to determine who would be whose valentine, pinning the lots on their bosom or sleeve and perhaps exchanging gifts.

24 St. Matthias the Apostle

— *Shrove Tuesday* (*Shrovetide*). Shrovetide was the day before Ash Wednesday, falling between February 3 and March 9. This holiday was the last day before the fasting season of Lent. On the Continent this day was celebrated with wild abandon, reflected in the modern Mardi Gras. The English version was more subdued but still involved ritual feasting and violence. On this day it was traditional to eat fritters and pancakes. It was also a day for playing football (a game much rougher than any of its modern namesakes), and for the sport of "cockthrashing" or "cockshys." In cockthrashing, the participants tied a cock to a stake and threw sticks at it: they payed the owner of the cock a few pence for each try, and a person who could knock down the cock and pick it up before the cock regained its feet won the cock as a prize. In towns, this was often a day for the apprentices to riot; their violence was often aimed against those who trangressed sexual mores, especially prostitutes. The two days previous were sometimes called Shrove Sunday and Shrove Monday.

— *The First Day of Lent* (*Ash Wednesday*). Lent began on the Wednesday before the 6th Sunday before Easter (between February 4 and March 10). The medieval church had forbidden the eating of meat other than fish during Lent. Although the religious basis for this restriction was no longer a factor, Queen Elizabeth decided to keep the restriction in place as a means of boosting England's fishing industry. The name Ash Wednesday was officially disapproved, as it smacked of Catholicism, but it was still commonly used. Lent was sometimes observed by setting up an effigy called a Jack-a-Lent and pelting it with sticks and stones: as this season was a season for fasting, the Jack-a-Lent symbolized all the hardships in the life of a commoner.

MARCH

In March the husbandman would sow his barley, the last of the Lenten crops. This was also the time to begin work on the garden, a task that generally fell to the woman of the house. She might also do the spring cleaning in this month.

1   *St. David.* David was the patron saint of Wales, and Welshmen traditionally wore leeks in their hats on this day.
2   *St. Chad*
7   *St. Perpetua*
12 *St. Gregory*
18 *St. Edward*
21 *St. Benedict*
25 **Feast of the Annunciation of Mary** (*Lady Day in Lent*). The number of the year changed on this day.
—   *Mid-Lent Sunday.* This was the Sunday three weeks before Easter (March 1 to April 4). This day was often called Mothering Sunday: it was traditional for people to visit their mothers on this day.

Breaking the ground. [Hindley]

APRIL

During this month the woman of the house would continue work on the garden, as well as beginning work in the dairy.

3   *St. Richard*
4   *St. Ambrose*
19 *St. Alphege*
23 *St. George.* George was the patron saint of England.
25 **St. Mark the Evangelist**

— **Palm Sunday**. This was one week before Easter Sunday, and it marked the beginning of the Easter Week. The ancient custom of bearing palm leaves or rushes into the church on this day had been suppressed by the Protestant church, although there may well have been conservative parishes where it was still observed.

— **Wednesday before Easter**

— **Thursday before Easter** (*Maundy Thursday*). This was traditionally a day for acts of charity.

— **Good Friday**

— **Easter Eve**

— **Easter**. Easter is a movable feast. It is based on the lunar Jewish calendar, which is why it does not always fall on the same day in the solar calendar we inherited from the Romans. Easter is the first Sunday after the first full moon on or after March 21; if the full moon is on a Sunday, Easter is the next Sunday. This places Easter between March 22 and April 25. Easter marked the end of Lent, and was an occasion for great feasting, as it was once again permissible to eat meat.

— **Monday in Easter Week**

— **Tuesday in Easter Week**

— *Hocktide* (*Hock Monday* and *Hock Tuesday*). The second Monday and Tuesday after Easter. On Hock Monday the young women of the parish would go about the streets with ropes and capture passing men, who had to pay a small ransom to be released; the men would do the same on Hock Tuesday. The money raised would go to the parish funds.

MAY

May was the first month of summer. Now the hard work of spring eased somewhat: this was a prime season for festivals, before heavy work began again with haymaking at the end of June. In this month it was time to weed the winter crops and to plow the fallow fields in preparation for the next season. The woman of the house would sow flax and hemp.

1   **Sts. Philip and Jacob the Apostles** (*May Day*). This day was often celebrated as the first day of summer. Both villagers and townsfolk might travel to the forests and fields to bring back flowers and branches as decorations—and this was notoriously an opportunity for young men and women to engage in illicit union in the woods. There might even be a full-scale summer festival, such as was often celebrated on Whitsunday (see below).

3   *Feast of the Invention of the Cross (Crouchmass)*

6   *St. John the Evangelist*

10 *St. Gordian*

19 *St. Dunstan*

26 *St. Augustine of Canterbury*
— *Rogation Sunday.* This fell five weeks after Easter (April 26 to May 30). This holiday was the time for "beating the bounds": the parishioners would gather with the local curate to walk around the boundary of the parish, reciting prayers and psalms, and asking God for forgiveness of sins and a blessing on the crops, which had by now all been sown. This ceremony helped to identify the traditional borders of the parish.
— **Ascension Day.** This was the Thursday after Rogation Sunday (April 30 to June 3). This was another popular occasion for summer festivals (see Whitsunday below).
— **Whitsunday** (*Pentecost*). Ten days after Ascension (May 10 to June 13). This was perhaps the favorite day for summer festivals, sometimes called "ales," or "mayings" (even when they did not fall in May). Each locality had its own customs, but certain themes were common. There were often folk plays and dramatic rituals, especially ones involving Robin Hood or St. George. Another typical activity was morris dancing, a ritual dance in which the dancers—often just men—wore bells, ribbons, and outlandish attire. The dance sometimes involved other ritual figures: a hobby horse (a man dressed up with a false horse to make him look like a rider), a Maid Marian (typically a man dressed as a woman), and a fool (a jester figure). The occasion might also be marked by displays of banners and by military demonstrations. The celebrants often elected a man and woman to preside over the festival under such names as Summer King and Queen, May King and Queen, or Whitsun Lord and Lady. Many

Morris dancers of the early seventeenth century. [Hatcher]

towns and villages erected a maypole, brightly painted and adorned
with garlands or flags, around which there might be a maypole dance.
Often a temporary hall or tent was erected where the parish would
sell ale, the proceeds going to the parish church.
— **Whitmonday**
— **Whitsun Tuesday**. The two days after Whitsunday, as official
  holidays, often continued the Whitsun festival, and all three days
  together might be called Whitsuntide.
— **Trinity Sunday**. One week after Whitsunday (May 17 to June 20). This
  was another popular day for summer festivals, like that described for
  Whitsun.

JUNE

June was the time to weed the Lenten crops and to wash and shear the
sheep—sheepshearing was often an occasion for merrymaking. At about
Midsummer began the mowing season: the men would go out to the
meadows, where the grass had been allowed to grow long, and cut it
down with scythes in preparation for haymaking.

3   *St. Nichomede*
5   *St. Boniface*
11 *St. Barnabas the Apostle*
17 *St. Botolph*
20 *The Translation of St. Edward*
24 **St. John the Baptist** (*Midsummer*). This festival was an important civic
    occasion, marked by a variety of festivities and displays of communal
    identity. There was often a huge bonfire on St. John's Eve, and it was
    common to stay up late that night. Midsummer was an occasion for
    parades featuring giants, dragons, explosions of gunpowder,
    drumming, military displays, and a march by the local watch and
    community officials.
29 **St. Peter the Apostle**. This holiday was sometimes observed with
    traditions similar to those on the feast of St. John.
30 *Commemoration of St. Paul*

JULY

During this month the mown grass was made into hay: it had to be
laid out in the sun to dry, stacked, and then carted away for storage. It was
crucial that the hay dry properly, as it would otherwise rot. Hay was very
important to the rural economy, since it was fed to horses and cattle,
especially during the winter when they could not graze. July was also a

time for a second plowing of the fallow fields and for gathering hemp, flax, and beans from the garden.

1   *Visitation of Mary*
3   *Translation of St. Martin*
15 *St. Swithun*
20 *St. Margaret*
22 *St. Magdalene*
25 St. James the Apostle
26 *St. Anne*

Making hay while the sun shines. The man on the right has stripped to his shirt in the heat. [Hindley]

AUGUST

August began the hardest time of a husbandman's year, with the harvest of the main crops. There was a great deal of work to be done in a short time, so the entire family was involved and temporary workers were often hired. The men went into the fields with sickles to harvest the grain. Then the cut grain was bound into sheaves, often given by the women and children. The sheaves were stacked and loaded onto carts to be taken away to shelter—as with the hay, it was very important to keep the grain dry lest it rot. The stalks of grain were cut towards the top, leaving the rest of the stalk to be harvested later with a scythe to make straw. The straw was sometimes fed to the livestock (although they did not generally care for it), and was especially useful for making baskets, stuffing beds, thatching roofs, and strewing on the floor.

1   *Lammas*
6   *Transfiguration of Christ*
7   *Name of Jesus*
10 *St. Laurence*
24 St. Bartholomew the Apostle (*Bartholomewtide*)
28 *St. Augustine of Hippo*
29 *The Beheading of St. John the Baptist*

Harvesting. The men have removed their outer garments in the heat; two women are also taking part. At bottom right are a basket and jug—harvest workers brought their food to the fields to save time. [Holinshed]

SEPTEMBER

At the end of harvest, the harvesters celebrated "harvest home," or "hockey." The last sheaf of grain would be brought into the barn with great ceremony, and seed cake was distributed. After the harvest was done, and on rainy days when harvesting was impossible, the husbandman threshed and winnowed. In threshing, the grain was beaten with flails so that the husk would crack open, allowing the seed to come out. Then it was winnowed: the winnowers waved straw fans, blowing away the straw and the broken husks (called chaff). Chaff had uses of its own: it could be fed to livestock, or used for stuffing beds. After harvest was over, the husbandman began work on the winter crop: the winter fields had to be plowed, and the husbandman would begin to sow the rye. This was also the season for gathering fruit from the orchard.

1   *St. Giles*
7   *St. Enurchus the Bishop*
8   *Nativity of Mary* (*Lady Day in Harvest*)

14 *Holy Cross Day (Holy Rood Day).* This was traditionally a day for "nutting," or gathering nuts in the woods.
17 *St. Lambert*
21 **St. Matthew the Apostle**
26 *St. Cyprian*
29 **St. Michael the Archangel** (*Michaelmas*). This day marked the beginning of the agricultural year: all the harvests were in, and the annual accounts could be reckoned up. The day was often observed by eating a goose for dinner.
30 *St. Jerome*

OCTOBER

October it was the time to sow wheat, which had to be done by the end of the month. The end of the wheat sowing was often marked by a feast. This was also a good time to brew ale for the winter.

1   *St. Remigius*
6   *St. Faith*
9   *St. Dennis*
13 *Translation of St. Edward the Confessor*
17 *St. Ethelred*
18 **St. Luke the Evangelist**
25 *St. Crispin*
28 **Sts. Simon and Jude the Apostles**
31 *All Saints' Even*

Sowing. [Hindley]

NOVEMBER

The dairy season ended during this month, and the livestock were brought in from pasture and stalled for the winter. This was the time to slaughter any animals the household planned to eat during the winter, as a means of conserving winter fodder. As the weather began to become too cold for agricultural work, the farmer took time to cleanse the privies, burying the muck in the garden as fertilizer; he might also clean the chimney before the chill of winter set in.

1   **All Saints** (*All Hallows, Hallowmas, Hallontide*)
2   *All Souls*
6   *St. Leonard*
11   *St. Martin.* This day was traditionally associated with the slaughter of animals for the winter.
13   *St. Brice*
15   *St. Machutus*
16   *St. Edmund the Archbishop*
17   **Accession Day** (*Queen's Day, Coronation Day, St. Hugh*). This was the only truly secular holiday: it commemorated Queen Elizabeth's accession to the throne in 1558.
20   *St. Edmund King and Martyr*
22   *St. Cicely*
23   *St. Clement*
25   *St. Katharine*
30   **St. Andrew the Apostle**
—   The season of Advent began on the nearest Sunday to the feast of St. Andrew (i.e. between November 27 and December 3). People were supposed to observe the same fast as in Lent, although few actually did.

DECEMBER

This was one of the least demanding times of the husbandman's year, and one of the principal seasons for merrymaking and sociability, especially around Christmas. Wood was split during this season; otherwise, relatively little outdoors work was suitable for this month, so it was a good time to sit at home maintaining and repairing tools in preparation for the next year. The winter snows arrived sometime in December.

6   *St. Nicholas*
8   *Conception of Mary*

13 *St. Lucy*
21 **St. Thomas the Apostle**
25 **Christmas**. Christmas, along with Easter, was one of the two most important holidays of the year. The Christmas season lasted for the full 12 days of Christmas, from Christmas Eve to Twelfth Day (January 6); it was a time for dancing, gymnastics, indoor games (especially cards), and folk plays. Elizabethan Christmas rituals in many respects resembled some of the traditions still in use today. People decorated their homes with rosemary, bay, holly, ivy, and mistletoe; and they enjoyed a great dinner, sang songs, and exchanged gifts. People often chose a Christmas Lord, Prince, or King to preside over the festivities. Nuts were a traditional food for Christmas, in addition to festive pies and cakes and "brawn," a type of pickled pork. Warmth and light were an important part of the Christmas festivities, as observed in the burning of a Yule Log and the lighting of many candles. Christmas Eve was a highly festive occasion when people often drank the Wassail (see its description under January 1).
26 **St. Stephen the Martyr**
27 **St. John the Evangelist**
28 **The Holy Innocents' Day** (*Childermas*)
29 *St. Thomas of Canterbury*
31 *St. Silvester the Bishop*

5

The Living Environment

THE HOME

"A man's house is his castle," wrote the jurist Sir Edward Coke in the early seventeenth century. The sentiment still resonates today, yet the meaning of one's house for people in Coke's day was not the same as it is for us. Today the house is a place of refuge, the place for private life. Although these trends had roots in the Elizabethan period, the distinction between a person's private and public life was much less obvious then than it is today. For the Elizabethan, the home was not just a private space: it was the focus of all aspects of life. People were born in their homes, they died in their homes, and often they worked in their homes too.

Then as now, the nature of one's dwelling varied between the city and the country, as well as between social classes. There were also distinctive building traditions in each area of the country, as well as differences of design between any one house and another. For the sake of simplicity, we will concentrate on three primary types: the rural cottage, the gentleman's manor house, and the town house.

The houses of the country folk were based on jointed frames of oak: instead of nails, which would be too weak, the timbers were carved with tongues (tenons) and slots (mortices) so that the whole frame fit together, with the tenons secured in their mortices by thick wooden pegs. Ideally the frame would rest on a stone foundation, since prolonged contact with moisture in the ground would eventually cause the timbers to rot. However, the

The Peasant House

cheapest sorts of structures simply had their main posts sunk into the ground.

The basic frame carried the weight of the house, and it had to be filled in to make the walls. The typical means of filling was a technique known as "wattle and daub." Wattling consisted of upright wooden stakes fixed at the top and bottom into the horizontal timbers of the house, with pliant sticks woven between them. The wattling created a rough base for the wall, which was then covered with daub—a mixture of clay and dung with straw or horsehair added for strength. The walls could be plastered on the inside and outside; sometimes the outside was whitewashed with a lime solution to prevent rain from washing away the clay too quickly.

Most English houses in this period were constructed according to some version of this technique. In some places, lath and plaster often took the place of wattle and daub: instead of wattling, the frame was filled in with horizontal strips of wood, which served as a base for a plaster covering. Those who had the money might use bricks to fill in the frame; this provided greater security against fire but it was much more costly. In areas where stone was plentiful, particularly the west and north, the house might be built of stone, but in other parts of the country stone was too expensive except for the very rich.

Shakespeare's house: a classic example of timber-framed construction.
[Gentleman]

The commonest form of roofing was thatch, a very thick covering made with straw or reeds. A thatch roof was the best for keeping the house warm, as the thickly layered stalks provided good insulation and kept the rising heat from escaping through the top of the house. Unfortunately, it could also be a haven for vermin, and it posed a serious fire risk as well. Alternatives were clay tiles, slate, or shingles, depending on the circumstances—tiles were expensive, as was slate (except in areas where it was naturally plentiful), while shingles were only readily available in regions with plenty of trees. Some wooden roofs were covered with lead to reduce the risk of fire, though again this increased the cost.

The peasant house was commonly just a two-room cottage. The front door led into an all-purpose hall, used for cooking, eating, and working. An inner door in the hall gave access to a parlor or chamber, which was typically the sleeping-room for the householder and his wife; young children slept here too. Slightly more prosperous households had an additional workroom for food preparation and similar tasks; this was separated from the hall by a narrow cross-passage running between the front and back doors.

The doors were made of wood and might be secured with bolts, although it was not uncommon even for ordinary people to have locks. An especially prosperous householder might even have glass windows, made of many small panes held together with lead. Most homes probably had wooden shutters, although thin layers of horn or oiled linen were alternatives that let in light while keeping out the wind.

The simplest form of cottage had an open hearth in the center of the room, with the smoke escaping through a hole in the roof. However, chimneys were becoming increasingly common. The chimney was sometimes made of wattle and daub, sometimes of brick to reduce the fire hazard. The hearth was lined with stones or bricks for the same reason. The existence of a chimney would make possible an upper floor (since otherwise a second floor would block the escape of the smoke). There was rarely a third floor; most homes probably had just one floor with perhaps some planking laid on the overhead beams to create a bit of additional space. Cellars were rare; in the simplest cottages the floor might be no more than packed dirt, although those who could afford them had wooden floors. Access to upper levels was provided by ladders in simpler cottages, or by permanent stairs in better cottages.

The country cottage was located on a small plot of land called a "croft." In regions of champion agriculture the croft **The Croft** was separate from the farmer's actual holding of agricultural land; in woodland areas the house typically stood in the midst of the holding. In addition to the house, the croft included outbuildings such as animal sheds and pens, storage buildings for tools and provisions, and— in the case of a more prosperous householder—perhaps a separate kitchen, brewhouse, dairy, or mill house. The croft also supported a small garden. Here the woman of the house raised flax and hemp for linen and canvas, hops for brewing, and whatever plants were needed for household use: trees to supply fruits and nuts, vegetables, herbs for cooking and for household medicines, and perhaps some flowers. Some crofts had cobblestone courtyards, and walkways might be covered with sawdust to prevent them from becoming too muddy.[1]

The Manor House

During this period the gap between the houses of the rich and the poor was increasing, as new and more elaborate styles of architecture evolved through which the wealthy could proclaim their social status. The compact medieval manor house, designed for defensibility, had given way in the sixteenth century to a more expansive and luxurious style that combined traditional medieval elements with new influences from Renaissance Italy. The stately Elizabethan home was typically based on an E or H shape, derived ultimately from the layout of medieval manor homes. The middle section (the vertical part of the E or the horizontal part of the H) was a large hall, the principal public space of the house. It was flanked on one side by the family wing, which included the various private chambers of the family, and on the other by the service wing, which housed the kitchens, stores, and other working areas. Manor houses might be built on a timber frame filled in with brick, or of solid brick or stone.

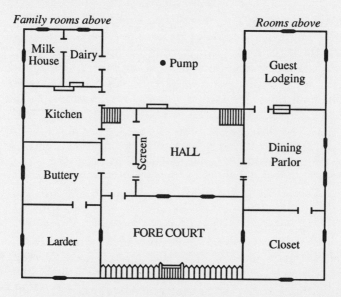

Plan of a country house for a prosperous commoner or a minor gentleman, after an early seventeenth-century design by Gervase Markham. The "closet" is a private room in the guest wing, the larder is for storing food, the buttery for drinks. Private meals would take place in the dining parlor, public ones in the hall. The screen is a wooden partition dividing the hall from the passageway to the main door, the service rooms, and the family's rooms above—it served to cut down on drafts. [Singman]

These homes were distinguished from their medieval predecessors by their open design. Aristocratic feuding and civil wars during the Middle Ages required a manor home surrounded by a stout wall, with the exterior walls of the house itself built to resist assault. By Elizabeth's time only a light wall would enclosed the grounds, and the building itself abounded in windows. However, many people continued to live in houses of medieval origin—the aristocratic manor hall of the Middle Ages had been solidly built, so that plenty of them still stood in Elizabeth's day, although owners often attempted at least superficial alterations to adjust them to contemporary tastes.

Building construction. [Holinshed]

Townhouses were similar in construction to those of country folk, save that they tended to be taller and closer together; they might even be built several in a row, since space was scarce in urban areas. Instead of wattle and daub, the walls were of wooden lathes covered with plaster; the best houses were of brick or stone. Two, three, or even four stories were typical; the upper floors might be built to jut out into the street over the lower ones, creating additional space. There was likely to be a proper floor and a cellar; however, there were still many simple cottage-type townhouses. The larger towns generally tried to forbid thatched roofs in favor of tile or wood covered with lead: a fire in the country might destroy only one house, but in the crowded conditions of the town it could lead to a major public disaster.

The Townhouse

If the owner was a tradesman or craftsman, the front of the ground floor might serve as a shop. The window shutter might swing downward into the street to create a kind of shop counter, with a canopy overhead to protect against rain. The family slept above the main floor. Additional space in the upper floors might be occupied by servants or apprentices, or rented to laboring folk too poor to have a house of their own—then as now, taking on boarders was a common way for a family to supplement its income. Boarders, like servants and apprentices, were likely to eat with the family, as there were probably no separate kitchen arrangements. Individual rooms were rather small, often as little as 10 to 15 feet on a side. The townhouse often had a garden in back.

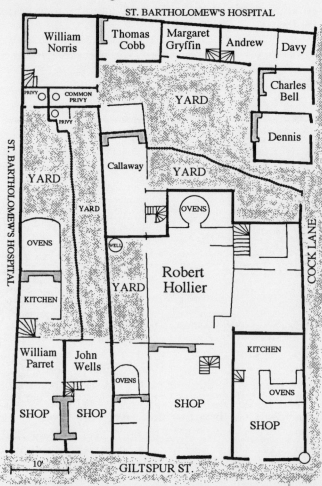

Plan of a block of London townhouses. Most of the rooms had a chamber above, sometimes another chamber or a garret above that. The first and third tenements on Giltspur Street belonged to bakers—hence the large ovens. The second was occupied by a maker of horse harnesses in the early seventeenth century. The tenement at the corner was a victualing house, the equivalent of a restaurant, with a hall above the main floor, probably for customers. The image of a pie was displayed as a shop sign at the corner, which gave the block the name of "Pye Corner." The small houses off the yard at the top shared the common privy.
[Singman]

The nature and use of the house allowed for very little privacy. Young children slept in their parents' room, servants sometimes in the same room as their masters. Four family members living in a two-room cottage had little private time, and a family living in town might share its space with servants, apprentices, or boarders. Tradesmen and craftsmen commonly worked at home, as did the woman of the house, whose domestic responsibilities were not limited to the immediate needs of the household but included the production of goods for sale. Of course, things were different for the wealthy and privileged, whose houses had many rooms and ample opportunities for private space. Even so, such houses always had a significant domestic staff; their responsibilities were both in the working areas of the house and in the private areas, where they served as personal servants to the householder and family. Furthermore, the upper classes were also likely to work at home. There were few public buildings, so that an aristocrat involved in government used his private house for public business; similarly, even a rich merchant's office was likely to be at home.

Conferring at a table. [Holinshed]

The floor of a room in a commoner's house might be covered with straw or rushes; better houses sometimes had **The Interior** rush mats, which would be patterned and quite attractive. Loose straw or rushes might be mixed with sweet-smelling herbs; herbs and flowers were sometimes strewn upon the floors in fine houses too. Wormwood was strewn as a means of discouraging fleas. Carpets were used as coverings for furniture rather than the floor, and only in well-to-do households. The walls might be plain or plastered; the wealthy would have them covered with wooden paneling, which were sometimes brightly painted. Plastered or paneled ceilings were also featured in rich people's houses. For decoration and extra warmth, the walls were often adorned with tapestries (for the wealthy) or with painted cloths (for the rest). These might depict biblical or legendary scenes; a painted cloth might even reflect folkloric themes such as the tale of Robin Hood. Alternatively, the walls themselves might be painted. Windows often had curtains, even in the houses of common folk.[2]

Although the average Elizabethan home was small and crude, it was not necessarily squalid. Even ordinary people were reasonably concerned to keep their houses in good order. The housewife used a broomstick (like the one now associated with witches) to keep the floor clean; if rushes or straw had been strewn, they were swept out periodically. When a goose died, the housewife saved the wing for dusting—the original featherduster!

Light and Heat   The homes of the wealthy, lavishly endowed with windows, were airy and bright; but in poorer houses, where glass would have been too expensive, window-openings had to be few and small to conserve heat; such houses were rather dark even in the daytime. After dark, light was provided by beeswax or tallow candles. Wax burned more brightly and cleanly but was very expensive. Tallow was a cheaper alternative, being derived from animal fats that were a natural by-product of cooking.

A candlestick. [Hoornstra]

Candles were not as simple to use as they are today. As the candle burned down, the wick remained long and and the candle receded from the flame, which became progressively weaker. To keep the light strong, the wick had to be trimmed at least every half-hour or so. This was a tricky procedure, as trimming it too close would bring the flame too near the candle, melting the candle and wasting precious fuel; one could even put the flame out in the process (the wicks in modern candles are designed to curl as they burn, so the end is burned away and the candle trims itself).

Materials for candlesticks included silver, pewter, brass, clay and wood. Other forms of light were the oil lamp, also fueled with animal fats, and the "rushlight," an iron clip holding a rush that had been dried and soaked in grease.

To provide light outdoors, people used lanterns of pierced metal or with horn or glass panes. It took quite a few artificial lights to provide any significant amount of light (as anyone who has tried to read by candlelight knows). Since the fuel was expensive, most people followed the schedule of the sun, the only source of light that was genuinely cheap and plentiful.

The late sixteenth century was a period of generally cool and wet weather, falling within what climatic historians call the Little Ice Age. Not only was the weather cold, but houses were drafty and poorly insulated. There was no central heating, although prosperous houses sometimes had tile stoves. Otherwise heating was provided by open fires, either on open hearths or in proper fireplaces. Wood or coal served as fuel, but wood was preferred since coal produced a foul smoke. Naturally, the best houses had fireplaces in as many rooms as possible, but ordinary people were unlikely to have more than one hearth. Hot coals from the fire might be placed in an earthen vessel to provide warmth in other parts of the house, but of course this increased the risk of fire.[3]

To the modern eye, an Elizabethan home would seem very sparsely furnished. Much of our furniture today serves **Furnishings** to store our personal possessions, and ordinary Elizabethans owned far fewer possessions—a person who has only two changes of clothing doesn't need a lot of wardrobe space. Furniture was wooden— mostly of oak and other hardwoods. Softwoods such as pine are cheaper nowadays, but pine was rare in Elizabethan England. Furniture was quite durable, since old oak becomes almost as hard as metal.

A boarded stool. [Singman]

Construction was of two general types. The cheapest furniture was "boarded," con-sisting mostly of boards pegged together with wooden dowels. Quality furniture was "joined," assembled with mortice and tenon joints. The wood might be brightly painted, carved, inlaid, or simply coated with a lin-seed-oil finish. Drawers were still quite rare in furniture at this time; doors, lids, and shelves were used instead.

The sparseness of furniture is illustrated by the inventory of a **The Hall** tanner in 1592, whose hall was furnished with a table, 5 joint stools, a chair, a bench, and painted cloths to hang on the walls. As indicated by the inventory, most people sat on stools or benches. Chairs (distinguished by having a back) were relatively rare: as in this tanner's hall, there was often just one, reserved for the head of the household (for this reason the term "chair" is sometimes used today to designate a position of authority, as in "chairman"). The nicest chairs were upholstered, but this was a luxury seen only in wealthy homes; cushions were the more usual means of making a seat comfortable. In the Middle Ages, chairs always had arms as well as backs, but the sixteenth century saw the emergence of the "farthingale" chair: fashionable women wore large hoop-skirts (farthingales) that were too big to fit between the arms of a chair, so the farthingale chair was made without arms. There were also benches with backs, called "settles."

The tanner's table mentioned above was probably a permanent and station- ary piece of furniture, although in some houses they were still using medieval style trestle tables—essentially a table- top mounted on two trestles that could be put up and taken down at will. This style was especially useful in small spaces and in large dining halls that sometimes had to be cleared for other

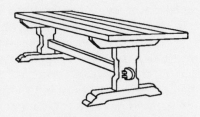

A pegged trestle table. [Singman]

uses. Midway between the two was the style of table illustrated here, which was pegged together but could be disassembled if necessary.

In addition to the items listed in the tanner's inventory, the hall might have a cupboard for storing table gear or some shelves for the same purpose. In some cases the hall would also serve as a kitchen and would be equipped accordingly.[4]

The Bedchamber Like the hall, the typical bedchamber was sparsely furnished. The tanner's inventory listed a table, an old carpet (probably used to cover the table), 2 joint-stools, 2 chairs, a clothes-press, 2 linen chests, 3 painted cloths to hang on the walls, a bed, a flock-bed, a featherbed, 2 bolsters, a pillow, 4 blankets, and a coverlet. The clothes-press was a cupboard fitted with shelves for storing clothes.

Otherwise, clothes would be kept in a chest, the commonest form of storage furniture. The simplest style was the boarded chest, consisting of boards nailed or pegged together. A more sophisticated design was the "paneled" chest, a jointed frame filled in with thin panels. This was considerably lighter than a boarded chest and less subject to cracking—the panels were set in grooves in the frame so they could freely expand and contract with

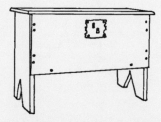

A boarded chest. [Singman]

changes in temperature and humidity that would otherwise strain the wood. A chest might have a small lockable box, or "till," set inside at the top; otherwise, valuables could be stored in a small coffer.

The tanner's bed fittings were typical for a well-to-do craftsman. The bed mentioned in the inventory was probably his wooden bedstead, which would support the mattress on slats of wood, on heavy webbing-type cloth, or—most likely—on a woven lattice of rope topped with a straw mat. The bedstead might hung about with curtains. This kept out the night air, which was considered unhealthy; it also kept in warmth, a very important consideration since the fires were put out at night and there was no heating in the room. The tanner's "flock-bed" would be made of canvas or ticking stuffed with wool; if quilted, it might be called a mattress. This particular tanner was obviously fairly prosperous, for on top of his flock-bed he had a featherbed, another mattress stuffed with feathers, which was much more comfortable than the flock-bed alone. Someone who lacked a featherbed might have a flock bed resting on a "pallet," a bed stuffed with straw, or a "chaff bed," filled with oat or wheat chaff. Poor people slept on the pallet or chaff bed by itself, which might lie directly on the ground. Ticking was of linen or canvas and was characteristically striped, as it has remained for centuries.

The tanner's bolsters were a kind of oversized pillow made like the flock-bed. A bolster went across the head of the bed, with the pillow (probably stuffed with feathers) on top. A person would sleep between two linen sheets covered by blankets or quilts, his back supported on the bolster and his head resting on the pillow. The bed was often covered with a decorative and protective bedspread. A full bedstead might have a "trundle" or "truckle" bed underneath for a servant or children; this could be rolled underneath the main bed during the day. Because nights were so cold, people sometimes used a "warming pan," a covered metal pan fitted with a handle and filled with warm coals, to heat up the bed. Beds were often shared by unmarried people of the same sex for reasons of space and economy—in an ordinary family, for example, young siblings were likely not to have beds of their own.[5]

One major difference between Elizabethan home life and our own was the lack of running water. In the country, water was fetched from a stream or well; in towns, there were also public fountains fed by water **Water, Washing, and Sanitation** pipes, and professional water-carriers who brought the water door to door. The house would have barrels or a cistern for storing water, from which the household could draw water as needed.

In the absence of faucets, people washed with a jug (often called a "ewer") and a basin. Those lucky enough to have servants could achieve the effect of running water by having it poured from the jug into the basin; otherwise you had to pour it yourself! Soap was a mixture of some sort of fat or oil with lye, an alkaline solution that the Elizabethans obtained by percolating water through wood ashes. Sometimes scents were added as well. After washing, people dried themselves with a linen towel. People were generally very good about washing their face and hands, which they generally did every morning; they also washed their hands before a meal and after defecating.

Bathing of the whole body was infre-
quent—this is hardly surprising considering the
drafty rooms and very real danger of catching a
chill, which in this period could be deadly.
When people did bathe, they used a wooden
tub before the fire, allowing for warmth and a
ready supply of hot water. Teeth were cleaned
with a linen tooth-cloth, and various recipes
existed for liquids and powders to help in cleaning them.[6]

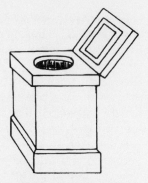

A sixteenth-century close-
stool. There would be a
chamber-pot inside.
[Singman]

The simplest Elizabethan equivalent of the
modern toilet was the metal or clay chamber-
pot (commonly called a "jordan"). The
chamber-pot could be used when needed and
emptied later into a cesspit. Slightly more elaborate was the close-stool, a
small stool with a hole in the seat under which was placed a chamber-pot
containing water. The close-stool was often built as a closed-in box to
conceal the chamber-pot within. The most substantial arrangement was
the privy (often called a "jakes"), which was similar to a close-stool, but
the seat was large, permanent, and set apart in a small room of its own (it
was called a privy from the French word for "private"). Sometimes the
privy would be built outside, with a cesspit underneath instead of a pot.
The function of toilet paper was served by a small piece of cloth, which
could be washed.

The disposal of human waste could be a major problem, especially in
the city. People in the country could rely on cesspits, which were
periodically emptied and used to fertilize the fields. In the city there were
public cesspits, which were cleaned out from time to time; the absence of
an effective means of removing sewage from the crowded city
environment was presumably a major factor in the poor health conditions
and high rate of urban disease and mortality.

VILLAGES AND TOWNS

The overwhelming majority of the population lived in the country,
typically in villages of 200 to 500 people. The village consisted of a cluster
of crofts around a central (unpaved) street; there might be a village green
and a parish church. If the village had a major landowning gentleman, his
manor hall might be nearby too. There was probably a good source of
water near the village center, whether a river or a well. Abundant water
was needed to support a village, so villages were typically near water

sources. Around the clustered crofts were the village fields, pastures, and meadows, and beyond that were waste areas such as woods or marshes.

Pillaging a village. [Holinshed]

The village was primarily a phenomenon of champion farmland. In areas of woodland agriculture, houses were likely to stand alone in the midst of their holdings, or in small clusters that were sometimes called "hamlets."

Village society varied greatly. Some villages were still dominated by a manor lord, who owned most or all of the local land and still held judicial powers over his tenants. Where the old manorial system had broken down, the village might be dominated by the local gentry or, in the absence of gentry, by the most substantial landholders.

Towns were generally of 500 to 5000 people, and only about 8% of the population lived in towns of more than 5000. London was the foremost city, with some 120,000 at Elizabeth's accession and 200,000 at her death, constituting about 5% of England's population. London overtook Venice in this period as the third largest city in Europe (after Paris and Naples) and far outstripped any other English town: Norwich, Bristol, and York all numbered between 10,000 and 25,000, while the rest had under 10,000.

Towns were primarily commercial centers. They invariably had at least one regular market, and in many cases an annual fair as well. Consequently, their location was a factor of transportation. The most important towns were located on navigable rivers, usually at the site of one or more bridges, and in general all towns lay at the intersections of major roads. The larger towns were usually walled, although there were a few exceptions. There were generally few public buildings. There might be a market cross in the square where the market took place, or even a covered market building. If there was a municipal government, there would be some sort of town hall. Otherwise, the only public buildings were churches and their associated buildings, which often served secular as well as religious functions: meeting hall, courtroom, school, business place, muster hall and armory. Specific crafts and trades tended to cluster in certain areas of the town, which facilitated guild administration.

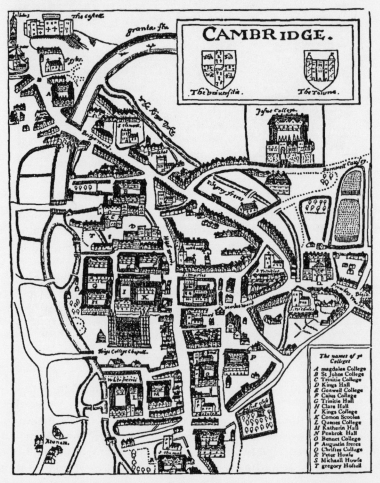

A map of Cambridge, typical of smaller towns of the period. [Furnivall 1877]

    Town streets had names, although houses were not numbered. Even London was rather small by modern standards, so it was possible to identify individual buildings by the name of their principal occupants or functions. Some city streets were surfaced with cobblestones, but many were unpaved and became quite difficult to use in wet weather when feet, hooves, and wheels churned them into a river of mud. A few streets were extremely broad, wide enough to be used as marketplaces or football fields.

A view of London looking northward across the Thames. Visible in the foreground are the Bear Garden, an amphitheater used for bear-baiting, and the Globe Theater, where many of Shakespeare's plays were performed. [Hatcher]

City streets were also the notorious haunts of pickpockets and cutpurses. The pickpocket was the more skilled thief, who would actually filch valuables out of his victims' pockets. The cutpurse typically wore a horn sheath on his thumb and carried a small knife, so that he could cut people's purses off their belts by slicing against his thumb. Such thieves especially frequented crowded places like markets, fairs, and public spectacles.

Waste disposal was a perennial problem in the towns. Refuse would be collected by "scavagers" once or twice a week, and there were rubbish tips, called "laystalls," outside the town. There were strict city ordinances against fouling the streets, but—as with many Elizabethan laws—they were not always effective.

Another major urban risk was fire. In spite of attempts to reduce the danger by passing laws against thatched or wooden roofs, fire remained an ever-present threat in an environment where most construction was of wood and light and heat were provided by fire. There was no official fire department, but churches and other public places often stocked fire-fighting equipment for neighborhood residents to use in case of emergency. These included buckets of leather for fetching water, and ladders and hooks with which to pull down burning buildings before the fire spread—the origin of the modern "hook-and-ladder" squad.[7]

TRAVEL

Local Elizabethan society tended to be very insular. Landholders did not often have need to travel, beyond visiting a nearby fair or market to purchase supplies: when villagers contrasted their "countrymen" with "foreigners," they were like as not speaking of people from the village as contrasted with non-locals. Yet overall, there was a surprising degree of mobility. In southeastern England, perhaps some 70-80% of the population moved at least once in their lives. For those who moved only once, the move was probably just local, as when young people left their parents' house for a new household either through marriage or employment.

A relocation was more likely to be bigger if it was a major career move. Craftsmen, tradesmen, and professionals might relocate in pursuit of advancement in their particular careers, and there was a constant migration of unskilled workers into the towns, especially London. Some livelihoods required ongoing travel: servants in search of a new master, pedlars selling their wares, and wage laborers following the market. Migration tended to be towards the south and east of the country, and from the countryside to the towns. Prosperous landholders were generally unlikely to migrate: it was the poor, the landless, and the young who most often had to move. The population of London was especially fluid: it was estimated in the 1580s that the population of any given parish was mostly changed over any given period of 12 years or so.

Travel was an important part of Elizabethan life and the Elizabethan economy, yet Elizabethan systems of transportation were so haphazard that it is misleading to call them systems at all. The roads were problematic: unpaved, and for the most part without foundations, they were difficult to use in adverse weather. Laws had been instituted in the mid-sixteenth century requiring each community to maintain its roads, but as with most far-reaching reforms of the period, the goals outreached the capacity for enforcement. In practice, conditions depended in the end on local custom and initiative. Moreover, weak law enforcement left travelers vulnerable to the depredations of highwaymen, many of whom lurked even just outside of London.

Although the roads were bad, traveling accommodations were surprisingly good. The better English inns had private rooms with fireplaces and food service; the lodger was given a key, and could expect clean sheets on the bed. Of course, people traveling on a tight budget might not be so well accommodated. If you weren't traveling on a main road, there might be no inns at all, in which case you would have to make arrangements with a local alehouse or at a private home. Even a seemingly good inn might have its drawbacks. It was generally known that inn employees such as tapsters (who served the drinks) and ostlers (who received guests at their arrival) were often in cahoots with nearby highway robbers, and would send report of particularly promising victims who stayed at their inn.

The speed of travel was just a fraction of modern rates. A person journeying on foot might cover 12 miles a day, on horseback twice or even four times as much, but this would exhaust the horse. Riders by "post," with regular changes of horses awaiting them at official "post-houses," could cover 10 miles an hour and as much as 100 or even 160 miles in a day. Post-houses were kept by "post-masters," typically innkeepers specially licensed by the Queen; the post-houses were located at about 10-mile intervals along major roads. They had originally been established as a network to ensure the speedy expedition of royal business, but private persons were also allowed to hire post-horses, although they also had to hire a post-boy or guide to bring the horses back. Those who wished might travel by a cart or coach. Both of these were slower than horses and neither had springs, so such rides were very rough. Overland transport of large volumes of goods was by cart, since the capacity of a packhorse was only around 200 pounds.

The system of posts provided the royal government with an effective means of transporting messages, but private citizens had to make shift as best they could. One might hire a courier; local letters might be entrusted to a servant; over long distances, the letter might simply be given to someone who was known to be traveling towards the letter's destination. The letter would be folded over, sealed with wax, and the recipient's name written on the outside, with some indication of where he or she might be found.

Given the limitations of travel by land, water played a much larger role in transportation than it does today—after all, rivers don't need maintenance! Water travel was not inherently faster than travel by land. The journey between Dover and Calais, a distance of about 25 miles, took 2 to 4 hours with favorable winds and could take as long as 7. The voyage to the New World required 1 to 2 months. However, it was a much more efficient means of transporting goods (which is why towns, as trading centers, were generally near navigable rivers). Since bridges were comparatively rare, boats were essential in some places as a means of crossing rivers. The outstanding example is London, which had only one bridge at this time: transportation along and across the Thames was provided by a multitude of small boats called "wherries," so that Elizabethan London had something of the flavor we associate with Venice. Water transport was of course especially important to England, an island nation which had no contact with the outside world except by sea.

An Elizabethan ship. [Holinshed]

Warships and commercial ships were much more similar to each other than is the case today. The seas were a dangerous place: commercial ships were generally fitted with at least a few guns, and were often pressed into military service. There were some differences. Ships built specifically for war tended to be narrower in proportion to their width, and the largest warships were much larger than any merchant ship. There were no passenger ships as such—travelers would book passage on a cargo ship of some sort. Merchant ships tended to be of about 200 tons, rarely reaching 300 or 350, and almost never anything above; the keel would be around 60 feet long. Warships might be of 500 tons or more, with keels of about 100 feet and beams of 35 feet, carrying 30-40 guns and crews of 200-300. Yet many ships were much smaller. The *Golden Hind*, on which Francis Drake circled the globe, was 100 feet long, 18 feet broad, displaced 140 tons, and carried 16 principal guns and 90 crew.

Hulls were rounded towards the fore, tapering towards the aft, and built up quite high and narrow at deck level. Sails were few: a 3-masted ship would carry 2 square sails each on the fore- and mainmasts, another square sail on the bowsprit, and a triangular lateen sail on the mizzenmast. Under favorable conditions, such ships might make some 4 to 6 knots (around 5 to 7 miles per hour).

A military encampment. [Holinshed]

During the Middle Ages, travel had been generally for professional or military reasons or for the purpose of pilgrimage. By the Elizabethan period, personal secular travel—tourism—had become a well-established activity. Within England one popular tourist attraction was Drake's *Golden Hind*, which was ultimately destroyed by visitors taking chips of wood from it. Another favored destination was the Tower of London, where privileged travelers might see the armories and the crown jewels. St. Paul's Cathedral and Westminster Abbey were also tourist sites. However, the favorite destination for English travelers was the Continent. A young man of the upper classes might follow his formal schooling with a journey to France and Italy, in the company of a tutor hired by his parents: such a trip, it was thought, gave the final polish to his education and breeding. Even older men and women were known to visit the Continent out of sheer interest. There was a growing volume of travel literature appearing in English, both as advice for those who went abroad and as information about the world for those who stayed at home. Then as now, tourism could be an expensive hobby: Fynes Moryson, one of the greatest travel writers of the day, recommended allowing expenses of £50-60 a year, several times the annual income of the middling sorts of commoners.[8]

6

Clothing and Accoutrements

Of all aspects of Elizabethan culture, the most distinctive may well be its clothing. It was a highly fashion-conscious age, and prized a look that was elaborate, artificial, stylized, and striking. Men and women alike were concerned to be wearing the latest and most fashionable outfits, and although the clothes we associate with the Elizabethans were worn primarily by the upper classes, their fashions influenced ordinary people as well.[1]

Fashionable men and women of the latter part of Elizabeth's reign. [Norris]

To the modern eye, Elizabethan clothing may look constrictive, hot, and uncomfortable. Clothing was indeed more heavy in the sixteenth century than it is today. England has never had a very warm climate, and Elizabeth's reign fell within a period of particularly cold weather known today as the Little Ice Age. At the same time, the clothing we usually associate with the Elizabethan period is the most formal attire of the aristocracy, and formal clothes are typically more constrictive than everyday wear. The ordinary clothes of working people had to allow for more mobility and were considerably more comfortable by today's standards.

Materials The basic components of Elizabethan clothing were linen and wool. Linen derives from the fibres of the flax plant; it is a very comfortable fabric, easy to clean and quick to dry, which made it ideally suited for shirts, underwear, collars, cuffs, hose—anything worn next to the skin. Linen was also used for lining and interlining garments. Sometimes, as an interlining, it was impregnated with gum (a sticky secretion derived from certain plants) to make it stiffer, in which case it was called buckram. A certain amount of linen was produced domestically, although the best linens were imported from the Continent, especially from northern France and the Low Countries. Table linen might be had for 5d. an ell (45 inches). Holland could cost 1s. 6d. for the coarser varieties, 5s. for the finer ones, and cambric could range from 2s. to 20s; both of these were finer linens often used for shirts. Lawn, an extremely fine linen used especially in neckwear and cuffs, cost 10s. and up.

Cotton was also used (although less widely, as it had to be imported from farther afield) and served similar purposes. One of its commonest forms was fustian, a blend of cotton and linen: it cost 1s. for coarse stuff, 3-5s. for fine. Fustian was often used to give the appearance of silk and was particularly used for stuffing padded garments.

Occasionally linen or cotton was used for outer garments such as breeches and doublets, particularly for reasons of economy. In such cases, it was generally of a heavier type than shirt-linen, such as linen canvas, which might range in price from 1s. to 3s. a yard. Canvas could also be made from hemp, the plant fiber used in making ropes. Canvas of this sort was very tough, suitable for such purposes as making sails and packing merchandise, but it might be used for clothing when economy or durability was more important than comfort. Hemp was also used to make lockram, a particularly coarse fabric used in shirts.

By far the most common fabric for the outer layers of clothing was wool, which was one of the principal sources of England's wealth in Elizabeth's day. Wool is sturdy and versatile—it resists rain, keeps the wearer warm in cold weather, yet is remarkably cool in the summer. It accepts dye readily but does not absorb moisture (such as sweat) or wash well. One of the cheapest sorts was called frieze, which cost 6d. to 3s. a yard; 2s to 4s. was a standard range for English wools. Woolen fabrics tended to be heavily felted, to the point that they could be cut without the edges fraying.

Finer fabrics were invariably made of silk and quite expensive. Satin was one of the cheaper luxury fabrics, ranging from 3s. to 14s. a yard; taffeta might cost 15s.; velvet, 31s.; and damask a princely £4, more than most people made in a year. Plain silk was used for fine shirts, satin and taffeta for outer layers and for lining, velvet for outer layers.[2]

Leather was also an important element in the Elizabethan's clothing. It was used not only for gloves, belts, and shoes, but also for a variety of garments, especially among men, including hats, doublets, and even breeches. Leather was often adorned with tooling.

Decoration The colors of Elizabethan fabrics were mostly based on natural dyes, the commonest being brown, grey, red, blue, yellow, and green. The various colors sometimes had specific associations, in many cases related to the expense of producing them. Brown and grey fabrics were generally inexpensive, and were associated with the poor. There were two types of red fabric. One was dyed with the plant madder, which yields a russet color. Such fabric was also relatively inexpensive, and was considered honest and homey. Bright red fabric, by contrast, had to be made with imported dyes, and was expensive. Blue was fairly inexpensive, and was often worn by servants and apprentices. The usual source for blue dye was the herb woad; its color tended to fade, so such people were often clothed in a lightish blue. Black was a difficult color to obtain with natural dyes and was consequently expensive: for this reason it was especially fashionable. Intense colors were difficult to produce, and natural dyes tend to fade quickly. Consequently, the colors of most Elizabethan clothing would have been rather muted.

Linen was generally undyed, although it was often bleached by exposing it to the sun. Sometimes it was block-printed or adorned with embroidery. Clothes could be further ornamented by slashing or pinking (piercing) the outer layer to reveal a fine contrasting fabric underneath. Other adornments included "guarding" (ribbon trim) and even gems or pearls on the most fancy outfits. A distinctive feature of Elizabethan clothing was the extensive use of padding, known as "bombast," to give the garments a fashionable shape. Bombast was especially common in men's clothes, and typically consisted of raw wool, cotton, or horsehair, but oats or bran were sometimes used instead.[3]

Cleaning As a rule, only the inner layers of clothing (such as shirts and underwear) were actually washed; evidence suggests that ordinary people probably washed clothing on a weekly basis, and donned a fresh shirt each Sunday. Detachable collars and cuffs might be changed more often. Such garments as were washed were most often made of linen. They would be saturated in soap and hot water, beaten with paddles, rinsed, and then left out in the sun to dry and bleach. They might then be pressed with irons. Outer layers of clothing, most often made of wool or richer fabrics, did not wash well, and were cleaned with a clothes-brush instead.

UNDERGARMENTS

An embroidered smock. [Gay]

The principal undergarment for both men and women was the shirt, which served as a comfortable, absorbent, and washable layer between the body and the outer clothes. Shirts had long sleeves and were pulled over the head. They were generally made of white linen, although the rich favored silk. Shirts tended to be simple in cut, with straight seams, but there might be a good deal of gathering at the collar and cuffs, sometimes even with attached ruffs. Fancy shirts were sometimes decorated with lace or adorned with black, red, or gold embroidery, especially about the collar, shoulders, and cuffs. Men's shirts typically reached to the crotch or thigh and were vented at the bottom of the side seams to allow for greater freedom of movement. Women's shirts, usually called "smocks," were normally between knee- and floor-length. Triangular gores of fabric inserted into the side seams allowed extra mobility. The neckline of a woman's shirt might be high or low. For many people the shirt also served as a nightgown, although wealthy people had special nightshirts for this purpose.

The shirt was more truly an undergarment than it is today. People who were not manual laborers were almost never seen in their shirt sleeves, although gentlemen might strip to their shirts for respectable physical exertion (such as tennis). Working people were sometimes seen in their shirts when they had to perform heavy labor, but women would at least wear a sleeveless bodice on top.[4]

In addition to the shirt, men often wore undershorts comparable to modern boxer shorts. These were generally called "breeches," an ambiguous term since it could refer to an outer garment as well. Women did not normally wear breeches in England, although they had started to do so in Italy. Breeches were made of white linen and might be adorned with embroidery, especially about the cuffs.[5]

WOMEN'S GARMENTS

On top of her smock an Elizabethan woman might wear any of three general styles of attire, sometimes in combination with each other. The first was the "kirtle," the second was a bodice and "petticoat" (skirt), and the third was a gown.

The kirtle was a long fitted garment reaching down to the feet, resembling a long fitted dress without any seam at the waist. It was a fairly simple style, closely related to medieval garments, and was not generally worn by itself among fashionable women, although it might be worn under another garment.

The bodice, or "pair of bodies," was a close-fitting garment for the upper body, normally made of wool. It kept the torso warm and was stiffened to mold the body into the fashionable shape. This shape was rather severe and masculine: flat, broad in the shoulders, and narrow in the waist. In effect, the bodice combined the functions of bra, girdle, and vest all in one. Its waistline was pointed in front. The neckline reflected the

A female commoner. [Norris]

trends of fashion: it was low towards the beginning and end of Elizabeth's reign, high during the middle years. A low bodice might be worn with a high-neckline smock; the decolleté look was normal only with young unmarried women and in some fashionable circles. The bodice had no collar.

The bodice could be sleeved or sleeveless. A sleeveless bodice was considered an adequate outer garment for working women, although they always wore a sleeved bodice or overgarment in less informal situations. Women of higher social status had no cause to be seen in their shirtsleeves, so a sleeveless bodice for them was solely an undergarment. A sleeved bodice might be worn on top of a sleeveless one. The sleeves were sometimes detachable, allowing for different sleeves to be laced or hooked in. If a sleeveless bodice was worn underneath, the outer bodice did not need to be as heavily stiffened. Bodices often had decorative tabs called "pickadills" about the waist; if worn on the outside, they might have rolls or wings of fabric around the armholes.

The degree of stiffening in the bodice depended on the wearer's station in life. Upper-class women wore stiffly boned bodices, but ordinary women needed more freedom of movement to perform everyday tasks (such as churning butter, baking bread, or chasing children), so their garments had to be less constricting. Stiffening might be provided by "whale bone" (baleen), bundles of dried reeds, willowy wood, or even steel. A less fashionable bodice might be shaped with just a heavy fabric interlining. For extra stiffening in front, a rigid piece of wood, bone, or ivory, called a "busk," might be inserted and held in place by a ribbon at the top; to this day women's undergarments often have a small ribbon bow just in the midpoint of the chest, the last trace of the Elizabethan busk.[6]

A bodice worn as an innermost garment took a fair bit of strain, so buttons would have been too weak a fastening. Instead, bodices were fastened with hooks and eyes, or else were laced up. Ordinary women's bodices usually laced up the front; side- and back-lacing bodices were worn by people who had servants to help them dress. The innermost bodice sometimes had holes to which a farthingale, roll, or petticoat could be laced.

On top of a sleeveless bodice, women sometimes wore doublets similar to those worn by men. Unlike a bodice, the doublet had a collar and buttoned up the front.[7]

Where the bodice served to flatten and narrow the upper body, Elizabethan fashion called

A roll. [Norris]

for volume in the lower body. This was generally achieved either with a "farthingale" or a "roll," or with a combination of the two. The farthingale had originated in Spain as a bell-shaped support for the skirts: it was essentially an underskirt with a series of wire, whalebone, or wooden hoops sewn into it. During the course of Elizabeth's reign, the "wheel farthingale" was introduced. This stuck directly out at the hips and fell straight down, giving the skirts a cylindrical shape. The wheel farthingale was often worn with a padded roll about the hips. Sometimes the roll was worn by itself to give a somewhat softer version of the wheel farthingale look. This style was particularly common among ordinary people, for whom it served not only to imitate the fashionable shape but also to keep the skirts away from the legs for greater ease of movement.[8]

A woman reveals her farthingale.
[Norris]

Skirts were known as "petticoats." Their shape was dictated by the shape of the undergarments. Bell-shaped farthingales required skirts of similar proportions, lightly gathered at the waist and made in several trapezoidal panels. Wheel farthingales required huge skirts, heavily gathered to the waist. Women who did not wear farthingales might wear many layers of petticoats to create volume (as well as warmth). The ordinary woman's outer petticoat was of wool; underpetticoats might be of linen, and were sometimes richly embroidered. Often hems were made of a different, more durable fabric that could be removed and replaced as they wore out.[9]

The other main style of female garment was the gown, which was essentially a bodice and skirt sewn together, usually worn on top of a kirtle or petticoat. The gown was the richest form of garment, and it took many forms. The bodice was frequently adorned with false sleeves which hung down at the back, and often the skirt was open in front to reveal the contrasting skirts underneath.

MEN'S GARMENTS

Lower-body garments for men changed substantially during the course of Elizabeth's reign. In the early years some people still wore the old-fashioned "long hose" and "codpiece," a style that had changed little since the late Middle Ages. The hose were roughly analogous to modern tights, but rather loose-fitting. They were made of woven rather than knitted fabric. The fabric was usually wool (which is naturally somewhat elastic) and cut on the bias (i. e., diagonally) to allow them to stretch, but they still tended to bag, especially around the ankles. The codpiece was a padded covering for the crotch, originally introduced for the sake of propriety. It also served the function of a modern trouser-fly: it could be unbuttoned or untied to allow the wearer to urinate.

This plain style of hose was already out of fashion by the time Elizabeth came to the throne. Well-dressed men had taken to wearing "trunkhose" over their long hose. These were an onion-shaped, stuffed garment that extended from the waist to the tops of the thighs. They were often slashed vertically to reveal a contrasting fabric underneath, or even sewn together from a large number of separate panes.

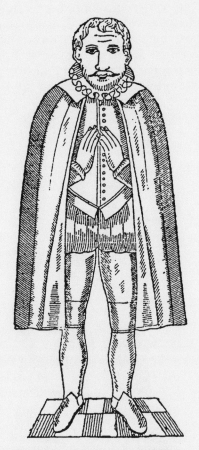

A prosperous man in trunkhose, doublet, and cape. [Ashdown]

Later in the reign, a new fashion arose of adding "canions" to these trunkhose. These were tight-fitting cylindrical extensions that reached from the bottom openings of the trunkhose to the top or bottom of the wearer's knees. At the same time, the trunkhose themselves became fuller and longer, reaching to mid-thigh, and were more likely to be of a solid fabric rather than slashed or paned. Such trunkhose were increasingly likely to have pockets, and were worn with stockings rather than long hose.

Codpieces continued to be worn on the outside of trunkhose. They were sometimes quite elaborate, and often in a shape that strikes the modern eye as downright obscene. Fashionable gentlemen occasionally had them made as pockets in which they could store candy and other knick-knacks! Codpieces became more subdued towards the latter part of the period, and had fallen out of fashion by the end of the century.

Ordinary men's clothes (the leg-bells worn by the man on the left indicate that he is a Morris dancer). [Furnivall 1879]

During the latter part of Elizabeth's reign a new style of lower-body garment appeared, known as "breeches." They were sometimes called "Venetian breeches" or just "Venetians" to distinguish them from underwear. Venetian breeches were essentially knee-length trousers, originally cut rather close to the body but becoming more voluminous towards the end of the reign. They normally reached below the knee, although some styles stopped short of it. The commoner's Venetians were made of wool and might be lined with linen. Even cheaper Venetians were made of linen canvas. Venetians were sometimes trimmed along the outseam and around the pockets. They could be fastened at the waist with buttons or with hooks and eyes. Venetians were not worn with codpieces; instead, they had a fly-opening that either tied or buttoned. Like the later styles of trunkhose, they were worn with stockings instead of long hose.[10]

Men's upper-body garments did not change nearly as much during the course of Elizabeth's reign. The characteristic upper-body garment was the doublet, a short, fitted jacket with a narrow waist. The doublet was made of wool, canvas, or a fine fabric, or sometimes of leather. It might be padded and quilted, or decorated with slashes. It either buttoned, hooked, or laced up the front. It was often adorned with wings at the shoulders and pickadills about the waist. As with women's bodices, the doublet might have detachable sleeves that hooked or laced in. Early in the reign the doublet was cut straight around the bottom edge, but in time it became fashionable for the front to dip downwards in a sharp V shape. In the latter half of the period doublets were cut with a distinctive "peascod belly," a padded protruding flare at the front that imitated the design of military breastplates (on a breastplate this shape helped to deflect blows). An additional garment called a "jerkin" could be worn over the doublet when temperature or fashion demanded. The jerkin was essentially of the same design as a doublet, except that it might be sleeveless.[11]

Fashionable and rustic men's clothing. [Furnivall 1879]

The doublet was worn by a very wide section of society, although the quality of the materials and the degree of tailoring and decoration varied enormously. People towards the lower end of the social scale might wear a coat instead. In its most elaborate form the coat resembled a plain doublet, except that it had long skirts. Fashionable men sometimes wore such coats over their doublets. The simplest form of coat was not fitted at all but dropped straight down from the shoulders; it might be belted at the waist.

OTHER GARMENTS

Stockings   Lower leg garments were called stockings or "netherstocks"; they were worn by women, and by men with trunkhose or Venetians. At the beginning of the reign, stockings were invariably made of woven cloth. During the course of the reign the English were first introduced to the technique of knitting stockings. Knit stockings were more expensive to produce and were originally a luxury made only with silk, but eventually knit woolen stockings appeared as well. However, cloth stockings of wool and linen continued to be worn throughout the Elizabethan period.

Stockings might be white or colored; they were sometimes decorated with silk embroidery about the top and down the sides—colors included red, green, and black. Knit stockings often had elaborate patterning in the same places. In addition, people sometimes wore heavy colored overstockings outside comfortable white ones. Riders might wear protective overstockings of heavy linen, known as boothose. If a man wore breeches that stopped above the knee, the stockings could be pulled up over the breeches; otherwise they went underneath.[12]

A good example of cloth hose. Note the seam up the back, and the single-bow tying the garter. [Holinshed]

Neither cloth nor knitted stockings were able to hold up reliably on their own, so both men and women held them in place with garters. Women gartered their stockings at the "gartering place," the narrow spot between the knee and upper calf. Men's stockings gartered there or just above the knee, depending on the length of the breeches or trunkhose. Another style for men was "cross-gartering," whereby the garter wrapped around the leg both above and below the knee, crossing behind it. Ordinary people's garters were made of woven or knit wool, or of leather straps with buckles. Fancier garters might be made of taffeta.[13]

Men's and women's shoes in the late sixteenth century were generally blunt-toed and flat: heeled shoes were not common **Shoes** until the seventeenth century. Most shoes were made of leather, although highly fashionable shoes for courtly use were sometimes made of fabrics such as velvet or silk. In the earlier part of the reign shoes generally slipped onto the foot, but in the latter part they tied on with laces or a buckle. Unlike modern shoes, Elizabethan shoes were "straight-lasted": left and right shoes were assembled on a single "last," or form,

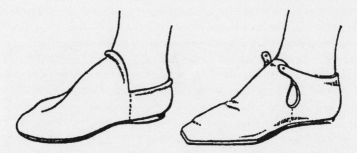

Typical shoe styles of the early and latter part of Elizabeth's reign. [Norris]

and only became differentiated with use. Decorations on fancy shoes included embroidery, cutwork, ribbon edging, pearls, gems, and slashes (sometimes puffed). Boots were generally worn only by men and only for riding, although working men sometimes wore low ankle-boots.[14]

Collars and Cuffs   Early in Elizabeth's reign, both men's and women's shirts were heavily gathered at the neck; this had given rise to the practice of sewing a ruff into the neckband. Eventually, a new style emerged in which a separate ruff was tied around the neck. Both men and women wore ruffs, which became progressively larger and more intricate in fashionable circles. In 1565 starch was introduced to the laundry process. This method of stiffening enabled the ruff to grow even larger, requiring meticulous care to set it properly. By 1580-85 ruffs were so large that they needed the support of a wire framework to fan them around the head. Ruffs were made of fine linen, sometimes edged with lace. They were often worn with matching hand ruffs at the wrists.

In the latter part of Elizabeth's reign, the "falling band" became fashionable among men. This had evolved from the neckband of the shirt; it was essentially a separate collar, which again tied around the neck. The simplest type was made of white linen of light to medium weight; fancier ones were adorned with lace or embroidery. Women did not wear falling bands, but they sometimes pinned a kerchief around their shoulders.[15]

A country woman wearing a chin-cloth and a kerchief over her shoulders. [Norris]

Elizabethan England was generally a chilly place, so
there existed a wide variety of garments for furnishing **Outer and Inner**
additional warmth; some of them were also crucial to the **Garments**
wearer's fashionable look. Between their shirt and outer
garments, people sometimes wore a knitted undergarment called a
"waistcoat."[16] Linen or knitted jackets were sometimes worn for extra
warmth indoors. Loose gowns were a very common garment for both men
and women. They were often open, reaching to the knee or ankle on men,
to the ankle on women. Gowns of this sort might be adorned with false
sleeves. Women were most likely to wear these indoors, whereas men,
especially older men of the middle and upper classes, might wear them
outside as well. They were typically made of very heavy fabric, often lined
or trimmed with fur. Another warm garment was the cassock, a flaring
coat especially favored by soldiers and sailors, but also worn by both men
and women in general, particularly commoners. Among fashionable men,
the circular or semi-circular cape was especially favored: it might be long,
or a merely decorative short cape reaching only to the waist.[17]

Men tended to wear their hair short in the early part of
Elizabeth's reign, but longer hair became fashionable in the **Hair and**
latter half. Although a few men were clean-shaven, the over- **Headgear**
whelming majority wore a moustache and beard, which might
be handsomely trimmed to a point. Men generally kept their heads
covered—the main exception was when they doffed their hats or caps as a
mark of respect before their social superiors.
An exclusively masculine form of headgear
was the brimless knitted cap, which resembled the modern toque. Men sometimes also
wore toque-style linen caps indoors.[18]

The flat caps that had dominated the first
half of the century were still in use, although
they became less fashionable as the reign
progressed and eventually became the mark
of the London citizen or apprentice. Common
cap materials were wool, felt, or leather, and
linen might be used to line the interior. Flat
caps were either knit of woolen yarn or sewn
of woven fabric. In an effort to support the
cap-knitting industry, it was mandated by law
in 1571 that male commoners wear knitted flat
caps on Sundays and holidays; for this reason
they came to be known as "statute caps." The

A gentleman in a finely
embroidered linen cap.
[Norris]

law was widely disobeyed and was repealed
in 1597, but the flat cap was nonetheless one

of the most common styles among ordinary men.[19]

Hats might be made of wool, woolen felt or leather; more expensive materials included velvet and silk. Some of the finest were made of animal pelts, particularly beaver. Straw hats were especially common among country folk. Hats became increasingly fashionable as the flat cap became less so, and among men in the latter part of the reign the height of fashion was represented by the high-crowned hats known as "copotains." Another style of hat had a somewhat lower crown and a broad brim. Hats were often decorated with a hatband, which might be cut long such that a tail hung down at the back. The hat might be adorned with a feather or a jeweled hat pin.[20]

Elizabethan women wore their hair long, although they generally pinned it up. It was kept off the forehead and was not cut into bangs. A young unmarried woman might sometimes have her hair uncovered, but it was customary to wear at least a simple cap known as a "coif." The coif was typically of linen, and some were ornately embroidered.[21] On top of the coif the woman might wear any one of a variety of head adornments. The simplest was the forehead-cloth, a triangular piece of linen with ties, which went over the front of the head and tied at the nape of the neck. Another form of headgear was the French hood, a fabric bonnet shaped with interior wires; it was especially fashionable in the early part of the reign. Women also wore flat caps. In the latter part of the reign, hats became increasingly common, in all the various styles worn by men.[22]

Fasteners The buttons of commoner's clothes were often made of wood covered with fabric scraps from the garment. Buttons could also be made of stuffed cloth, plain wood, bone or horn. Metal buttons—pewter, silver, or gold—were a luxury.[23] In general, buttons were spherical, small, and numerous, rather than large and widely spaced. In contrast with modern garments, they were generally sewn along the edge of the fabric rather than slightly in from the edge.

One characteristic feature of Elizabethan clothing was the "point," a ribbon or lace made of fabric or leather with metal tips (called "tags" or "aglets"). Points were used to attach the breeches to the doublet or the skirt to the bodice, to lace in a pair of sleeves, or to serve the function of buttons on a doublet or jerkin.[24] They were passed through matching pairs of circular holes worked into the two pieces, and tied in a half-bow. Hooks and eyes were also in use.[25] In addition, Elizabethans depended heavily on pins to hold their clothes together: a man's ruff or falling band was often pinned in place, while a woman would use pins extensively for her headgear, neckwear, and other garments.

The belt, known as a "girdle," was a common and important part of people's attire, not for holding up garments but as a place from which to hang personal possessions. Gentlemen's girdles were thin, with a fixed buckle in the front, and a sliding buckle on the side to adjust for size, with hooks for a hanger to hold a rapier.[26] Ladies were likely to have chain girdles or girdles made of fine fabric. Among ordinary people, thin leather girdles or girdles of woven tape were common. A girdle might support a knife in a leather sheath; often it held a purse, closing with a drawstring or a flap. Purses might hold one or more small knit or cloth pouches.[27] Towards the end of the century, belt-purses became less important for men, as pockets became more common.

Belts, Knives, and Purses

A man with a fashionable rapier and rapier-belt. [Castle]

Gentlemen, and many of lower station, often carried swords and fighting daggers on their girdles. The fashionable sword of the period was the rapier, which featured a blade about a yard long and weighed some $2\,^1/_2$ to 3 pounds. Rapiers made in the latter part of Elizabeth's reign often had elaborately swept hilts to protect to the hand. The rapier was an Italian innovation; it contrasted with the more traditional English sword in that it was longer and thinner (although not much lighter), being designed for thrusting with the point whereas the sword relied on blows with the edge. The fighting dagger was easily distinguishable from a civilian knife by its larger size and its crossguard, or "quillons." These weapons could be of actual use in a society where street-fights and brawls were known to break out in broad daylight, but for gentlemen they served primarily as an expression of social status and were likely to be highly ornate.

Handwear ranged from functional, heavy work gloves or mittens used by laborers to the heavily embroidered and perfumed gloves with tassels and gold beads worn by noble ladies. Handwear was particularly fashionable among the aristocracy, who were rarely without them. Both gloves and mittens tended to have long flaring cuffs.[28]

Miscellaneous Accessories

Working women commonly wore long aprons made of linen, and fashionable women had aprons made of rich fabrics. Tradesmen also wore aprons, and blacksmiths had leather ones. Handkerchiefs were used in this period; among the wealthy, they might be richly adorned.[29] Travelers often wore canvas or leather satchels, and perhaps a small wooden cask or leather bottle for drink slung over the shoulder. Fashionable ladies owned fans, which had long, straight handles, and were often made of ostrich feathers. In 1590 folding fans were introduced as the latest fashion accessory from France. Mirrors were sometimes suspended from the belt, even by women of fairly ordinary station.[30]

A man wearing a flat cap and spectacles. [Norris]

Spectacles of the pince-nez type were used in Elizabeth's day, although they were only for close activities like reading. Sometimes they were made more secure by strings that passed around each ear.

Men and women alike wore jewlery, including rings, earrings, bracelets, necklaces, and pendants. Miniatures (small portraits set in a frame) were fashionable, as were watches, usually suspended on a chain around the neck or incorporated into other pieces of jewelry.[31]

Cosmetics were widely used among fashionable women, and sometimes even by men. The favored look for women called for a very pale face, often with a touch of red in the cheeks and perhaps a tinting of the eyelids. The make-up used to achieve the fashionable whiteness was rather toxic, being based on lead. Fashionable men and women also used perfumes.

Bathing may have been rare, but grooming was frequent, at least among those who aspired to social respectability. Children were taught to clean their nails and comb their hair every morning. Combs were made of ivory, horn, or wood, and had two sides: one broad-toothed for preliminary combing of tangled hair, the other fine-toothed for combing out smaller knots once the larger tangles were removed. Brushes were usually reserved for cleaning clothes. The very fastidious even owned "ear-spoons," small ivory tools for getting rid of earwax. People of high social standing often carried small grooming kits in "comb cases." Mirrors, or "looking-glasses," were used in wealthy households, but were still a relative luxury. Most people never saw their own faces except by looking into still water.

CLOTHING PATTERNS

The instructions on the following pages will enable you to create a complete Elizabethan outfit, male or female, in a style appropriate to the latter part of Elizabeth's reign. All the patterns are based as far as possible on surviving originals. Of course, this approach has some disadvantages. The survival of original pieces has been haphazard, and surviving pieces are not always well documented in published sources. To make things even harder, it is generally the unusual examples that have survived. Nonetheless, the patterns here will allow you to make an ordinary Elizabethan outfit with a degree of historical accuracy that is very rare in practical costuming books.

The instructions here presuppose a basic knowledge of sewing. You may want to consult an experienced seamster for additional help. Another useful source is *Singer Sewing Step-by-Step* (Minnetonka MN: Cy de Cosse, 1990), which has brilliant instructions and illustrations to assist the home sewer.

The first step in successful costuming is making the right choice of fabrics. The instructions here suggest the fabrics from which the garments were most likely to be made. Even if you do not choose to use linen or wool, you can still use them as a guide in choosing an alternative fabric. You might also wish to line and/or interline overgarments. Lining would normally be of linen, interlining of heavy linen, canvas, or buckram, depending on the desired stiffness. Anything originally made of wool could also have been made of linen or canvas.

Unless specified otherwise, the patterns do not include a seam allowance: remember to add an extra $1/2$" around the edges. Be sure to press seams as you sew them.

With any of the more complex patterns, it can be helpful to make a mock-up, or fitting, of cheap material first—muslin is ideal for this purpose. You can make the necessary adjustments to this fitting, and proceed to the real fabric when you are satisfied with the fit.

Smock

This pattern is based on a Swedish man's shirt of the late 1560s, but it is intended here as one of the easiest styles of women's shirts to reproduce.[32] The pattern has been altered by the addition of side-gores. This smock should require $3 1/2$ yds. of white linen; the ruffs might be of finer linen.

The exact measurements will depend on the wearer. The collar (**c-d**) should be about 2" longer than your neck size (including seam allowance). The distance from the ends of the neck to the edge of the fabric (**a-b** and **e-f**) should be a bit longer than your shoulders. The length of the sleeve should equal the distance from your shoulder to your first knuckles, measured around your bent elbow. Adjust the overall length if desired—the smock should be fairly long, between knee-length and ankle-length. The neckline slash on the body is cut only on the front piece.

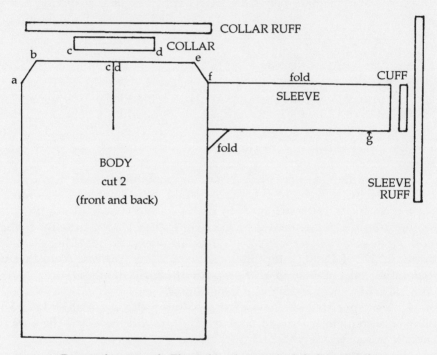

Pattern for a smock. The right side is as the left. [Hadfield]

Hem back the top and sides of the collar ruff. Hem back the side edges of the collar. Gather the collar ruff to the top of the collar (right sides together) and stitch in place. Press the seam allowances towards the collar so that the ruff stands up.

Hem back the front slit on the body front and take in a small dart at the base of the slit. Sew the side gussets to the body. Sew the body front to the body back at **a-b** and **e-f** (right sides together). Gather the top opening of the body (**c-b-e-d**) into the bottom of the collar (right sides together), matching **c** and **d** on the body to **c** and **d** on the collar. Stitch.

Treat the sleeve ruffs and cuffs as with the collar ruff and collar. Hem back the sleeve from **g** to the cuff edge. Gather the sleeve into the sleeve cuff (right sides together) and stitch. Stitch up the bottom edge of the sleeve from **g** to the beginning of the gusset, and stitch the gusset to the sleeve. Stitch the sleeve/gusset piece to the body. (For a more complete description of the gusset, see the pattern for the man's shirt below.)

Sew the outside edge of the side gussets on each side together. Hem the bottom edge and add ties at the base of the cuff and collar.

Bodice

This design is based on a late sixteenth-century noblewoman's bodice.[33] A sleeveless bodice should require about 1 yd. of wool for the outer shell, 1 yd. of linen for a lining, and 1 yd. of canvas or buckram for an interlining. Add another 1 yd. of wool if you want sleeves (plus as much again for lining, if you want it).

The first step is to generate a pattern. Take a piece of denim-weight cloth and wrap your torso from armpit to hips, lifting your bust (it may help to wear a bra while doing this). Pin yourself in snugly, especially at bust and waist. Take the following measurements:

- —Bust
- —Waist
- —Armpit to Waist
- —Across Front (armpit to armpit)

Fold your fabric as shown and pin it in place. Rough-cut your pieces as shown—remember to allow $1/2$" seam allowance. Note that the total measurement of the bottom of the back piece at the waistline (from point **d** to point **d** on the other side) is $1/5$ of your waist measurement.

Cut the fore pieces from the back piece along a line midway between lines **a-b** and **c-d**. You will now have two fore pieces and one folded back piece. Pin line **a-b** to line **c-d**, and do the same with the other fore piece and the other side of the back piece. Remove all other pins, wrap the bodice around your torso, and pin the fore pieces together along CF line. Make sure each time you don the garment that you line up the waistline to your own waist.

Insert a new pin at CF waist to make the waist fit tightly. Measure the distance from the original CF waist pin to the new one, then remove this pin. Remove the bodice, and shift point **b** on each fore piece forward by this distance, so as to take in this amount at the side opening. On both · sides, redraw the new line **a-b** and pin the new **a-b** to **c-d**.

Put the bodice on again. Redraw the armholes to fit your arms—they angle slightly from bottom front to upper back. Draw your neckline in front and back, and the bottom edge of your bodice as shown. Unpin CF and remove. Adjust your armholes, neckline, and bottom edge as needed to make them symmetrical. (The shaded area indicates the location of boning on the original—you can make this garment with boning if you choose.)

To design the shoulder straps, cut an 11x11" piece and pin it to the back piece as shown. Put the bodice on, then pin the shoulder piece to the front. Mark the desired shape for this strap—the outside edge should run along the edge of your shoulder.

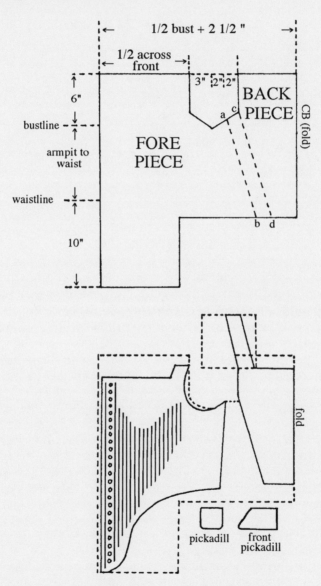

Pattern for a bodice. [Hadfield/Singman]

At this point you have your patterns—you may want to make a paper copy in case you make another bodice in the future.

You can now cut your fabric. For the bodice, you will want a total of 2 fore pieces and 1 back piece cut of wool for the outer layer, 2 fore pieces and 1 back piece of linen for the lining, and 2 fore pieces and 1 back piece of canvas or buckram for the interlining (if you use boning, it will go between the lining and interlining). For the shoulder straps, you will want 2 straps of the wool, 2 of the lining, and 2 of the interlining. Remember to allow $1/2$" for seams all around.

You can now assemble the pieces. Pin the interlining pieces to their corresponding lining pieces, wrong sides together. Sew the lining/interlining fore pieces to the back pieces along the line **a/c-b/d**, right sides together. Sew the outer fore pieces to the outer back pieces in the same manner. Sew the top and CF line of the outer layer to the top and CF line of the lining layers, right side of the outer layer to the right side of the lining (leave the armholes unsewn if you plan to add sleeves), *taking in a seam allowance of 1" at the CF line*—you will want to have the lacing holes pass through the seam allowance, and this will also create a 1" gap at the front, giving you some play when lacing up.

Of your outer fabric, cut 2 front pickadills, and as many ordinary pickadills as will be needed to reach around the bottom edge of the bodice (the 2 front pickadills are mirror images of each other). Do the same with the lining fabric. Pin each outer piece to its lining piece, right sides together, and sew along the bottom and sides. Turn each pickadill right side out. Pin the pickadills to the bottom edge of the outer layer of the bodice, right sides together (the two front skirts flank the CF opening, with the slanted side forward). Stitch. Turn in the bottom seam allowance of the lining-interlining and finish.

For the shoulder straps, pin the lining pieces to the interlining pieces, wrong sides together. Then pin the lining/interlining pieces to the outer pieces, right side of the outer layer to the right side of the lining, and stitch along the ends and one long side. Turn right side out. Pin the straps to the place where they meet the back piece, with the raw edge facing outwards. Put the bodice on, and pin the straps to the place where they meet the fore pieces. Remove the bodice, and sew the straps in place. If the bodice is sleeveless, press under the remaining seam allowance and sew shut.

Stitch lacing holes or apply grommets, at a spacing of about 1", at CF; lacing holes will work best if you stitch small rings onto the fabric around the holes. You might choose to insert rigilene boning on either side of the lacing holes, even if the rest of the bodice is not boned. (Rigilene boning is available from many sewing-supply stores.)

If the bodice will be worn as an outer layer, you may want a placket to cover the gap at CF. Cut a strip of the outer fabric 5" wide and as long as the front opening, plus 1" for seam allowances; cut a lining piece and an interlining piece of the same size. Sew these to each other along the long sides and one short side, right side of the outer fabric to the right side of the lining. Turn right side out, press, finish the open end, and sew it into the inside of the bodice to one side of the CF opening (behind the lacing holes, so that it doesn't get in the way of the lacing).

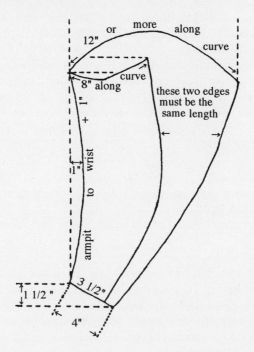

Pattern for a bodice sleeve. [Hadfield/Singman]

To make a sleeve, cut two pieces as shown (the two pieces are depicted one on top of the other: they share the same left edge). You can also cut lining pieces if you choose to have a lining. The actual length of the top curve on the larger piece will depend on how much gathering you choose to have; the total length of the top curve on the larger piece plus the top curve on the smaller piece must be at least 1" greater than the armhole it will be gathered into. Stitch the sleeve right sides together along both side edges. Gather the sleeve to the armhole, right sides together, lining up the front seam (the left one on the illustration) with the foremost point of the armhole. Stitch the sleeve to the armhole, finish the shoulder seams, and hem the cuff. The other sleeve is a mirror image of the first.

Roll

This pattern for a roll is based on visual evidence, as no originals are known to survive. Cut a piece of sturdy linen or light canvas **a-b-c-d** as shown above. Sides **a-b** and **c-d** will be equal to your hip measurement, **a-d** and **b-c** will be 12". Solidly hem sides **a-d** and **b-c**. Sew line **a-b** to line **d-c**, right sides together, creating a tube of fabric. Turn right side out. Pass a lace through the hems at the two ends. Tighten the lace and one end, gathering it shut, and stuff the roll with fabric scraps. Gather the other end shut, and use the laces to tie it on. It is worn slightly below the waist to accentuate the hips.

Pattern for a roll. [Hadfield/Singman]

Petticoat

This design for a woman's petticoat derives from an example of the early seventeenth century.[34] It should be ankle-length or toe-length, requiring about 8' of fabric: medium to heavy wool for an outer petticoat, linen or lighter wool for an underpetticoat. If you plan to wear a roll, make it first, as it will affect the design.

The easiest style to make is a drawstring petticoat. Cut the fabric crosswise into two panels as shown and sew them selvage to selvage (**c-d**). Sew the other selvages together (**a-b**), leaving the top 6" open. You now have a loop of fabric.

If the overall circumference of this loop is greater than three times your waist measurement, you will need to trim the panels into trapezoids, until the measurement **a-c-a** is no greater than three times your waist (otherwise it will be too difficult to gather). This does not need to be done if the fabric will be pleated into a waistband, but it does need to be done if it is gathered to a waistband or drawstring.

Fold over 2" at the top of the loop and sew it down, creating a channel. Open a hole in the channel at the seam at point **a**, and thread a drawstring through. Put the roll on, put the skirt on, and draw the string tight, then have someone pin the bottom edge so that it reaches your ankle or toes. Remove and hem.

A more comfortable design in the long run (to which the drawstring petticoat can be converted) involves a waistband. Cut a strip of wool 4" wide and as long as your own waist size plus 2" for an overlap plus 1" for seam allowances. Fold the waistband as shown, right sides together, stitch up the ends, and turn right side out. Insert a strip of buckram or some other reinforcement. Gather or pleat the top edge of the petticoat to the seam allowance on the outside of the waistband, right sides together, leaving an extra 2" at one end of the waistband for the overlap. Stitch. Fold the waistband over, folding in the inside seam allowance, and stitch it closed. Use hooks to close the waistband—the petticoat can also be hooked or tied to the bodice to prevent gaping at the waist. You may add a placket to cover the opening in the petticoat.

Alternatively, you can use cartridge pleating, finishing the waistband first and sewing the pleats to it afterward.

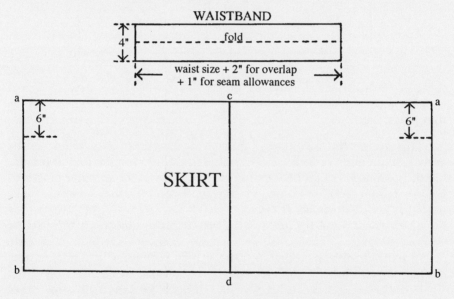

Pattern for a petticoat. [Hadfield/Singman]

Breeches

This design for a man's breeches is based on the photograph of a surviving Italian example of the late sixteenth century.[35] It will require 1 yd. of white linen.

Cutting: Cut two of each piece as shown.

—**a-b** = **a-f** = half waist measurement

—**b-c** = small of the back to mid-crotch
—**d-e** = a bit more than half the circumference of the thigh
—**a-e** = hip to thigh (anywhere from mid-thigh to just above the knee)
—**f-c** = small of back to mid-crotch

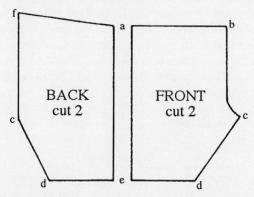

Pattern for a man's breeches. [Hadfield/Singman]

<u>Sewing</u>: Sew outseam of each leg (**a-e**), right side together. Sew inseam of each leg (**c-d**), right side together. Sew front and back seam (**f-c** and **b-c**), right sides together. Hem the cuffs. Fold over the top to make a channel for the drawstring: sew it down, open a hole at the front seam (at point b), and thread the drawstring through.

Shirt

This pattern is based on a man's shirt of the late sixteenth century.[36] It is shown without seam allowances. The shirt should require $3^1/_2$ yds. of white linen.

Adjust the measurements as necessary. The collar should be 1" longer than your neck size (including seam allowance). The distance from the ends of the neck opening (**a**) to the sleeve should be a bit longer than your shoulders—narrow the neck opening if necessary. The length of the sleeve should equal the distance from your shoulder to your first knuckles, measured around your bent elbow.

Stitch the sleeve gusset to one side of the sleeve along **d-e**. Stitch the sleeve-gusset piece to the body. Do the same with the other sleeve. Fold the body-sleeve piece over crosswise and stitch up the sides (leaving open at the bottom as shown), stitching **f-g** on the gusset to **f-g** on the body. Stitch **g-e** on the gusset to **g-e** on the sleeve, and stitch up the rest of the sleeve from the gusset to the arrows. Do likewise with the other sleeve. Fold over $^1/_8$" of the side reinforcements all around, and stitch to the point where the side seams end, as shown.

Hem back the open section of the sleeve seam. Fold the cuff along the dotted line, stitch up the ends, and turn right side out. Gather the cuff edge of the sleeve to the seam allowance on the outside of the cuff, right sides together. Stitch. Fold the cuff over, folding in the inside seam allowance, and stitch it closed.

Stitch the neck gussets into the ends of the neck openings, right sides together, matching points **a-b-c**. Hem back the front slit, and take in a small dart at the bottom. Fold over the collar and stitch as you did with the cuffs, and gather the neck opening into it as with the sleeves and the cuffs. Hem the bottom and the open edges of the sides, and add ties to the bottom edge of the collar and the sleeve edge of the cuffs. The original is heavily embroidered on the upper torso, collar, sleeves, and cuffs.

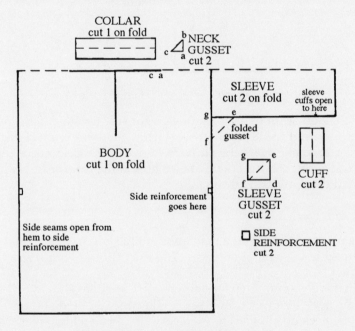

Pattern for a man's shirt. [Singman]

Venetian Breeches (Venetians)

This pattern for a man's Venetians is based on a pair from the early seventeenth century, probably of German origin.[37] The Venetians should require about 2-3 yds. of wool (and as much again for lining, if used) and a small amount of linen for the pockets (although these can be made of wool).

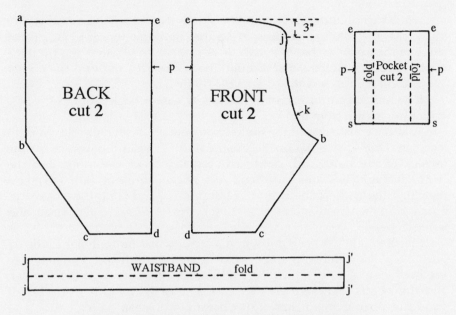

Pattern for Venetian breeches [Hadfield/Singman]

Pattern: The easiest way to proceed is to don a pair of trousers and take a few measurements to draft a pattern based on the one shown here.

—a-e = e-j = $1/3$ to $1/2$ hip measurement, depending on how full you want them
—a-b = top rear of trousers to crotch
—b-c = crotch to 3" below the knee along inseam
—c-d = $1/2$ bottom cuff opening
—e-d = top of trousers to 3" below the knee along outseam
—j-i = top front to crotch
—j-k = 7"
—e-p = 7"
—j-j^1 = waist size (remember to add seam allowances)
—j-j = j^1-j^1 = 3" (remember to add seam allowances)
—e-s = 16"
—e-e = s-s = 13"

Cutting: You will need 2 of each piece except the waistband.

Sewing: On the back and front pieces, sew point **e** to point **e**, and sew the outseam of each leg (**p-d**), leaving pocket slit open (**e-p**). On the pocket, sew point **e** to point **e** and **p-s** to **p-s**, leaving a slit from **e** to **p**. Fold the pocket along the dotted lines and sew across the bottom. Turn the pocket so the seam allowances are inside. Pin the slit of the pocket to the pocket slit in the outseam of the Venetians (**p-e**), right sides together and from the outside of the Venetians. Sew around the pocket slit, and turn the pocket in (you will have to sew the ends of the slit by hand).

Sew the inseam of each leg (**b-c**). Sew center back seam (**a-b**). Sew center front seam from **b** to **k**.

Fold the waistband on the dotted line, sew up the ends, and turn right side out. Gather the top of the breeches to the seam allowance on the outside of the waistband, right sides together, with the top end of the pockets caught into the waistband (the pockets are not gathered), and matching the ends of the waistband to points **j** and **j**^{1} on the Venetians. Stitch. Fold the waistband over, folding in the inside seam allowance, and stitch it closed.

Finish the fly (**j-k**) and cuffs, add 3 buttons and buttonholes to the fly opening, and attach hooks and eyes to fasten the waistband. You may also use hooks and eyes to attach the waistband to the bottom of the doublet, and at the cuffs to make them fit your leg more tightly (this works best if you leave open a few inches of the inseam or outseam at the bottom). A placket can also be added at the fly.

Doublet

The design given here is based primarily on an Italian doublet of the 1570s.[38] You should need about 3 yds. of wool for a man, 2 to $2^1/_2$ for a woman (and as much linen for lining, if used). It may be advisable to use a fairly stiff fabric or to reinforce it with a stiff lining, perhaps including an interlining. Use a medium weight wool and a sturdy lining fabric for best results. The same basic design can be used for a sleeveless jerkin.

Pattern: The surest means of making a doublet fit properly is to make the pattern from an old fitted shirt.

> —Cut off the collar of the shirt.
> —Cut off the bottom of the shirt to shape of the doublet as shown. Point **c** is 4" below the waist, **b** is at the waist.
> —Cut the shirt in two down the middle of the back.
> —Cut off the sleeves at the armhole seams.
> —Cut the sleeve down the seam to give the sleeve pattern.
> —Cut the shoulder seam of the shirt body (this is normally at the front of the shoulder panel on the shirt).
> —Cut the underarm side seam of the shirt to give the fore and back pieces.

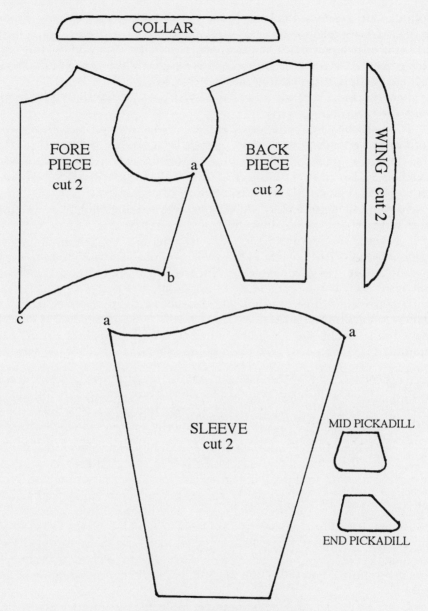

Pattern for a doublet. [Singman]

—The length of the collar will be equal to the distance around the neckline, plus 1" for seam allowances.
—The wings and pickadills are optional.

<u>Cutting</u>: Cut 2 each of the fore, back, and sleeve pieces (omit the sleeve pieces for a sleeveless jerkin). If you want a lining, cut 2 each of the fore, back, and sleeve pieces. If you use an interlining, cut 2 each of the fore and back pieces. If there is no lining, allow a 1" seam allowance at the front opening to support the buttons and buttonholes.

For wings, cut 4 of the outer fabric. Cut 2 of the interlining (without seam allowances) if you have it.

For pickadills, you will need 2 end pickadills to go on each side of the front opening, and as many mid pickadills as are needed (measure the total bottom edge of the body, subtract 4" for the two end pickadills, and divide by 3). For each pickadill, cut 1 of the outer fabric and 1 of the lining fabric. The end pickadills are mirror images of each other.

For the collar, cut 1 of the outer fabric and 1 of the lining. Cut 1 of the interlining (without seam allowances) if you have it.

<u>Sewing</u>: Sew the front pieces to the back piece at the shoulder seam, right sides together. Sew the sleeves to the armholes of the body, matching point **a**.

If you want wings, you will need to insert them *before* sewing the sleeves to the armholes. To make a wing, sew two outer pieces along the curved side, right sides together, and turn right side out. Insert the interlining if you have it. When you pin the sleeves to the body, insert the wing between the right side of the body and the right side of the sleeve, lining up the raw edges of all three pieces together and making sure the midpoint of the wing lies at the shoulder seam. When you sew the sleeve to the armhole, you will also be sewing the wing in place.

Sew up the sleeve and side seams.

If you have a lining, assemble it as you did the outer layer (it will not have wings). Sew it to the outer piece along the CF, right sides together. Turn right side out, and push the lining sleeves through the outer sleeves.

For the collar, sew the outer fabric piece to the lining piece, right sides together, leaving the bottom edge open. Turn right side out. Insert the interlining, if you have it. Sew the neckline of the body to the outer seam allowance of the collar, right sides together, matching the raw edges. Fold the collar over, folding the inner seam allowance in, and stitch it shut. If you have a lining, you will stitch the lining of the collar to the lining of the body.

If you want pickadills, see the instructions for them under the bodice pattern. Otherwise fold over the bottom seam allowance and finish. Fold over the cuff seam allowance and finish.

The doublet normally buttons up the CF; buttonholes would be 1" to $1^3/_4$" apart (depending on button size). You may also add hooks around the waist to support eyes to hold up the breeches; if you are ambitious, you could consider matching rows of paired eyelets in the doublet and in the waistband of the Venetians for points. The sleeves could also be attached with hooks and eyes or laces to make them removable.

Coif

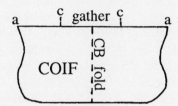

Pattern for a coif. [Hadfield/Singman]

The original on which this coif is based is said to have belonged to Queen Elizabeth; it is made of white linen and is heavily adorned with embroidery.[39] The piece measures 17" by $8^3/_4$". After cutting, hem the entire coif. Fold on the dotted line, and sew **a-c** to **a-c**. Thread a small string through the top from **c** to **c**, gather, and secure the ends of the string. Gather the bottom edge in the same manner, or use a lace, the ends of which can be used to hold the coif on your head.

Flat Cap

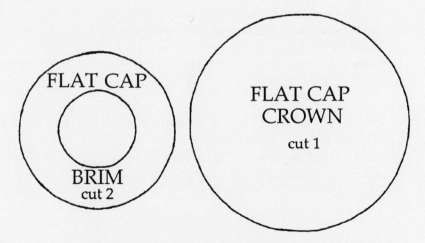

Pattern for a flat cap. [Hadfield/Singman]

The flat cap is the easiest type of male Elizabethan headgear to reproduce. It might also be worn by women over a coif. Use wool for the outer layer, with linen for a lining if you want one, and sturdy canvas or buckram to stiffen the brim. The design is based on an Italian man's flat cap of the 1560s.[40]

The diameter of the hole in the brim piece is such that it will fit snugly over the head—probably around 6". The brim should be about $1^1/_2$". The diameter of the crown piece will be the diameter of the brim piece plus twice the width of the brim. Cut 2 brim pieces and 1 crown piece; cut another crown piece of lining fabric if you want lining. Sew the outside edges of the brim pieces together, right sides together, and turn right side out to make the brim. You may wish to insert a third brim piece of stiffer fabric to make the cap less floppy—canvas or buckram are two possibilities. Then gather the outside edge of the crown piece into the inside edge of the upper brim piece to make the crown. Finish the edges, and the cap will be complete.

Netherstocks and Garters

Woolen socks that reach the knee are available for cross-country skiing and mountain climbing. For knitters, patterns are also available.[41] If you choose to make hose of a woven fabric, the weave should be loose and cut on the bias to allow for a snug fit. The following design is based on a number of surviving examples.[42] They can be made with 2 yds. of fabric ($1^1/_2$ yds. for a woman). Wool will give the best fit; linen is also possible, although it will not have the same stretch.

Draft your hose as follows:

—**a-a** = the measurement around heel and instep

—**c-c** = **d-d** = half the measurement around the broad part of your foot

—line **a-b** is drawn at a slight angle

—**b-c** = **c-d** = half the distance from anklebone to anklebone measured under the sole

—lines **b-e** and **d-d** on the sole intersect at the broadest point of the foot (measure its distance from the toe)

—**b-e** = the distance from heel to toe less **a-b**

—**d-e-d** on the body is the same as **d-e-d** on the sole

—the measurements on the gussets are the same as the measurements on the body and sole

Extend the body upwards as follows:

The distance from the calf line to the top is the distance from the thick of the calf to the knee + 6".

When cutting, do not worry about the lack of a seam allowance in the slashes on the body: just stitch them close to the edge.

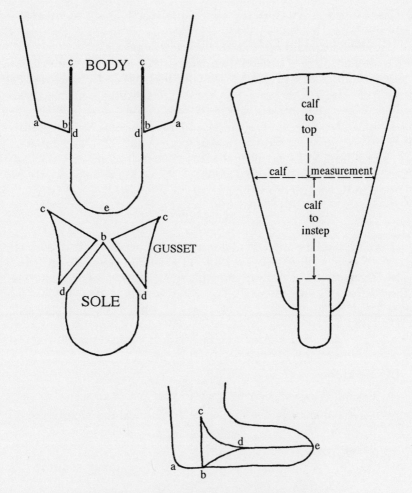

Pattern for cloth hose. [Hadfield/Singman]

Using zig-zag stitch to prevent breakage of the thread, sew up the stocking, right sides together:

  —Sew around the slashes, close to the edges, to prevent raveling.
  —Sew the gussets to the sole.
  —Sew the gussets to the slashes on the body.
  —Sew the foot of the body to the sole.
  —Sew up the heel and body, curving the seam around the heel.

Try the stockings on the opposite feet, still inside out. Repin seams (primarily the long heel-leg seam) to fit them as closely to your leg as you can without making it impossible to pull the stockings on and off. Remove, and restitch, using the new seam-lines. Cut away the excess seam allowance and finish seams and top. Don't worry about the tendency for these stockings to bag at the ankle and twist around the leg: cloth stockings by nature did not fit as snugly as knitted ones.

Garters are strongly recommended, as they can save the aggravation of having your stockings slide down your legs. They can be made of strips of fabric at least 39" long and 1-4" broad. If the fabric is springy, so much the better, as it will allow a better fit. This can be achieved by cutting a woven fabric on the bias; a quick and easy route is to use bias tape. Alternatively, you could knit a strip of wool about 1-2" wide and at least 2' long, alternating knit and purl stitches in both directions. Cross-garters, which wrap around the legs twice, once above the knee and once below, will have to be considerably longer.

Shoes

Shoes are much harder to make, but certain styles of bedroom slipper strongly resemble the plainer style of Elizabethan shoe. Tai-chi shoes are an alternative, with or without the strap: the design is again similar to that of Elizabethan shoes, although they would normally have been of leather instead of cloth.

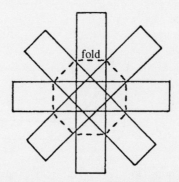

Pattern for a shoe rosette. [Hadfield/Singman]

Your shoes can be given a more distinctively Elizabethan look by adding rosettes, which can be made with four ribbons (preferably 2 each of 2 contrasting colors) roughly 7" x $^3/_4$". Sew them together in the middle as illustrated. Fold the ends over so that they overlap each other in the center back, and sew them in place. Then attach them to the shoe.

Falling Band

This design for a man's falling band derives from visual evidence and surviving examples from the early seventeenth century.[43] The band should be of linen. The collar piece is 25" long, $4^3/_4$" deep at the ends, and $3^3/_4$" deep in the middle. The neckband is 4" deep before folding, and as long as your neck measurement (remember to add $^1/_2$" at each end for the seam allowance).

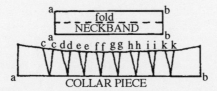

Pattern for a falling band. [Hadfield/Singman]

The 8 pleats on the collar piece are evenly spaced and deep enough to make the curved edge equal to your neck measurement. The first pleat on each end is $^1/_4$ of your neck measurement away from the edge, so that it lies over the midpoint of your shoulder. Pin the pleats up and press: each pleat folds forward, so that the opening faces the back of the neck (the pleats lie on the underside of the collar). Hem the bottom and sides of the collar piece by $^1/_8$". Sew the pleats shut on top with a hemming stitch.

Fold the neckband along the dotted line, and sew up the sides. Turn right side out. Sew the collar piece to the outside seam allowance of the neckband, right sides together. Fold the neckband over, fold back the inside seam allowance, and stitch shut. Attach flexible ties, about 5" long, to the top of the fore-edge of the neck piece.

The collar should be pinned to the doublet and folded down over the doublet collar. Cuffs can be constructed in the same manner as the falling band.

Cassock

The cassock is a good warm garment for both men and women. The design given here is based on a mid-seventeenth-century Swedish example, adjusted to make it closer to sixteenth-century illustrations.[44] The cassock should require 2 yds. of wool. Two of each piece will be needed. Sew the back pieces together at the CB seam. Sew the fore pieces to the back at the shoulder seams. Sew the sleeve to the armhole, and stitch up the sides and sleeve seam. Hem the neckline and cuffs; if the wool is sufficiently felted, you will not need to hem the bottom edge.

The cassock can fasten with buttons all the way down the front, or just a few at the top, with the remainder of the front sewn up. The side seams can be sewn shut, left open, or fastened with buttons or ties. The sleeves could be omitted. If you decide to add a lining, remember not to sew the lower edge of the garment to the lining: this will attract rainwater.

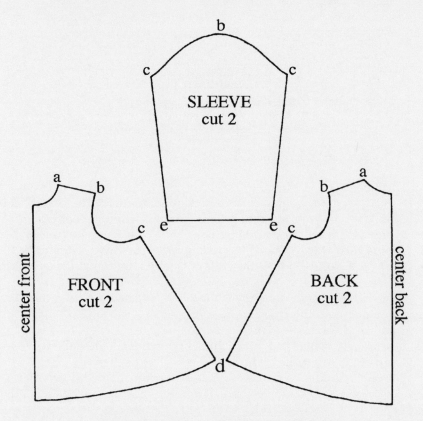

Pattern for a cassock. [Hadfield/Singman]

Buttons

Buttonmaking kits are an easy means of reproducing the look of Elizabethan cloth-covered buttons, although the originals would have been more round. Try to get small ones— Elizabethan buttons tended to be under $3/_4$" in diameter. When choosing a button kit, try to be sure that the shank comes attached to the face rather than to the back-plate; buttons of the latter type are less sturdy. You can also make an Elizabethan button entirely of cloth: cut a $1^1/_2$" diameter circle, then sew a 1" diameter gathering stitch around it. Gather the stitch, stuffing the edge of the circle into the center as you do, and sew it up. Buttons were generally sewn to the edge of the garment, rather than slightly in from the edge as is usual today.[45]

A royal hunting party. [Ashdown]

7

Food and Drink

Food ranks among the most important of human needs, a fact of which the Elizabethans were more acutely aware than we generally are today. By contemporary standards, the Elizabethans were well fed. Travelers from the Continent were often impressed by the Englishman's hearty diet: even the husbandman ate reasonably well compared to the Continental peasant. Yet in England as elsewhere during the sixteenth century, food production was a laborious and precarious endeavor. Agriculture was back-breaking work, which by modern standards yielded only low returns in produce. Worse, it was extremely susceptible to natural misfortunes: mysterious illnesses could devastate livestock, and a summer with too much or too little rain would lead to poor harvests, skyrocketing food prices, and famine. The harvests of Elizabeth's reign were relatively good, but severe shortages in 1586-88, 1594-95, and 1596-98 led to widespread hunger and mortality. Even in a good year, poverty and malnutrition were never wholly out of sight of those who had steady sources of income: the poor were always highly visible in Elizabethan England. Not surprisingly, there seems to have been less waste of food: when an aristocratic family finished eating, the leftovers were given to the servants; when the servants were done, the remains were brought to the door for distribution to the poor, who gathered outside to receive it.[1]

The first meal of the day was breakfast, which was generally an informal bite on the run rather than a sit-down meal. Many **Meals** people did not take breakfast at all but waited until dinner in the late morning. Those who did have breakfast might eat right after rising or up to several hours later. A simple breakfast might consist of porridge or pottage (stew), or even scraps and leftovers. A more hearty breakfast could include bread with butter or cheese, ale or wine, fruit, and some sort of meat—beef, mutton, or chickens.

Merrymaking at the table. [Hindley]

The real meals were dinner, served around 11 or noon, and supper in the evening, somewhere from 6 to 9. For ordinary people, the midday dinner was probably the larger meal of the two, but those of the privileged classes may have had their principal meal in the evening. A simple meal might be served all at once, but in wealthy households—or on special occasions like holy days—a meal might consist of many courses, each containing several dishes, with cheese and fruits at the end of the meal. Sweet dishes would be included in each course, rather than served only at the end. One contemporary cookbook offers the following sample menu:

The First Course: Pottage or stewed broth; boiled meat or stewed meat, chickens and bacon, powdered [salted] beef, pies, goose, pig, roasted beef, roasted veal, custard.

The Second Course: Roasted lamb, roasted capons, roasted conies [rabbits], chickens, peahens, baked venison, tart.[2]

These formal meals were not the only times people ate. Those who felt hungry during the day might have a bit of bread or cold food, and perhaps a bit of ale. During haymaking and harvesting seasons, rural folk took their food into the fields; common harvesting fare included bottled beer, apple pasties (a sturdy, hand-sized pastry), bread, cheese and butter. At the other end of the social scale, an aristocratic hunting party might bring along cold meats, pies, and sausages.

       Bread, a prominent feature of everyone's diet, was always present **Diet**   at meals, although contemporaries agreed that it was less important in England than on the Continent. Wheat was the favored grain for bread, and whiter breads were preferred to dark ones, although even the whitest Elizabethan bread was almost as brown as a modern whole-wheat loaf. The finest bread was the small hand-loaf called a "manchet." Commercial manchets typically weighed 8 oz. when they went into the oven and 6 oz. when they came out—the price of bread was fixed by law, but the weights were allowed to change according to the current price of grain. Next came "cheat," which was less refined; a cheat loaf weighed 18 oz. going into the oven and 16 oz. when it came out. Poorer people often made do with rye, barley, or mixed-grain bread; beans, peas, and oats were used in times of dearth. Breads were not baked in pans, so they were low and round rather than tall. Bread would go stale after a few days, since there were no plastic bags or refrigerators to keep it fresh. However, nothing was wasted: stale bread could be used to make bread puddings, and bread crumbs served to thicken soups, stews, and sauces. An alternative to bread was biscuit, which kept longer and was especially useful aboard ships. Unground oats and barley were used in pottages and stews, as was imported rice.[3]

Contemporaries agreed that just as bread was less prominent in the English diet than it was on the Continent, meat was correspondingly more so—according to the Elizabethan traveler Fynes Moryson, England was particularly noted for the quality of its roast meats. A greater variety of meat was consumed in the sixteenth century than is common today. Red meats included beef, mutton, veal, lamb, kid, and pork. For poultry there were chickens, ducks, geese, and even pigeons. Game meats included deer, rabbit, and an enormous variety of wildfowl—for example, larks, sparrows, pheasants, partridge, quail, crane, plovers, and woodcocks. Another distinctive feature of Elizabethan cuisine was that very little of the animal went to waste: cookbooks for prosperous households include recipes for pigs' and calves' feet, lamb's head, and tripe.[4]

Seafood was another important source of protein—in fact, fish were a much larger part of the Elizabethan diet than is generally the case today. English fishermen exported a great deal of cod and herring, the coasts abounded in oysters and mussels, and the rivers supplied freshwater fish and eels. Popular seafood included flounder, mackerel, carp, pike, salmon, trout, shrimp, crab, and even the occasional porpoise or seal. During the season of Lent people were supposed to abstain from eating meat, relying on fish instead: this was no longer a religious requirement, as England was a Protestant country, but the ban was reinstated by Elizabeth as a means of supporting English fisheries (and thereby English sea-power in general). The same rule applied on Wednesdays, Fridays, and Saturdays, as well as throughout Advent and on the eves of certain holy days; in total, it accounted for over a third of the year. This fasting was not rigorously observed by Elizabeth's subjects—indeed, the Queen herself refused to be bound by the law, although she saw to it that everyone else at her court was served no meat on fast-days. Nevertheless, seafood was a handy staple: it was relatively cheap, it was available fresh in much of the country, and it could be preserved by salting, drying, or pickling.[5]

The truly poor probably derived most of their protein from "white meat": milk, eggs, butter, and cheese. Cheese was featured in the aristocratic diet too, being commonly served at the end of a meal. Nuts were another source of protein: chestnuts, walnuts, and hazelnuts were all common.

Vegetables probably had a larger part in the Elizabethan diet than is sometimes supposed today. It was common for houses to have gardens, even in the middle of London; such gardens provided a variety of vegetables for the household, including artichokes, asparagus, cucumbers, endive, radish, spinach, lettuce, beans, cabbage, carrots, leeks, parsnips, peas, and turnips. Fruits were also a regular part of the diet: they were used flavor dishes, and were often served at the end of a meal. They too were likely to be grown in the garden. Domestically produced fruit included apricots, grapes, figs, strawberries, raspberries, apples, pears, plums, currants, mulberries, and cherries. England also imported certain fruits, especially oranges from the Mediterranean.

Fruits were probably the principal source of sugar for most people. Refined sugar was expensive—about a shilling a pound—although still within the reach of people of means. Honey, although not cheap, was also a common sweetener. People at the top of the social scale liked to indulge in a variety of sweet foods, including gingerbreads and cakes, candies, marzipan, conserves, and marmalade—ordinary people probably had such foods only on special occasions, such as holy days.

Spices, like sugar, were quite expensive. Then as now, they were mainly imported from exotic places, but their transport was much more difficult, dangerous, and time-consuming than it is today. Consequently, the use of spices was a good way to demonstrate one's social position. Elizabethan recipes call for a distinctive range of spices, particularly cinnamon, nutmeg, cloves, mace, saffron, ginger, and pepper. Other imported flavoring agents were capers, olives, and lemons.

Ordinary people relied more on the seasonings that grew in their household gardens, such as cress, fennel, mint, onions, scallions, marjoram, parsley, rosemary, sage, savory, thyme, and tarragon. Mustard was a particular favorite, especially in sauces for dressing meats. Vinegar and oil were popular, as was "verjuice," the sour juice of the crabapple. Salt was the commonest flavoring agent of all; it appears in many Elizabethan recipes, and it was always set out on the table at mealtimes. One last additive worth noting is flowers, which provided both flavor and coloring: marigolds, primroses, and violets were commonly used in this way.[6]

Some staples of the modern table were either rare or wholly unavailable in Elizabethan England. This is especially true of New World plants such as coffee, vanilla, and cocoa. Tomatoes were used in southern Europe but not in England. Potatoes were first imported to England during Elizabeth's reign: they were an extremely expensive delicacy!

The content of a meal depended very much on the season, since fresh food did not keep or transport well. In November, people at the low end of the economic scale would slaughter any livestock they planned to eat during the winter: it was expensive to keep animals fed after they had to be taken in from pasture. The meats were preserved by smoking or salting; bacon, ham, and sausage were all familiar winter fare. Fish were likewise smoked, dried, or salted. Salted meats were soaked before cooking to remove some of the excess salt, but they tended to be fairly salty nonetheless. Butter was also preserved by salting. Another means of preservation was pickling, especially for seafoods and vegetables. Fruits, peas and beans could be preserved by drying; fruits were also made into preserves.

Regardless of one's place in Elizabethan society, the conditions under which a meal were prepared were **The Kitchen** primitive by modern standards. All cooking involved an actual fire. There were three principal ways of cooking a main dish: boiling, roasting, or baking. Of these, boiling was the easiest and probably the most common. It involved placing the food in a pot over hot coals or an open flame. Many pots had legs so they could be set directly on the fire, and fireplaces typically had chains and hooks for suspending pots; sometimes a ratchet allowed the pot to be moved up or down to adjust the cooking temperature. Once the food was set to boil it needed relatively little attention, so boiled soups, pottages (stews) and meats were convenient dishes. Frying was a similar procedure: the pan was placed on a gridiron over the flames or hot coals.

Roasts were turned on a spit next to the fire, with a dripping-pan below to catch the grease—a by-product that might be used in other recipes or in providing domestic lighting. Roasting was a laborious procedure, since the spit had to be turned constantly. Some kitchens had automatic devices for this job, powered by the rising heat of the fire, but usually it was done by hand, often by the children of the house or the lowest-ranking kitchen servants.

Baking involved an enclosed clay or brick oven, sometimes a separate structure outside the home. A fire was lit inside the oven and allowed to burn until the interior was sufficiently hot, at which point the coals were raked out, the baking surface wiped with a damp "malkin" (a mop made of rags tied to a long handle), and the food slid inside with a "pell" (a flat long-handled wooden shovel) to bake in the residual heat. Those who could not afford a proper oven might bake under a crock turned upside down and covered with coals. Probably the commonest form of baked dish was the pie, which might stuffed with meat, poultry, fish, shellfish, fruit, or vegetables.

Cooking utensils were typically made of clay, iron, copper or brass. Because copper and its alloys (such as bronze and brass) are less susceptible than iron to rust, and can transmit heat very quickly, they are good for heating water. Iron, on the other hand, transmits heat more slowly but spreads it more evenly, and after long use it acquires an oily coating that keeps food from sticking to it. For these reasons, iron was the better material for cooking food. Clay pots were also useful for cooking, since they could be placed very close to the fire and conduct heat quite evenly.

A well-appointed kitchen would also have a wooden kneading-trough for making bread, a mortar and pestle for grinding. Flour was kept in legged wooden bins called "meal arks." Spices and dried fruits might be stored in small boxes or clay pots; vinegar, oil, and other liquids in leather, earthenware, or glass bottles. Additional storage was provided by baskets and linen and canvas bags and sacks. Spices were normally stored whole, to be ground as needed. Salt was kept in special salt-boxes. The kitchen would be provided with cupboards and shelves for storing all of these utensils and provisions.

Drinks   Water was not a particularly healthy drink in Elizabethan England due to poor sanitation in the cities, and natural impurities in country water. Under the circumstances, fermented drinks were actually the healthier choice. The traditional English beverage was ale, made of water, malted barley, herbs and spices; it lacked hops, so it tasted little like what we call ale today, and its shelf-life was short. Already, beer—similar to ale but brewed with hops—had come to be favored in the cities. Beer was lighter and clearer than ale; it also kept longer, and was therefore cheaper. The best beer was 1 to 2 years old, but usually it was consumed after just a month of aging.

Ale varied greatly in strength, from the watery small ales to "double ale," or even the rather expensive "double-double," often known by such evocative names as "Mad Dog," "Huffcap," "Father Whoreson," and "Dragons' Milk."[7] Ale was the staple drink of Elizabethan England, having

A tapster or tavernkeeper. He holds the glass by its base in the characteristic manner of the period. [Hindley]

properties as well as being a source of water for the body. As a daily staple it was generally consumed in forms with very low alcohol content: children drank it as well as adults, and people would drink it when they breakfasted and throughout the working day. A gallon a day seems to have been a normal ration for a grown man.

Wine in Elizabethan England was invariably imported, since English grapes were unsuitable for winemaking. What the Elizabethans called "French" wine came from the north of France; wines from southern France, such as the modern Bordeaux, were known to the Elizabethans as "Gascon" wine, or "claret." Rhenish wines, both red and white, were also enjoyed in England; other wines came from Italy and even Greece. The favorite imports appear to have been the sweet fortified wines of the Iberian peninsula, especially "sack," imported from Jerez (whence its modern name, "sherry"), and "madeira" and "canary," respectively from the Madeira and Canary Islands off the northwest coast of Africa. The English liked their wines sweet and would often sugar them heavily. Because it was imported, wine was quite expensive—typically twelve times the cost of ale—so it was primarily a drink for the privileged. For reasons of health (and perhaps expense), many people would add water to their wine.

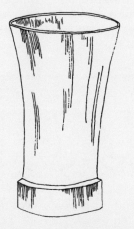

A pewter beaker. The original is about 6" high. [Singman]

Although English grapes were not used for winemaking, other English fruits yielded a range of alternative drinks. These included cider from apples, perry from pears, and "raspie" from raspberries. Other fruits used in winemaking included gooseberries, cherries, blackberries and elderberries. Mead and metheglin, made with honey, were common in Wales and had some aficionados in England. Distilled liquors were also in use, albeit mostly for medicinal purposes: the commonest was known as aqua vitae. There were also mixed drinks, notably posset, an ale drink vaguely comparable to eggnog, and syllabub, a similar concoction soured with cider or vinegar. Both wine and beer might be seasoned with herbs and spices—spiced wine was often called "hippocras." Nonalcoholic drinks included milk, whey (the watery part of milk that remains after coagulated curds are removed), and plain water, but these were generally not favored by adults.

The Elizabethans closely associated drink with tobacco, which was served along with beer in alehouses. In fact, it was common to speak of "drinking" tobacco smoke. Tobacco was first brought to England from the New World during Elizabeth's reign; it was much more narcotic than its modern descendant. Some, like King James of Scotland (soon to be king of England as well), reviled the new weed, but most authorities believed it had great medicinal powers. In the words of one contemporary author, "Our age has discovered nothing from the New World which will be numbered among the remedies more valuable and efficacious than this plant for sores, wounds, affections of the throat and chest, and the fever of the plague."[8]

Tableware   In the Middle Ages the dining table had most often been a temporary board set upon trestles, but by the late sixteenth century the trestle table had generally been supplanted by the permanent "table dormant." At mealtimes this table was covered with a white linen tablecloth. A typical place setting consisted of a drinking vessel, a spoon, a trencher (wooden plate), a bowl and a linen napkin.

Elizabethan drinking vessels were quite varied. Some were plain beakers of wood, horn, or pewter; others were fine goblets of pewter or richer materials. Very poor folk might drink from a wooden bowl (a custom observed by many at Christmastime when drinking the wassail, or spiced ale). Some of the finest vessels were made of glass, which might be produced domestically or imported from the Continent. Pewter tankards were common, normally in a lidded form, and ceramic mugs were also used. One of the most distinctive Elizabethan drinking vessels was the "black jack," a mug made of leather and sealed with pitch. Drinks were generally poured from jugs, which were made of the same range of materials as the drinking vessels themselves.

A pewter spoon.
[Hoornstra]

The least expensive spoons were made of horn or wood; finer spoons were cast in metals such as pewter or silver. The characteristic spoon of the period had a thin handle, round in cross-section, and a large fig-shaped bowl. The handle of a metal spoon sometimes had a decorative ending called a "knop." Designs for knops included various sorts of balls, acorns, and even human figures: one form was the "Apostle Spoon," which had a knop in the figure of one of the Twelve Apostles. Pewter and silver spoons were among the commonest luxuries in ordinary households, and were frequently given as gifts at weddings and christenings.

The ordinary form of plate was the trencher, a square piece of wood with a large depression hollowed out for the food and a smaller one in the upper righthand corner for salt; fancier round plates might be made of pewter or silver. The trencher was smaller than a modern dinner plate, more like a modern salad plate. Ordinary bowls were likewise made of wood. In addition to the plates for the diners, empty plates called "voiders" were often set out to receive bones, shells, and other scraps.

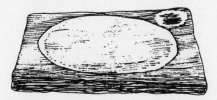

A wooden trencher. The original is of sycamore, about 7 1/2" broad and 6" deep. The depression on the right is for salt. [Singman]

Missing from the typical place setting was the knife and fork. In ordinary households it was widely expected that diners would be carrying their own knives. The Elizabethan table knife was invariably pointed—the blunt form of modern knives was introduced during the seventeenth century to reduce the danger of mealtime brawling. The blade was of carbon steel; unlike modern stainless steels, it had to be kept dry and oiled to prevent rust. The handle might be of wood, horn, bone, or ivory. Forks, on the other hand, were not a feature of the Elizabethan table at all. The Italians were using forks in this period, but in England the fork was exclusively a kitchen utensil. Food was cut on either the cook's bench or the serving platter, so by the time the food hit the trencher it did not need to be held down and cut.

A knife. [Hoornstra]

Salt was put out in salt-cellars, and the diners transferred it with their knives to the salt-depression on the trencher. Silver salt-cellars were a common luxury, pewter being a cheaper alternative. Condiments (such as mustard) and sauces were also set out for the diners. Valuable tableware was one of the likeliest luxuries for a person to own, as it could be brought out to impress guests: a poor man might well invest in some pewter, and a man of limited means might own some silver or glass.[9]

Eating and drinking are among the most ritualized aspects of daily life, and this was as true in Elizabethan England as in other societies. It was customary to begin the meal by washing hands—a particularly important ritual in an age when people used their fingers in eating much more than we do today. This generally involved one of the servants or children passing among the guests with a pitcher of

Etiquette

A Prayer to Be Said before Meat

All things depend upon thy providence, O Lord, to receive at thy hands due sustenance in time convenient. Thou givest to them, and they gather it: thou openest thy hand, and they are satisfied with all good things.

O heavenly Father, which art the fountain and full treasure of all goodness, we beseech thee to shew thy mercies upon us thy children, and sanctify these gifts which we receive of thy merciful liberality, granting us grace to use them soberly and purely, according to thy blessed will: so that hereby we may acknowledge thee to be the author and giver of all good things, and above all that we may remember continually to seek the spiritual food of thy word, wherewith our souls may be nourished everlastingly, through our Saviour Christ, who is the true bread of life, which came down from heaven, of whom whosoever eateth shall live for ever, and reign with Him in glory, world without end. So be it.

A Thanksgiving after Meals

Glory, praise, and honour be unto thee, most merciful and omnipotent Father, who of thine infinite goodness hast created man to thine own image and similitude; who also hast fed and daily feedest of thy most bountiful hand all living creatures: grant unto us, that as thou hast nourished these our mortal bodies with corporal food, so thou wouldest replenish our souls with the perfect knowledge of the lively word of thy beloved Son Jesus Christ; to whom be praise, glory, and honour, for ever. So be it.[10]

water, a basin, and a towel. When everyone had washed, someone would recite a prayer. Then the meal would begin.

Adult men generally kept their hats on at the table, unless one of their fellow diners was clearly higher in social status; women wore their coifs, while children and servants were bareheaded out of respect for their superiors.[11] In large and wealthy households there might be a substantial number of servants to bring the food to the table and clear it away, as well to pour drinks when they were called for. In the best households drinks did not sit on the table but on a sideboard: a thirsty diner would summon a servant to provide him with a cup, which was taken away once he had drunk from it. The bond created by sharing of food and drink was emphasized by the custom of toasting and pledging with one's drink. In humbler homes it was common for children to serve their parents before sitting down to eat, and they were likewise expected to clear away the food at the end of the meal.

Men draped their napkins across one shoulder, while women kept their napkins on their laps. Manners books warned children not to smack their lips or gnaw on bones, to keep their fingers clean with their napkins, and to wipe their mouths before drinking. Once the meal was over, it was customary to recite another prayer and to wash hands again. People might clean their teeth at this point with a toothpick made of wood or ivory, turning away from the company and covering the mouth with a napkin while doing so.

A family at the table in the early seventeenth century. [Hindley]

When not at home, Elizabethan folk obtained food and drink at taverns, inns, alehouses, and "ordinaries." An inn **Eating Out** was primarily a place for lodging and catered to the upper classes; it also offered food, ale, beer, and wine. The tavern generally provided respectable lodging, and served wine but not food; its clientele was largely middle to upper class. The alehouse offered ale and beer, and sometimes simple food and lodging on the side. The alehouse was by far the most common sort of establishment, and the only one at which ordinary folk would be welcome. It was recognizable by the "ale-stake" displayed over the door: either a pole with a bush attached at the end, or a broom, such as was used to sweep the yeast from the top during brewing—when a batch of ale was ready, the broom was set out to alert passersby. An establishment that primarily served food was called an "ordinary," so named because it served a fixed fare at a standard price. According to the Swiss tourist Thomas Platter, women were as likely to frequent taverns and alehouses as men: one might even invite another man's wife to such an establishment, in which case she would bring several other female friends and the husband would thank the other man for his courtesy afterwards.[12]

RECIPES

The following recipes are all based on original sources: Gervase Markham's *The English Housewife*, first published in 1615; Thomas Dawson's *The good huswifes iewell* and *The second part of the good huswifes iewell*, first printed in the 1580s; and the anonymous *The Good Huswifes Handmaide for the kitchin*, printed in 1594. In each case the original text is given in italics (with spelling modernized), followed by an interpretation for the modern cook.

Bread

Of baking manchets [small loaves of fine flour].

First your meal, being ground upon the black stones if it be possible, which make the whitest flour, and bolted through the finest bolting cloth, you shall put it into a clean kimnel [kneading trough], *and, opening the flour hollow in the midst, put into it of the best ale barm the quantity of three pints to a bushel of meal, with some salt to season it with: then put in your liquor reasonable warm and knead it very well together both with your hands and through the brake* [a board with one end of a rolling pin hinged to it]; *or for want thereof, fold it in a cloth, and with your feet tread it a good space together, then, letting it lie an hour or thereabouts to swell, take it forth and mould it into manchets, round, and flat; scotch about the waist to give it leave to rise, and prick it with your knife in the top, and so put it into the oven, and bake it with a gentle heat. . . .*

And thus . . . you may bake any bread leavened or unleavened whatsoever, whether it be simple corn, as wheat or rye of itself, or compound grain as wheat and rye, or wheat and barley, or rye and barley, or any other mixed white corn; only, because rye is a little stronger than wheat, it shall be good for you to put to your water a little hotter than you did to your wheat. [Markham, Ch. 9, nos. 15-17]

Sift **3 cups unbleached flour**; use white flour for manchets, whole wheat for a household loaf, or any combination of wheat, rye, and barley as Markham suggests. Dissolve **1 teaspoon active dry yeast** in **1 cup lukewarm water or beer** and stir in **1 teaspoon salt**. Make a well in the flour and pour the yeast mixture into it. Mix and knead for 5 minutes. Since the wheat can vary in initial moisture, you might have to add water or flour to ensure that it is moist to the touch but not sticky. Let the dough rise in a warm place for about an hour. The loaf should be round and flat, and pricked on top with a knife. Let it rise until it has doubled in volume, about 45 minutes to an hour. Preheat the oven to 500° F. When the dough has risen, put it in the oven and reduce heat to 350° F. After about 20 minutes the bread should be golden brown and ready to remove from the oven.[13]

Pottage

To make the best ordinary pottage, you shall take a rack of mutton cut into pieces, or a leg of mutton cut into pieces; for this meat and these joints are the best, although any other joint or any fresh beef will likewise make good pottage: and, having washed your meat well, put it into a clean pot with fair water, & set it on the fire; then take violet leaves, endive, succory [a salad herb, closely related to endive], *strawberry leaves, spinach, langdebeef* [oxtongue], *marigold flowers, scallions, and a little parsley, and chop them very small together; then take half so much oatmeal well beaten as there is herbs, and mix it with the herbs, and chop all very well together: then when the pot is ready to boil, scum it very well, and then put in your herbs, and so let it boil with a quick fire, stirring the meat oft in the pot, till the meat be boiled enough, and then the herbs and water are mixed together without any separation, which will be after the consumption of more than a third part: then season them with salt, and serve them up with the meat either with sippets* [a small slice of bread, toasted or fried, used to sop up gravy or broth] *or without.* [Markham, Ch. 2, no. 74]

Cut **1 1/2 lb. mutton** into 1-inch cubes. Add **6 cups water**. Bring to a boil. Chop together **1 cup endive, 1 1/2 cup spinach, 1 1/2 cup scallions, 1 cup parsley,** and **2 cups rolled oats** (if you can find yourself the violet leaves, succory, strawberry leaves, oxtongue, and marigold flowers, then so much the better). Stir the herbs and oatmeal into the liquid, cover and simmer gently for about 1 hour or until meat is tender, stirring periodically. Add **salt** to taste. Makes 4-6 servings.

This dish is fairly representative of the ordinary fare of the Elizabethan commoner, relying on mutton and domestically grown grain and herbs.

Roast Chicken

Preheat oven to 450°. Clean **1 4-5 lb. chicken or capon**. Stuff with **1 recipe stuffing** (see below), truss up the legs, and sew the body cavity shut. Place the bird on a roasting pan in the oven and reduce temperature to 350°. Baste frequently with the juices from the bird; you may begin the process by basting with **2 teaspoons salt** dissolved in **1 cup water**. Roast for about 20 minutes a pound (the bird will be done when its juices run clear and there is no redness left in the meat). Pour **1 recipe capon sauce** (see below) on the bird just before serving.[14]

Stuffing

To farse all things. Take a good handful of thyme, hyssop, parsley, and three or four yolks of eggs hard roasted, and chop them with herbs small, then take white bread grated and raw eggs with sweet butter, a few small raisins, or barberries, seasoning it with pepper, cloves, mace, cinnamon, and ginger, working it all together as paste, and then may you stuff with it what you will. [Dawson, *The second part*, p. 10]

Take the yolk of 1 hardboiled egg, and chop it up with 1/2 teaspoon thyme and 2 tablespoons parsley. Work together in a bowl with 2 cups bread crumbs, 2 raw eggs, 2 tablespoons unsalted butter, 2 tablespoons raisins, 1/8 teaspoon pepper, 1/8 teaspoon cloves, 1/8 teaspoon mace, 1/8 teaspoon cinnamon, and 1/4 teaspoon ground ginger.

Capon Sauce

To make an excellent sauce for a roast capon, you shall take onions, and, having sliced and peeled them, boil them in fair water with pepper, salt, and a few bread crumbs: then put unto it a spoonful or two of claret wine, the juice of an orange, and three or four slices of a lemon peel; all these shred together, and so pour it upon the capon being broke up. [Markham, Ch. 2, no. 79]

Peel and dice **1 small onion**. Add to **1 3/4 cups boiling water**, along with **1/4 teaspoon pepper**, **1/2 cup bread crumbs**, and **salt to taste**. Boil for 5 minutes, then remove from heat, and add **1 tablespoon red wine**, **3 tablespoons freshly squeezed orange juice**, and **1 teaspoon grated lemon rind**. Pour it on the roast and serve.

Salads and Vegetables

Your simple sallats are chibols [wild onion] *peeled, washed clean, and half of the green tops cut clean away, so served on a fruit dish; or chives, scallions, radish roots, boiled carrots, skirrets* [a species of water parsnip], *and turnips, with such like served up simply; also, all young lettuce, cabbage lettuce, purslane* [the herb *Pastalaca oleracea*], *and divers other herbs which may be served simply without anything but a little vinegar, salad oil and sugar; onions boiled, and stripped from their rind and served up with vinegar, oil and pepper is a good simple salad; so is samphire* [the herb *Crithmum maritimum*], *bean cods, asparagus, and cucumbers, served in likewise with oil, vinegar, and pepper, with a world of others, too tedious to nominate. Your compound salads are first young buds and knots of all manner of wholesome herbs at their first springing, as red sage, mints, lettuce, violets, marigolds, spinach, and many other mixed together, and then served up to the table with vinegar, salad oil and sugar.* [Markham, Ch. 2, no. 11]

The term "salad" as used by Markham covers a range of vegetable dishes. His description suggests several possibilities, of which two are offered here.

(1) Chop **3 carrots, 2 parsnips,** and **1 turnip** into 1-inch cubes. Bring **4 cups water** to a brisk boil and add the chopped vegetables. Chop together **1 tablespoon chives, 2 radishes,** and **1 tablespoon scallions.** When the vegetables are tender, drain them, mix them with the chives, radishes, and scallions, and serve.

(2) Wash and tear up **1/2 head leaf lettuce** and an equal quantity of **spinach.** Add **3 tablespoons mint leaves** and, if possible, **3 tablespoons violets** and **3 tablespoons marigolds.** Mix **3 tablespoons olive oil** and **3 tablespoons vinegar** with **1/2 teaspoon sugar** to make a salad dressing. This salad can be varied with the addition of **sliced cucumber, endive, radishes, spinach,** or **mint.** The salad oil could be made with **1/4 teaspoon pepper** instead of the sugar.

Pies

Pie Crust

Your rye paste would be kneaded only with hot water and a little butter, or sweet seam [animal fat] *and rye flour very finely sifted, and it would be made tough and stiff that it may stand well in the rising, for the coffin thereof must ever be very deep: your coarse wheat crust would be kneaded with hot water, or mutton broth and good store of butter, and the paste made stiff and tough because that coffin must be deep also; your fine wheat crust must be kneaded with as much butter as water, and the paste made reasonable lithe and gentle, into which you must put three or four eggs or more according to the quantity you blend together, for they will give it a sufficient stiffening.* [Markham, Ch. 2, no. 109]

Sift together **2 cups unbleached white flour** with **1 cup whole wheat flour.** Make a well in the flour, and shave **1/2 cup butter** into it. Mix into a finely crumbling consistency. Work **2 eggs** into it, then work **1/2 cup water** into it bit by bit (you may need slightly less or more water—the dough should be just elastic enough to be worked). Divide the dough in half, and roll it out into two circles for a pie shell and a lid. Pour the **1 recipe fruit or spinach filling** (see below) into the pie shell, and cover with the lid.

Fruit Filling

To make all manner of fruit tarts: You must boil your fruit, whether it be apple, cherry, peach, damson [plum], *pear, mulberry, or codling* [a kind of apple], *in fair water, and when they be boiled enough, put them into a bowl and bruise them with a ladle, and when they be cold, strain them, and put in red wine or claret wine, and so season it with sugar, cinnamon, and ginger.* [Dawson, *The good huswifes iewell*, p. 18].

Preheat oven to 450°. Cut **6 peaches** into eighths, removing the pits, stems, and skins. Bring **4 cups water** to a boil, add the peaches, and boil for 5-10 minutes or until tender. Remove the mixture from the heat and crush the peaches with a ladle. Let the mixture cool, and strain it to remove excess water. Add **1/2 cup red wine, 1/2 cup sugar, 1 teaspoon ground cinnamon**, and **1 teaspoon ground ginger**. Place in pie shell and cover. Bake at 450° for 10 minutes, then reduce to 350° and take it out when the crust is golden brown, which should be approximately 45 minutes later.

Spinach Filling

To make a tart of spinach: Boil your eggs and your cream together, and then put them into a bowl, and then boil your spinach, and when they are boiled, take them out of the water and strain them into your stuff before you strain your cream, boil your stuff and then strain them all again, and season them with sugar and salt. [Dawson, *The good huswifes iewell*, pp. 20-21]

Preheat oven to 375°. Stir **4 eggs** into **1 1/2 cups cream**, bring to a boil, and remove from the heat. Boil **6 cups spinach** in **4 cups water** for 1 minute. Strain the spinach, add it to the egg and cream mixture, boil, and season with **1/2 tablespoon sugar** and **salt to taste**. (Other recipes replace the salt with cinnamon and ginger—you can use a teaspoon of each.) Place in pie shell and cover. Bake at 375° for 35-40 minutes, and take it out when the crust is golden brown.

This dish is essentially an Elizabethan quiche.

Spiced Cake with Currants

To make a very good Banbury cake, take four pounds of currants, & wash and pick them very clean, and dry them in a cloth: then take three eggs and put away one yolk, and beat them, and strain them with barm [froth from ale-making], *putting thereto cloves, mace, cinnamon, and nutmegs; then take a pint of cream, and as much morning's milk and set it on the fire till the cold be taken away; then take flour and put in good store of cold butter and sugar, then put in your eggs, barm, and meal and work them all together an hour or more; then save a part of the paste, & the rest break in pieces and work in your currants; which done, mould your cake of what quantity you please; and then with that paste which hath not any currants cover it very thin both underneath and aloft. And so bake it according to the bigness.* [Markham, Ch. 2, no. 172]

Preheat oven to 350°. Dissolve **1 teaspoon dry active yeast** in **1/4 cup lukewarm water or beer**, and allow to sit for 10 minutes. Add **1 beaten egg, 1/4 teaspoon cloves, 1/4 teaspoon mace, 1/2 teaspoon cinnamon**, and **1/4 teaspoon nutmeg**. Warm **3/4 cup half and half**, and stir it into the yeast mixture. Mix **2 cups sifted unbleached flour** with **3/4 cup sugar**, and work in **1/2 cup butter**. Work the yeast mixture into the flour mixture. Work in **1 cup dried currants**.   Bake in a greased breadpan for about 1 hour; when the cake is done, the surface will be golden brown and a knife stuck into it will come out dry.

An Elizabethan cake, like bread, was leavened with yeast, since baking soda had not yet been introduced.

Spiced Beer

Take three pints of beer, put five yolks of eggs to it, strain them together, and set it in a pewter pot to the fire, and put to it half a pound of sugar, one pennyworth of nutmegs beaten, one pennyworth of cloves beaten, and a halfpennyworth of ginger beaten, and when it is all in, take another pewter pot and draw them together, and set it to the fire again, and when it is ready to boil, take it from the fire, and put a dish of sweet butter into it, and brew them together out of one pot into another. [*The Good Husewifes Handmaide*, p. 62]

Add **1 egg yolk** to **1 pint of beer**, and warm. Stir in **1/4 cup sugar** and a pinch each of **ground nutmeg, ground cloves**, and **ground ginger**. When it is on the verge of boiling, remove it from the stove, add a spoonful of **butter**, and stir.

A pewter jug. [Hoornstra]

This sort of drink was often consumed as part of the festivities of the Christmas season.

Hippocras

Take a gallon of wine, an ounce of cinnamon, two ounces of ginger, one pound of sugar, twenty cloves bruised, and twenty corns of pepper big beaten, let all these soak together one night, and then let it run through a bag, and it will be good hippocras. [*The Good Husewifes Handmaide*, p. 54]

Take **1 bottle red wine**; add **1/4 teaspoon ground cinnamon, 1/2 teaspoon ground ginger**, and **5 crushed whole cloves, 5 peppercorns**, and **1 cup sugar**. Stop up and let it sit overnight, then the next day strain it through a coffee filter.

Mulled wine was also consumed during the Christmas season, but hippocras was drunk cold at any time of the year. It was considered medicinal; its name derived from the ancient Greek physician Hippocrates.

8

Entertainments

ELIZABETHAN PASTIMES

Leisure, no less than work, played an important part in the lives of Elizabethans. The landowning classes were not obliged to work at all. Many of them did work quite hard, whether in government, estate management, or some other aristocratic calling; but all of them had plentiful opportunity to pursue leisure activities. Ordinary people had much harder schedules, laboring from dawn to dusk most days of the week, yet they eagerly pursued entertainments in such free time as was allowed them. For such people, the principal leisure time was after church on Sundays and holidays, although religious reformers increasingly objected to Sunday games as a violation of the Sabbath.

The Elizabethan traveler Fynes Moryson commented on his countrymen's devotion to their pastimes:

> It is a singularity in the nature of the English, that they are strangely addicted to all kinds of pleasure above all other nations. . . . The English, from the lords to the very husbandmen, have generally more fair and more large Gardens and Orchards, than any other nation. All Cities, Towns, and villages swarm with companies of musicians and fiddlers, which are rare in other kingdoms. The City of London alone hath four or five companies of players with their particular theaters capable of many thousands, wherein they all play every day in the week but Sunday. . . . Not to speak of frequent spectacles in London exhibited to the people by fencers, by walkers on ropes, and like men of activity, nor of frequent companies of archers shooting in all the fields, nor of Saints' days, which the people not keeping (at least most of them, or with any devotion) for church service, yet keep for recreation of walking and gaming. What shall I say of dancing with curious and rural music, frequently used by the better sort, and upon all holidays by country people dancing about the

Maypoles with bagpipes or other fiddlers, besides the jollities of certain seasons of the year, of setting up maypoles, dancing the morris with hobby horses, bringing home the lady of the harvest, and like plebeian sports, in all which vanities no nation cometh anything near the English. What shall I say of playing at cards and dice, frequently used by all sorts, rather as a trade than as recreation. . . . As the English are by nature amorous, so do they above other nations assert and follow the pleasant study of poetry. . . . To conclude with hawking and hunting, no nation so frequently useth these sports as the English.[1]

An aristocratic feast with music and dancing. [Holinshed]

Theater   The Elizabethan period witnessed the first emergence of a genuine entertainment industry, especially in the theaters of London. At the beginning of Elizabeth's reign, theatrical performances took place in the courtyards of large inns. In 1576 London's first public theater was built—outside the city limits, to escape the stringent regulations imposed by hostile city authorities. This theater was not at first successful, but by the end of the 1580s such theaters had become a permanent fixture in London.

The early theaters resembled the innyards from which they had evolved. They were built around courtyards, with three-story galleries on three sides, facing a stage that projected out into the yard. People sat in the galleries, while the less privileged stood on the ground; a few ostentatious young gentlemen might sit on the stage itself. The plays were attended by all manner of people. Aristocrats were often to be found in the galleries, while standing room on the ground was certainly within the means of most people. General admission cost only a penny, the price of two quarts of beer—the price of going to the theater was analogous to going to the cinema today, although the low wages of working people meant they could not do it very often.

The plays had to be licensed, and authorities were always wary of the overcrowding, plague, and disorder associated with play-going. In fact, laws against vagrants were often used against actors and other performers, who lived wandering lives, unattached to any employer or household. In response, theatrical companies placed themselves under the patronage of the great noblemen of England, which allowed players to avoid punishment by becoming, technically, servants of the lord.

There was a constant and insatiable demand for plays, and actors became very popular figures—the first "stars." The plays' action combined humor and violence along with musical interludes and dazzling special effects; in these respects they were very similar to modern popular films. Playwrights were typically university graduates, and their lives were often short and turbulent. Christopher Marlowe took Elizabethan audiences by storm. His *Tamburlaine the Great*, full of violence, ambition, and horror, was a true blockbuster. William Shakespeare began his theatrical career late in Elizabeth's reign, in the early 1590s; Ben Jonson entered the scene later in the same decade.

In addition to the theaters in London, there were less formal settings for theatrical performances. The London companies occasionally brought their plays to the provinces, and there were plenty of minor performers, part-time folk players, puppeteers, acrobats, and other entertainers.

The other principal form of commercial public entertainment was literature. Elizabethan presses churned out **Literature** all manner of texts: technical works, political and religious tracts (some of which were considered highly seditious by the authorities, who punished the authors severely if they were caught), ballads, almanacs, histories, and even news-reports. These texts varied in format from lavish volumes richly illustrated with fine woodcuts or engravings— sometimes even colored by hand—down to cheap pamphlets and "broadsides" (single printed sheets) produced for the mass market and selling for just a penny. Reading was often a more public activity than it is today—people sometimes read aloud in groups.

If theater and literature were predominantly consumer entertainments, most other Elizabethan pastimes involved people **Music** as producers as well as consumers. Perhaps the most prominent example is music. The Elizabethans, like people today, liked to hear music. Unlike people today, they had no access to recording technology: all music had to be performed live. To some degree, people made use of professional musicians to satisfy their desire for music. A wealthy householder might hire musicians to play during dinner, and major towns had official musicians known as "waits" who sometimes gave free public concerts—such as took place at the Royal Exchange in London after 7 p.m. on Sundays and holidays.

For the most part, people made their own music. Laborers and craftsmen often sang while working; gentlefolk and respectable townspeople frequently sang part-songs or played consort music after a meal. The ability to hold one's own in a part-song or a round (known to the Elizabethans as a "catch") was a basic social skill. In fact, musical literacy was expected in polite society, and well-bred people could often play or sing a piece on sight. Even those of Puritanical leanings who frowned on most forms of music found pleasure in singing psalms.[2]

A fiddler and a viol-player. [Hindley]

Favored instruments among the upper classes included the lute, the virginals (a keyboard instrument in which the strings are plucked rather than struck), the viol (resembling a modern viola or cello), and the recorder. Among common folk the bagpipe was popular, especially in the country; other common instruments were the fiddle and the pipe-and-tabor (a combination of a three-hole recorder played with the left hand and a drum played with the right). Public music was most often performed on loud instruments such as the shawm (a powerful double-reeded instrument) and sackbut (a simple trombone). In the countryside, the ringing of church-bells was a popular form of entertainment.

Dancing Dancing was also a popular activity. It was considered a vital skill for an aristocrat (the Queen was said to look favorably on a man who could dance well), but was equally important to ordinary people: it was not merely a pleasant diversion but one of the best opportunities for interaction between unmarried people. The Puritan moralist Phillip Stubbes complained in his *Anatomy of Abuses,*

What clipping and culling, what kissing and bussing, what smooching and slavering one of another, what filthie groping and uncleane handling is not practised in those dancings?

The preferred type of dancing varied between social classes. Those of social pretensions favored the courtly dances imported from the Continent, especially Italy. These dances were mostly performed by couples, sometimes by a set of two couples; they often involved intricate and subtle footwork. Ordinary people were more likely to do the traditional "country" dances of England, which were danced by couples in round, square, or rectangular sets, and were much simpler in form and footwork. The division was not absolute: ordinary people sometimes danced almains, which were originally a courtly dance from France, while Elizabeth herself encouraged the cultivation of country dances among the aristocracy. In addition to social dances, there were performance and ritual dances. Foremost among these was morris dancing, characterized by the wearing of bells, and often performed as a part of summer festivals.

Elizabethan pastimes were not all as gentle as music and dance. One of the preferred sports of gentlemen was hunting—particularly for deer, sometimes for foxes or hares. Birds were also hunted, in two different ways. One **Hunting and Animal Sports** was the ancient and difficult sport of falconry in which trained falcons were sent after the prey. However, guns were increasingly used instead. Rather more sedate was the sport of fishing, enjoyed by many who found hunting too barbarous or expensive. All these sports might be enjoyed by women as well as men. Ordinary people did not generally hunt or fish for

Fishing. [Furnivall 1879]

sport. Indeed, they were not allowed to do so. The rights of hunting and fishing were normally reserved for landowners, although poaching was still common as a means of obtaining extra food.

Hunting was a relatively mild pastime in comparison with some Elizabethan sports, especially bull-baiting, bear-baiting, and cockfighting. Cockfighting involved pitting roosters against each other in a "cockpit," a small round arena surrounded by benches—sometimes a permanent structure was built for the purpose. In bull-baiting, a bull was chained in the middle of a large arena with one or more bulldogs or bull mastiffs. The dogs were trained to clamp their jaws closed on the bull's nose or ears and hang on until the bull fell down exhausted; the bull meanwhile tried to shake the dogs free and gore them to death. Bear-baiting was very similar, with the bull replaced by a bear. In all of these sports the onlookers would place wagers on the outcome of the combat.

Martial Sports
While some sports pitted animals against each other, others involved human combatants. The aristocracy sometimes practiced the medieval sport of jousting; jousts were sometimes the centerpiece of major public festivals. Fencing was popular both as a spectator entertainment and a participatory sport.

Fencing weapons had blunted edges and rounded ends but the sport was dangerous nonetheless. The rapier used in fencing was a great deal heavier than a modern fencing weapon; the only protective gear was a padded jacket, and occasionally a large rounded "button" placed over the tip of the blade to reduce the risk of putting out an eye. Sometimes the rapier was supplemented by a small round shield, called a "buckler," or by a larger one, either round or square, called a "target." Alternatively the fencer might use a rapier in one hand and a dagger in the other, or even two rapiers.

The rapier was considered an Italian weapon; those who preferred English traditions might fight with a sword instead. The sword was a slightly heavier weapon with a thicker blade, designed to deliver cutting blows instead of thrusts with the point. Sometimes the fencers used wooden swords called "wasters." Combat with the quarterstaff was another popular sport.

Fencers with sword and dagger. [Castle]

These martial arts had some practical application. There was a certain amount of lawlessness in Elizabethan England: even in London, streetfights and brawls were known to break out in broad daylight. For many people, the ability to defend oneself was an important life skill.

Other martial sports were geared towards military rather than civilian purposes. By law, every English commoner was to practice archery regularly. The law was originally introduced in the fourteenth century, when archery was still very important on the battlefield. By Elizabeth's time archery had declined in importance, but Elizabeth encouraged it nonetheless (she sometimes engaged in the sport herself, as did many English aristocrats). There were archers in the militia, and some military theorists still preferred the bow to the gun. Laws promoting archery were not strictly observed, but the sport remained popular among all classes and was widely seen as an especially patriotic pastime.

More useful for the national defense was the practice of military drill with pike and shot. Elizabeth's government made a concerted effort to improve England's defenses by training a national militia known as the Trained Bands. Sixteenth-century warfare required more training of the ordinary soldier than had once been the case. The matchlock musket

Elizabethan soldiers. [Scott]

required less physical strength and skill than the bow, but it was a fairly complex weapon to fire, requiring 20 to 30 seconds for each shot and some two dozen distinct motions—all of this while holding a slowly burning piece of treated rope (called the "match") and charging the weapon with gunpowder. An error could be fatal.

The pike, a 16- to 24-foot spear designed to ward off cavalry, was less dangerous but even more demanding. There were about a dozen positions in which the pike might be held, and the pikemen had to learn to move from each position to all the others in precise formation with the rest of the pikemen or else the pikes would strike each other and become hopelessly tangled. The government's efforts to promote military training met with extraordinary success, for military drill actually became a fashionable pastime, as well as a popular spectator entertainment.

Physical Games
Even games that were not basically martial could be quite perilous. The most characteristic English outdoor game of the period was football, especially favored by the lower classes.

Football was traditionally violent, loud, and dangerous to bystanders as well as players. As described by the Puritan social critic Phillip Stubbes, "Football playing . . . may rather be called a friendly kind of fight, than a play, or recreation; A bloody and murdering practice, then a fellowly sport or pastime."[3]   Football was roughly the same as modern European football (called "soccer" in America), but with fewer rules. Two teams would try to kick a ball through their opponents' goal. The ball was made of a farm animal's bladder, inflated and tied up and sewn into a leather covering. A major part of the game was the subtle art of tripping up one's opponents on the run. Even more violent were the versions known as "camp-ball" in England, "hurling" in Cornwall, or *cnapan* in Wales. In these games, a ball or other object was conveyed over open country to opposing goals by any means possible—even horsemen might be involved. These games frequently led to serious injuries.

Football was exclusively a male sport, but there were games with some violent content which might be played by both sexes. In Hot Cockles one player hid his head in another's lap while the others slapped him on the rear—if he could guess who had slapped him last, the two traded places. Blindman's Buff, also known as Hoodman Blind, was a similar game in which a blinded player tried to catch the others while they dealt him "buffs" (blows). If he could identify the person he caught, they would trade places. In both of these games, men and women might play together, although they were more commonly played by boys and girls.

One piece of equipment most people carried at all times was a knife, and these were used in several games. In Penny Prick, a peg was set in the ground with a penny on top; players would throw their knives at it, trying either to knock the penny off or to lodge their knife in the ground closest to the peg.

Similar to football in concept if not equipment was the game of bandy-ball, the ancestor of modern field hockey. The object of the game was to drive a small, hard ball through the opponents' goal with hooked clubs (almost identical to field hockey sticks).

Stoolball was an ancestor of cricket and baseball in which a stool was set on its side and players tried to hit the seat with a ball. In this game, women were expected to hike up their skirts and play with the men. In the game of trap or trapball the ball was placed on a device for casting it up in the air to be hit with a stick.

Tennis, a game introduced from France during the Middle Ages, called for expensive equipment and an equally expensive court, so it was popular only among the rich. The tennis ball was made of fabric scraps tightly wrapped in packing thread and encased in white fabric; the rackets were made of wood and gut. Tennis was perhaps the most athletic game played by the upper classes, and it was only played by men. The plebeian version of this game was Handball: as the name suggests, the ball was hit with the hands rather than with a racket. A similar game was shuttlecock, comparable to modern badminton. The shuttlecock was a cylinder of cork rounded at one end with feathers stuck in it; it was batted back and forth with wooden paddles known as "battledores."

A less demanding outdoor game was Bowls, similar to the modern English game of that name, or to Italian *bocce*. Bowls involved casting balls at a target with the goal of having your balls end up closest to the target. It was a very popular pastime. There were even commercial bowling alleys; as played in such settings, Bowls could be quite sophisticated, involving different shapes of balls, an elaborate terminology for describing the lay of the ground and the course of the ball, and a formalized system of betting. Moralists often criticized the game, yet when betting was not involved it was played by even the most respectable men and women.

A slightly more dangerous form of this game was quoits, in which a stake or spike was driven into the ground and players tossed stones or heavy metal disks at it. The game seems to have been played with vigor rather than finesse, and serious injury was known to result. The modern game of horseshoes is a variant of this game.

Similar to modern American bowling was the game known by such names as nine-pegs, ten-pins, skittle pins, skittles, or kittles. Nine conical pins were set up on the ground, and players would try to knock them down with a wooden ball. In a related game called kayles or loggats, the pins were knocked down with a stick instead of a ball. Country folk sometimes used the leg bones of oxen for pins.

Some games involved a great deal of running and little or no equipment. The game known in modern schoolyards as Prisoner's Base was played under the name Base or Prison Bars. A particular favorite in this period was Barley Break, a chasing game in which two mixed-sex couples tried to avoid being caught by a third couple, with the couples changing partners each time. Footraces were also a popular entertainment.

Other athletic sports included leaping and vaulting, swimming, and throwing weights. Riding was a favorite sport among the wealthy, and wrestling was popular among common folk. People also liked simply to take walks for exercise; members of the upper classes were especially fond of strolling in their gardens after a meal.

Many games were specifically geared for indoor recreation.

Table Games Among table games, chess was the most prestigious. Its rules were essentially the same as they are today. Chess was unusual among table games in that it did not normally involve betting.[4] For those who wanted a simpler game, the chess board could be combined with "table men" (backgammon pieces) for the game of draughts (now known in North America as checkers), again with essentially the same rules as today.[5]

Cards were widely popular throughout society, and inexpensive block-printed decks were readily available. Elizabethan playing cards were unwaxed, and the custom had not yet evolved of printing a pattern on the back to prevent marking. The cards were divided according to the "French" system, essentially the same one used in English-speaking countries today. The French suits were the same as in a modern deck, and each suit contained the same range of cards. The first three were called the Ace, Deuce, and Tray, and the face cards were called King, Queen, and Knave (there was no Joker). The cards had only images on them, no letters or numbers. The images on the face cards were very similar to modern ones, save that they were full-body portraits (without the mirror-image of modern cards).

Many Elizabethan card games have disappeared from use, but some still have modern equivalents. One and Thirty was the equivalent of the modern Twenty-One, except that it was played to a higher number. Noddy was an earlier variant of Cribbage (which first appeared in the early seventeenth century). Ruff and Trump were ancestors of modern Whist, and Primero was an early version of Poker.

There were several games in the family known as Tables, played with the equipment used in modern backgammon. Backgammon itself was not invented until the early seventeenth century, but the game of Irish was almost identical to it. Games at tables varied enormously. The childish game of Doublets involved only one side of the board: each player stacked his pieces on the points of their side, then rolled dice first to unstack them, then to bear them off the board. Perhaps the most complex game was Ticktack, in which the general idea was to move all one's pieces from one end of the board to the other, with several alternative ways of winning the game at single or double stakes en route.

Dice were the classic pastime of the lower orders of society—they were cheap, highly portable, and very effective at whiling away idle time (for which reason they were especially favored by soldiers). Dice games were played by the aristocracy as well; Elizabeth herself was known to indulge in them. The dice were typically made of bone, and the spots were called the "ace," "deuce," "tray," "cater," "sink," and "sise"—thus a roll of 6 and 1 was called "sise-ace."

Shovelboard or shove-groat was an indoor game in which metal discs (often groats—4d. pieces) were pushed across a table to land as close as possible to the other end without falling off. Various horizontal lines were laid out on the board, and points were scored according to which set of lines the piece stopped between. Wealthy households sometimes had special tables built for this game. Another coin game was Cross and Pile, identical to Heads or Tails—the "cross" was the cross on the back of English coins, the "pile" the face of the Queen on the front.

Fox and Geese and Nine Men's Morris were two simple board games in which each player moved pieces about on a geometric board, trying to capture or pin his opponent's pieces. Boards for these games could be made by cutting lines into a wooden surface or by writing on it with chalk or charcoal.

One of the simplest of games involved the tee-totum, a kind of top, used exactly like a Hannukah dreidel. It had four sides, each bearing a letter: *T* for "take," *N* for "nothing," *P* for "put," and *H* for "half." Depending on which side came up, the player would take everything, get nothing, put another stake into the pot, or take half the stakes out of the pot.

A few new table games appeared during Elizabeth's reign. Billiards appears to have been introduced to England during this period. The Game of Goose came to England from the Continent in 1597. This was the earliest ancestor of many of today's commercial board games. The Game of Goose was a commercially printed sheet bearing a track of squares spiralling towards the center. Players rolled dice to move their pieces along the track. Some of the squares bore special symbols: the player who landed on such a square might get an extra roll or be sent back a certain number of squares. The first player to reach the end won.

Some entertainments involved nothing more than words. Jokes were as popular then as now—there were even printed joke books. Riddles were another common word game. In general, Elizabethans greatly enjoyed conversation and were especially fond of sharing news: in a world without mass or electronic media, people were always eager for word of what was going on in the world around them.

Games and Life

As in modern times, the custom of game-playing began in childhood. Children played many of the games described above; other children's pastimes included tag (called Tick), leap-frog, hide-and-seek (called All Hid), hobby-horses, whip-tops, see-saw, blowing bubbles, swings, mock drilling with drums, banners, stick pikes, muskets and swords, and cup-and-ball. In the autumn when nuts began to harden, children would play at Cob-Nut: nuts on strings were stuck against each other, the one whose nut broke first being the loser. However, where modern-day people tend to lay aside much of their childhood game-playing when they enter adulthood, games remained an integral part of the life of Elizabethan adults.

Games were often segregated by gender. Women did not engage in martial, dangerous or extremely vigorous sports such as fencing, football, or tennis. However, they might take part in lighter physical games such as Blindman's Buff or Barley Break. Games with minimal physical activity such as Bowls and card games were especially common pastimes for women; and they often participated as spectators at sports which they did not play themselves, even violent sports like bear-baiting.

Most Elizabethan games were less rules-oriented and standardized than is true today. Rules were often minimal and might vary from one locality to the next. This was especially true of children's games and folk games, less true of table games and games of the upper classes, which were generally more elaborate and formalized.

One last distinctive feature of Elizabethan games was the prevalence of gambling, which pervaded Elizabethan culture. A wager might be laid on almost any game, and in many cases betting was an integral part of the game itself. Even children gambled, playing for lacing-points, pins, cherry stones, or various sorts of counters.

RULES FOR ELIZABETHAN GAMES

Almost no rules for games survive from the late sixteenth century, but there are quite a few from the late seventeenth century. As games tend to be conservative, these rules are probably quite close to their Elizabethan forms; most of the rules given below are interpretations of such sources.[6]

Physical Games

BARLEY BREAK

Barley Break is played by 3 mixed-sex couples, AB and EF at the ends of the field, and CD in the middle, called "Hell." All 3 couples hold one another by the hands. To initiate play, AB shout "Barley!" and EF respond "Break!" All three couples drop hands. AB and EF break, B and F running to meet each other, and A and E likewise. C and D try to catch any one of them.

A   C D   E

B   F

If C and D can catch anyone before that person meets his or her new partner, those two must go in the middle next time. If both new pairs meet each other before any of them is caught, C and D remain in Hell. Both C and D must catch their target before the new partner reaches them, or it does not count. The new pairs go to the ends of the field for the next round.

Another variation is to have just one person from each end run towards the opposite side, with the middle couple trying to catch that person before he or she reaches the players on the far side. This variation can be played with more than six people, with the one who just ran going to the end of the line at the far side.

STOOLBALL

Equipment

—1 leather ball (see instructions below)
—2 sturdy sticks for staves, approximately 2' long and 2" in diameter
—2 stools or similar targets

Stoolball is another running game in which both men and women participated. It seems to have been played in several versions; the version here is a close relative of English cricket and American baseball.

The first step is to make a ball. Cut 4 pieces of leather (designated I, II, III, and IV) in the shape shown.

Right sides together, stitch **abc** on I to **adc** on II; do likewise with III and IV. You will now have two roughly hemispherical pieces. Right sides together, stitch III to I/II, with the two hemispheres at 90° to each other (so that the point **a** on III matches with **d** on I, **d** on III matches with **a** on I and II, **c** on III matches with **b** on II). You will now have a single sphere, with one seam still open. Turn the sphere right side out. Grab a bundle of fabric scraps (preferably wool, since it is springy). When squeezed, they should be about the size to stuff the sphere. Too many is better than too few.

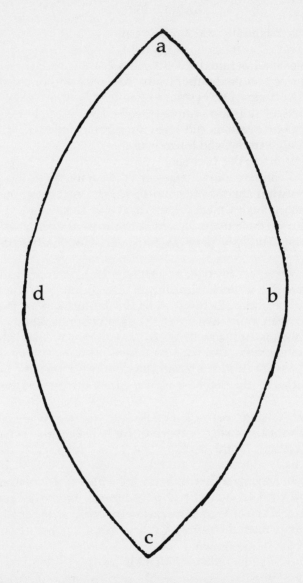

Tie a piece of twine tightly around the scraps, and pass it around a few times in various directions, pulling tightly (you may want to wear gloves). Check the fit. If the bundle is too big, pull a few pieces out, wrap tightly a few more times and try again. If it is significantly too small, you will have to untie the twine, add some more pieces, and try again. Once the fit is reasonably close, wrap the twine tightly many times about the fabric so that most of the surface is covered. Squeeze the stuffing into the cover, and stitch it shut. A well-made ball will actually bounce on a hard surface (this is essentially what tennis balls were like in the days before rubber).

To play stoolball, set up the two targets 7 or 8 yards apart. The ideal is a pair of stools laid on their side, but any pair of objects of comparable size will suffice. The basic game is played with two teams of two players. One team stands as defenders, one at each of the targets, each holding a staff. One of their opponents stands by each target, one of them holding the ball. (Toss a coin to determine who defends first.)

The player with the ball casts it at the opposite target, and the defender standing there attempts to ward it off with the staff.

If the caster hits the target, the defender is "out," and the two sides change positions, the defenders becoming the casters.

If the defender misses the ball, he must touch the target with his staff before the opponent next to him can touch the ball to the target, or else he will be out.

If the defender hits the ball, he and the other defender run to change positions while the other two try to retrieve the ball. If the opponents manage to touch the ball to either of the targets before the defender reaches it, the defenders are "out." The defenders must try to change places at least once and may do so as many times as they choose. Each time they change places (touching the targets with their staves each time), they score one point. If at any point the opponents manage to touch the ball to a target while the defenders are between the targets, the defenders are "out."

If neither defender is put "out" in any of these ways, play begins again, with the other caster throwing the ball at the other defender's target. Play continues until one side reaches 63 points. The game can be played with any even number of people. There will always be as many targets as there are players on each team, arranged in a triangle, square, and so on, and the ball is cast from one target to the next. The game can also be played with two targets and just two people—this version involves a lot of running to fetch the ball!

BOWLS/QUOITS

Equipment

—2 hardwood balls for each player, about 3 1/2" in diameter (each pair of balls should be color-coded to distinguish them from other pairs)

—1 "Mistress" (a stake that can be set upright in the ground) or 1 "Jack" (a ball smaller than the others, preferably of a bright contrasting color)

A point is designated as the casting spot and is indicated with some sort of mark, such as a piece of wood or metal called a "trig." If using a Mistress, it is set up on the ground some distance away—the distance will depend on the players. Two Mistresses can be set up, each serving as the other's casting spot; this will save walking back and forth. If using a Jack, the first player casts it out onto the ground. Each player in turn casts one ball, trying to get it as close to the Jack or Mistress as possible; then each in turn casts the second ball. The player whose ball is closest at the end scores 1 point, 2 points for the two closest balls. A ball touching the target counts double. Balls can be knocked about by other balls, and the Jack can be repositioned in this way. The first player to reach a certain number of points (generally 5 or 7) wins the game.

Quoits is played in the same manner, save that the bowls are replaced by quoits, large flat stones or pieces of metal. The Mistress in quoits is an iron stake or "hob" driven into the ground; the Jack is a smaller quoit.

Board and Dice Games

FOX AND GEESE

<u>Equipment</u>

—1 game board. This could be as small as 4" square or as big as you like. It can be made by carving a board, by drawing, painting, and so on.

—15 "Geese." These are small counters: they can be pegs (in which case the board needs to have holes at all the intersections), stones, or other small items.

—1 "Fox." This is a counter visibly larger than the Geese.

One player has the Geese, which start on points **a, b, c, d, e, f, g, h, i, j, k, l, m, n, o**. The other player has the Fox, starting on point **z**. Each player moves in turn, along the lines to adjacent intersections. The Geese can move only sideways, downwards, or diagonally downwards. The Fox can move in any direction. The Fox can also jump over a Goose and capture it, as in checkers; multiple jumps are allowed in a single move. The Geese win if they pen up the Fox so that it cannot move; the Fox wins by capturing all the Geese.

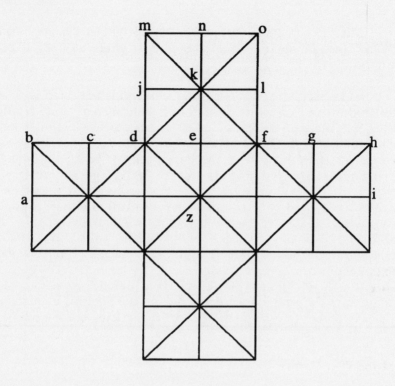

IRISH

Equipment

—1 backgammon set

Irish was one of the commonest "games at tables" (i.e., games played on a backgammon board). The rules are exactly the same as for modern backgammon, save that the special rules for doubles do not apply. The 15 "men" are placed as indicated by the numbers on the diagram, the upright numbers belonging to player 1, the upside-down ones to player 2. Player 1 moves his men clockwise around the board from z towards a (his "home point"), player 2 counterclockwise from a towards z (his home point). The 6 points from a to f are player 1's home points, the 6 from z to t are player 2's home points.

The players each roll 1 die, and the higher roll moves first (if the rolls are equal, roll again). The first player rolls 2 dice for his move and may move one man for the number on each die (the same man may move for both). Once touched, a man must be played. After the first player has moved, it is the second player's turn.

A man cannot be moved onto a point already occupied by 2 or more opponents. If a man is left alone on a point and an opponent's man lands on it at the end of 1 die's move, that man is removed from the board and must be played on again from the far end.

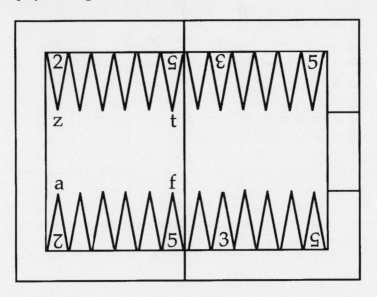

Any player who has a man off the board must play it on before he can move any other men. This means that if the roll would require placing the entering man onto a point already occupied by 2 or more opponents, he must forfeit his turn. If a player has 2 or more men on all of his 6 home points and his opponent has a man to enter, one of those points must be "broken": both players roll 2 dice, and the higher chooses a point from which all but one of the men are removed. The removed men must re-enter the board again.

The player who removes all his men from the board first wins. No man may be played off the board until all of the player's men are in the 6 home points. It does not require an exact roll to play a man off the board.

HAZARD

This was by far the most popular and enduring game at dice. The rules here derive from seventeenth-century sources.

Order of play is determined by the roll of 1 die—the highest roll goes first.

The first player rolls 2 dice until he gets a "Main," which can be any number from 5 through 9.

He then rolls again.

—On a 2 or 3, he loses (a roll of 2 was called "ames-ace").

—If the Main is 5 or 9 and the player again rolls the Main, he wins. This is called a "nick." If he rolls an 11 or 12, he loses.

—If the Main is 6 or 8 and the player rolls the Main or a 12, it is a nick. If he rolls 11, he loses.

—If the Main is 7 and the player rolls the Main or an 11, it is a nick. If he rolls a 12, he loses.

—Any other roll is called the "Mark." The player continues to roll until he gets the Mark and wins, or gets the Main and loses. If the player wins, he starts again rolling for a Main; if he loses, play moves clockwise to the next player.

Card Games

To determine order of play in any card game, each player lifts a random number of cards from the deck and looks at the bottom card. The highest card deals; ties lift again. As in modern usage, cards are shuffled and cut before play. The player to the left of the dealer is called the "eldest." The eldest hand plays first and will be the next dealer.

PUT

This game had a particularly low reputation as an alehouse pastime. All cards are used, of which the 3 ranks highest, the 2 next, and then the Ace, King, Queen, and so on. Suits are irrelevant to this game. This game is usually played with 2 players but can be played with more.

Each player is dealt one more card than there are players. The eldest leads a card, and the other players play cards to it until all players have laid down a card. Whoever plays the highest card takes the trick. Ties go to nobody. Each round consists of as many tricks as the players have cards, and whoever wins 2 of the tricks scores 1 point. If nobody wins 2 tricks, nobody scores a point. Once the round is played, the next player deals. Play is normally to either 5 or 7, as agreed on by the players before the game.

At any point a player may knock on the table and say "Put!" If the other says "I see it," whoever wins that round wins the game, regardless of the score, and takes the stakes. If the other does not see, the first player automatically wins the round and scores a point.

MAW

This is perhaps the simplest of trick-taking games involving suits. Each player pays 1 chip or coin to the pot and receives 5 cards. The aim is to either sweep the pool by winning 3 or more tricks, or, at least, to prevent anyone else from doing the same, thereby carrying the pot into the next round. The ordinary ranking of cards is Ace high and Deuce low.

The eldest hand plays a card to the table. Each player in turn must "follow suit," if possible, by playing any card of the same suit led by the eldest. If the player does not have a card of that suit, he may play any card he chooses. The highest card in the suit led wins the "trick." That player places all the cards from that trick next to him to keep score, and leads the first card of the next trick. Once the current hand is played out, the deal passes to the eldest hand.

A player winning the first 3 tricks may claim the pot without further play, but if he leads to the fourth he is said to "jink" it, thus undertaking to win all 5 tricks. If he succeeds, all players must pay a second stake; if he fails, he loses the pot and it carries over into the next round.

This basic idea can be elaborated with all sorts of complications to make it more amusing to play. One version involves ranking 2 of the suits (usually the black suits or the red suits) in reverse order (Deuce high and Ace low).

Trumps can also be added. When the cards have been shuffled and dealt, turn over the top card of the deck. The suit of that card is the trump suit, and cards of that suit will beat cards of the suit led in any trick, with higher trumps beating lower trumps. Another variation is to have the top 3 cards of the deck be the Five of Trumps (called "Five Fingers"), Jack of Trumps, and Ace of Hearts (regardless of current trump suit), in that order.

PRIMERO

To judge by contemporary references, this appears to have been one of the most popular card games in Elizabethan England. It is obviously related to modern poker.

Discard the 8s, 9s, and 10s of each suit. All players ante in. The dealer deals 2 cards to each, proceeding counterclockwise. Starting on the dealer's right, each player may choose to bet or to trade in 1 or both cards. As soon as 1 player bets, no one else may trade in cards. Once a player trades cards, the play passes to the next player. If all players trade cards (including the dealer), the hand is redealt.

Once a player bets, the others may play with the cards they have or drop out of the hand. However, if no other player chooses to continue, the last player after the one who laid the bet must match it and continue.

Except for the ante and the above provision, any bet may be refused. If each subsequent player refuses the bet, it must be withdrawn and play continues with the betting at the previous level.

French playing cards of the late sixteenth century. [Hoornstra]

After the initial round of betting, each player remaining receives 2 more cards. At this point there is another round of betting, during which players declare the rank of their hands as they place their bets. Players may declare their hands at a level equal to or higher than what they actually have, but not lower. The one exception is if a previous player has declared a Flush or Primero and your hand is a Chorus (see hand rankings below), in which case you may declare your hand to be equal to the hand already declared.

After this round of betting, players may trade in 1 or 2 cards. Finally all remaining players reveal their hands, and the highest hand takes the pot.

The ranks of hands are as follows:

Numerus, the lowest hand, consists of 2 or 3 cards of the same suit. The point value is equal to the sum of the cards in that one suit.
Primero, or *Prime*, ranks next, consisting of 1 card of each suit. The value of a Primero is the sum of the cards in the hand.
Supreme, or *Fifty-Five*, is a hand containing the Ace, Six, and Seven of one suit. The value of this hand is always 55.
Flush consists of 4 cards of the same suit. Its value is the sum of the cards in the hand.
Chorus, the highest hand, is 4 of a kind.

Card values are as follows:

Seven:	21
Six:	18
Ace:	16
Five:	15
Four:	14
Three:	13
Two:	12
Face Cards:	10

If two hands tie, the one closest to the right of the dealer wins.

SONGS

Quite a large number of songs of the Elizabethan period survive, including popular and folk-type songs. The following pages offer a selection of a few fairly simple ones, mostly from Thomas Ravenscroft's collections *Pammelia, Deuteromelia*, and *Melismata* [1609-11].

LORD WILLOUGHBY

(Chappell)

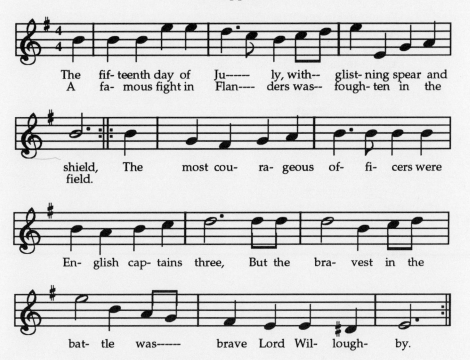

The fif- teenth day of Ju----- ly, with-- glist- ning spear and
A fa- mous fight in Flan---- ders was-- fough- ten in the

shield, The most cou- ra- geous of- fi- cers were
field.

En- glish cap- tains three, But the bra- vest in the

bat- tle was------ brave Lord Wil- lough- by.

"Stand to it, noble pikemen,
And look you round about,
And shoot you right, you bowmen,
And we will keep them out.
You muskets and calivermen,
Do you prove true to me,
I'll be the foremost man in fight,"
Said brave Lord Willoughby.

Then quoth the Spanish general,
"Come let us march away,
I fear we shall be spoiled all
If we here longer stay,
For yonder comes Lord Willoughby
With courage fierce and fell,

He will not give one inch of way
For all the devils in hell."

And then the fearful enemy
Were quickly put to flight,
Our men pursued courageously
And caught their forces quite,
But at the last they gave a shout
Which echoed through the sky,
"God and St. George for England!"
The conquerors did cry.

To the soldiers that were maimed
And wounded in the fray
The Queen allowed a pension
Of eighteen pence a day,
And from all costs and charges
She quit and set them free,
And this she did all for the sake
Of brave Lord Willoughby.

Then courage, noble Englishmen,
And never be dismayed,
For if we be but one to ten
We will not be afraid
To fight the foreign enemy
And set our country free,
And thus I end the bloody bout
Of brave Lord Willoughby.

This patriotic song commemorated a victory by Peregrine Bertie, Lord Willoughby, in the Netherlands in the 1580s. The words are preserved in a seventeenth-century broadside, but the music is found in sixteenth-century collections.

TOMORROW THE FOX WILL COME TO TOWN

(Ravenscroft)

To- mor-row the fox will come to town, *Keep, keep,*

keep, keep, keep! To- mor-row the fox will come to town, *O-----*

keep you all well there! I must de- sire you

neigh- bors all To hal-low the fox out of the hall, And

cry as loud as you can call, Whoop whoop whoop whoop whoop! And

cry as loud as you can call, *O-----* *keep you all well there!*

He'll steal the Cock out from his flock!
Keep, keep, keep, keep!
He'll steal the Cock out from his flock!
O keep you all well there! etc.

He'll steal the Hen out of the pen!
Keep, keep, keep, keep!
He'll steal the Hen out of the pen!
O keep you all well there! etc.

He'll steal the Duck out of the brook!
Keep, keep, keep, keep!
He'll steal the Duck out of the brook!
O keep you all well there! etc.

He'll steal the Lamb e'en from his dam!
Keep, keep, keep, keep!
He'll steal the Lamb e'en from his dam!
O keep you all well there! etc.

The fox was a constant problem for the Elizabethan husbandman—traditionally, when such an animal was found prowling in the village, all the villagers would be called out to pursue it.

OF ALL THE BIRDS THAT EVER I SEE

(Ravenscroft)

Of all the birds that e- ver I see, the

owl is the fair- est in her de- gree, for all the day long she

sits in a tree, and when the night comes a- way flies she. *Te-*

whit te whoo! **To whom drinks thou?** *Sir Knave, to you!* This

song is well sung, I'll make you a vow, and he is a knave that

drink- eth now. Nose, nose, nose-------- nose and

who gave thee that jol- ly red nose? *Cin- na- mon and gin- ger,*

nut- meg and cloves, and that gave thee thy jol- ly red nose!

"Of all the birds that ever I see" was a common traditional opening for a song—this silly song was a send-up of the type. Cinnamon, ginger, nutmeg, and cloves were used to make spiced ale and wine. This song was originally set for several voices; if you have several singers, all should sing the plain text, and divide into half to sing the italic and bold texts.

HOLD THY PEACE

(Ravenscroft)

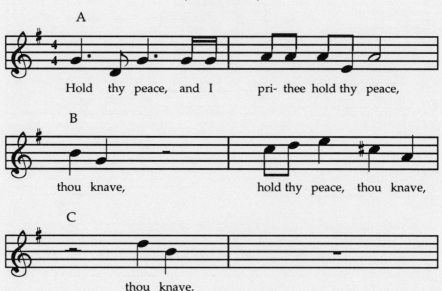

This is a "catch," or round, for three voices—it appears in Shakespeare's *Twelfth Night*. "Thou knave" was a common insult, and "Hold thy peace" was essentially the Elizabethan for "Shut up!" This round was obviously intended to be silly and loud.

HEY HO NOBODY AT HOME

(Ravenscroft)

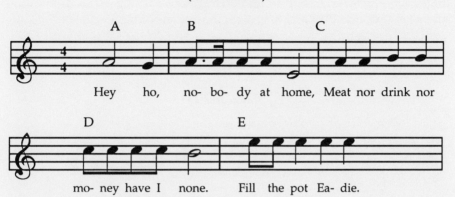

This is a catch for five voices, a version of which is sometimes heard today.

DANCE

Elizabethans tended to categorize dances according to the country of origin. Italian dances were particularly fashionable; French dances also had a long history in England; and dances of the native English style were known as "country" dances. Our principal source for English country dancing is *The English Dancing Master*, a collection of dances published by John Playford, which went through ten editions between 1651 and 1700 and several more in the eighteenth century.[7]

Elizabethan sources mention quite a number of country dances by name, nearly 20 of which were later to appear in Playford. Three of these appear here. We cannot be certain that these dances were the same in the sixteenth century as in Playford's day, but Playford's versions probably correspond in general to the Elizabethan form even if they may have differed in detail.

Of the courtly dances imported from France, perhaps the most popular was the almain, which is often found in country as well as courtly contexts. Quite a few almains are described in Elizabethan manuscripts from the Inns of Court, including those printed here: the versions here try to follow Bodleian MS. Douce 280, a manuscript dating to around 1600. The "measure" was an English development of French dances, and probably similar to the almain in style.

It is relatively easy to recreate the steps of dances; it is harder to recreate their feel. Many Elizabethan dances were rather simple and sedate, and we may presume that they did not rely on exciting choreography for their appeal. There was probably a lot of communication of one sort or another; and there was doubtless considerable emphasis on skill and grace, rather than mere memorization of complex patterns.

Symbols

[A],[B], etc. designate sections of the music.

[Ax2] means that section is performed twice.

[A1] and [A2] are two repetitions of the same music.

LF Left Foot

RF Right Foot

H   Honor

s   Single

d   Double

"Up" means the "top" of the hall, normally where the musicians are. All dances begin on the left foot. The man normally stands on the lady's left. Couple dances begin with partners taking near hands; if necessary, couples may be arranged in a processional circle, with "up" being clockwise.

Steps

The numbers on the left of each step description are beats of the music ("*and*" is a half-beat).

Honor (Reverence)

As the music begins, take hands: hands are held low for a country dance, forearms are held horizontal for a measure or almain.

1-2 Slide the right foot back, bending the right leg, and remove the hat with the left hand (women do the same, but do not move the right foot as far or remove the hat).

3-4 Return the right foot to place and replace the hat.

An Honor should always be done at the beginning and end of any dance. For this purpose, the musicians should play the last few measures of the tune to start, and hold the last note at the end.

The reverence. [Norris]

Double (Country Dance)

1   Step onto the left foot

2   Step onto the right foot

3   Step onto the left foot

and   Rise on the toes of the left foot

4   Close the right foot to the left foot as you lower your heels.

The next double starts on the right foot. A double can be done in any direction.

Double (Measure or Almain)

1   Step onto the left foot

2   Step onto the right foot

3   Step onto the left foot

4   Kick the right foot forward, either with or without a hop.

The next double starts on the right foot. Doubles may be done in any direction.

Single/Set (Country Dance)

1   Step onto the left foot

and   Rise on the toes of the left foot

2   Close the right foot to the left foot as you lower your heels.

The next single starts on the right foot. A single can be done in any direction: in country dances, a single to the side is called a "set."

Single (Measure or Almain)

1   Step onto the left foot
2   Kick the right foot forward, either with or without a hop.

The next single starts on the right foot. Singles may be done in any direction.

Slip Step ("French slide")

1   Step left foot to the left
and Move the right foot next to the left as you hop onto it.

The next slip steps will be onto the left foot again—they do not alternate.

"French" Dances

EARL OF ESSEX MEASURE

[Cunningham 26; Pugliese & Cassaza 17]

[A] Double forward, single back. Repeat a total of four times.

[B] Slow set left and right, double forward, single back.

MADAM SOSILIA ALMAIN

[Cunningham 27; Pugliese & Casazza 29]

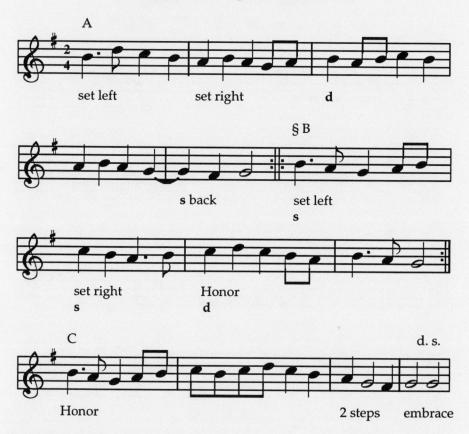

[Ax2] Set left and right, and a double forward, then a single back.

[Bx2] Turn to face partner, dropping hands: Set left and right, then Honor on LF. Then two singles and a double forward, passing right shoulders to partner's place and turning to face each other.

[C] Honor, then take two steps forward and embrace.

[Bx2] Repeat B above, returning to your places.

[C] Repeat C above.

BLACK ALMAIN

[Cunningham 27, 33; Pugliese & Casazza 31]

A

d

d   d (falling back)
                                     turn left: d

d
turn back: d

C

s   s   d (men or women)

D

d to change places

slip   slip   slip   slip   d to change places

slip   slip   slip   slip

d back   **d** forward

[A] All dance four doubles forward.

[B1] Turn to face partner and drop hands: double back, then double forward.

[B2] All make a quarter-turn left: double forward. All make a half-turn right: double forward.

[C] All turn to face partner. Men do two singles and a double, turning in place. Women do likewise on the repeat.

[D] All take both hands: double clockwise to partner's place. All do 4 slip-steps up the hall. All double clockwise back to own place, and do 4 slip-steps down the hall. All drop hands: double backwards, then double to meet again.

The second time through the dance, the women set first, then the men.

Country Dances

STEPS AND TERMS

Unless indicated otherwise, steps are a lively walking step. According to one late seventeenth-century Continental observer, English country dances were noteworthy for the dancers' freedom in choosing such types of steps as pleased them.

Set: A single step to the side.

Turn single: The dancer turns alone in place with a double step. The feet trace out a small circle on the floor, and the dancer ends up where he started.

Turn each other: Partners take one or both hands and turn around each other, giving weight (i.e., leaning or pulling back slightly) as they go around.

Lead a double and back: Partners take near hands and do a double step forward in the specified direction and a double backwards.

Partners, Corners, Opposites: Partners stand with the man on the left, the woman on the right. The "corner" is the dancer of the opposite sex on the other side of you from your partner. The "opposite" is the person of the opposite sex across from you in the set.

Numbering of Couples: The "1s" are the couple closest to the top of the hall, the "2s" the couple next to them, and so on.

Circle: All join hands in a circle and slip-step around for a certain number of steps (clockwise first).

Cast: The dancer turns away from the set and goes around the outside.

Arming: The two dancers link arms, left arms for "arm left" and right arms for "arm right," and walk around once in a circle, ending back in their original places.

Siding: The two dancers move towards each other with a small double step, to meet left shoulder to left shoulder (for "side left"), or right shoulder to right shoulder (for "side right").

TRENCHMORE

(The Hunting of the Fox)

[Playford (1653) 103; Millar 85]

This dance is mentioned as early as 1551 and seems to have been extremely popular for a very long period. Any number may dance: partners stand in a longways set, men on the left side, women on the right.

The melody is that of "Tomorrow the Fox Will Come to Town" (page 173).

Top of Hall	
M	W
M	W
M	W
	etc.

1st Verse

Partners lead up a double and back twice [Playford: 3 times]. 1s, followed by the rest, cast off, going separately down the outside, then meet at the bottom to lead back up to their original place [Playford: 3 times].

2nd Verse
Arched hey: All take hands; 2s make an arch, which 1s pass under; 1s make an arch, which 3s pass under; 1s pass under 4s while 2s pass under 3s, etc., until all are back in their original places [Playford: "Do this forward and back twice or thrice"].

3rd Verse
1s cross to set to the 2s (the first man setting to the second woman, and the first woman to the second man), then to each other, then to the 3s, then to each other, and so on down the line. Once all the way through the set, they turn back and arm the last couple by the right (the man arming the last woman, the woman the last man), then each other by the left, and so on back up the set to place.

4th Verse
1s turn each other by the right hand, then the 2s by the left, the 3s by the right, and so on to the bottom of the set. The dance begins again with a new couple at the top.

The version here is somewhat shortened from Playford's. The dance has also been adjusted to make the 3rd and 4th verses work; from the way Playford describes it, it is obviously not too rigidly structured anyway. Millar offers a slightly shorter version in which the 3rd verse consists of arming to the bottom, and the 4th verse is omitted.

SELLENGER'S ROUND

(The Beginning of the World)

[Playford (1675) 1; Keller & Shimer 96; Millar 8]

This dance is first mentioned in 1593 but was probably popular for some time before that; the melody is recorded in sixteenth-century collections. Any number of couples stand in a circle facing inwards, with each man on his partner's left.

1st Verse

[A]   All circle eight steps clockwise and eight steps back.

Chorus

[B]   All do two single steps advancing towards the middle of the circle, then fall back a double to places, face partners, then set and turn single. Repeat.

2nd Verse

[A] Partners lead in a double and back. Repeat.

[B] Chorus.

3rd Verse

[A] Partners side right and left.

[B] Chorus.

4th Verse

[A] Partners arm right and left.

[B] Chorus.

Playford's version of the first chorus omits the double in and back, but the music seems to demand it.

HEARTSEASE

[Playford (1651); Keller & Shimer 45; Millar 20]

This dance is attested as early as 1560. Two couples stand facing each other in a square, each man with his partner on his right, and his corner in front of him.

M W

M W

<u>1st Verse</u>

[A] Partners lead forward a double and back. Repeat.

<u>Chorus</u>

[B1] All face partners, fall back a double, then forward a double. Then face corners and turn your corner once around by the right hand.

[B2] Still facing corners, fall back a double, then forward a double. Then face partners and turn your partner once around by the left hand.

2nd Verse

[A1] Partners side right.

[A2] Face your corner. Corners side left.

[B] Chorus.

3rd Verse

[A1] Partners arm right.

[A2] Face your corner. Corners arm left.

[B] Chorus.

Glossary

alderman A member of a city council.

ale An early form of beer made without hops.

apprentice A young person learning a craft or trade.

archdeacon A church officer assigned to assist the bishop in administering his bishopric, having especial authority for church courts.

breeches underwear, shorts.

broadside A single printed sheet, often a ballad, sold for a penny.

burgess See **citizen**.

cassock A sleeved cape.

champion settlement A system of agricultural organization in which each holding consists of strips of land scattered about a village, as contrasted with **woodland settlement**.

churchwarden A parish officer chosen periodically from among the inhabitants of the parish and responsible for upkeep of the parish church.

citizen An inhabitant of a town having the full rights and privileges of the town.

clothes-press A shelved cupboard for clothing.

coif A linen cap worn by women.

commoner Anyone not of the gentlemanly class; a person obliged to work for a living.

communion The religious ceremony in which the communicants receive wine and/or bread as representing the blood and body of Christ.

confirmation The religious ceremony by which a young person is fully admitted as a member of the church.

constable A local officer chosen periodically from among local residents and responsible for law and order.

cottager The smallest sort of landholding commoner, holding insufficient land to support a family without doing additional labor.

cutwork A form of decoration combining cutting of the fabric and embroidery.

deacon A church officer responsible for assisting a priest.

distaff A long staff used in spinning flax fibers into linen thread.

doublet A fitted jacket with buttons worn by both men and women.

esquire A substantial gentleman, especially one who has a knight among his ancestors.

falling band A detachable collar.

fallow field A field out of use for a season to allow it to recover for future crops.

farthingale An underskirt made to flare by means of hoops.

freeholder The most privileged class of common landholder, holding his land in perpetuity, generally for insignificant rent.

garter A strip of leather or fabric used to hold up one's stockings.

gentleman A man of the class traditionally holding sufficient lands not to be required to work for a living; any man of a gentlemanly family.

gentleman-usher A personal servant of gentle birth, serving in an aristocratic household.

guild An organization regulating the practice of a craft or trade in a particular town. "Guild" is the modern term; the Elizabethans usually called it a "company."

holding A parcel or quantity of land rented to a holder in accordance with the custom associated with that holding. Also called a **landholding**.

husbandman A small but self-sufficient landholding commoner.

joint stool A stool made with mortice-and-tenon joints, superior to a "boarded" stool made without joints.

journeyman A craftsman or tradesman who has completed apprenticeship but does not possess a business of his own, working instead for others.

justice of the peace A gentleman empowered by the crown to administer minor legal matters in a locality.

kirtle A long fitted garment for women.

lady-in-waiting A female servant of gentle birth, serving in an aristocratic household.

landholding See **holding**.

lay peers The secular aristocracy of the House of Lords in Parliament, as opposed to the bishops who also sat in the House of Lords.

Lent The period from Ash Wednesday until Easter, during which Elizabethans were supposed to abstain from eating meat and poultry.

master A craftsman or tradesman who has his own shop.

master of arts A university graduate.

page The lowest rank of servant, usually a young boy.

petticoat A skirt.

pickadill One of a row of decorative tabs on the edge of a garment.

Privy Council The committee of royal officers with primary responsibility for advising the Queen and carrying out her policies.

roll A padded roll of fabric worn about a woman's hips.

saint's day A holy day traditionally commemorating a particular saint.

squire See **esquire**.

Statute of Artificers A law regulating work and wages, passed by Parliament in 1563.

Whitsun The Sunday 7 weeks after Easter (Pentecost), traditionally an occasion for summer festivals.

winnowing The process of separating cracked grain husks from the seed.

woodland settlement A system of agricultural organization in which each holding is a discrete parcel of land, as contrasted with **champion settlement**.

yeoman The upper rank of landholding free commoners.

Appendix A:
The Elizabethan Event

The text on which this book is based was originally written as a living history manual for the Elizabethan period. It has since been expanded and reworked to provide an introduction to Elizabethan daily life for the general-interest reader, but it can still be used for organizing a period event such as an Elizabethan fair, festival, or feast. It can also prepare the individual reader to participate in such an event.

For the individual preparing to take part in an event, the first steps will be to choose what sort of character you will be representing and to assemble an appropriate kit of personal equipment. A character towards the lower end of the social scale would be easier to portray well: an upper-class character would not only have expensive clothing but would probably be attended by a servant and would certainly be well versed in all manner of social graces. A minimum outfit for a man would be a **shirt, hose, garters, Venetians, doublet, hat** or **cap**, and **shoes**. For a woman, it would be a **smock, petticoat, bodice, coif**, and **shoes**. Depending on the circumstances of the event, you may also need to provide basic eating equipment such as a **bowl** and/or **trencher, knife, spoon**, and **drinking vessel**. To assist in this process, Appendix B lists suppliers of goods and materials useful for Elizabethan living history.

ORGANIZING AN EVENT

To host a successful event, you will need to attend to the following:

Define and Disseminate the Goals. First, decide precisely what you are trying to achieve, as this will govern the balance struck between practicality and authenticity. Every group must make its own decisions about the degree of authenticity it wishes to achieve. If the principal goal is entertainment of yourselves or your guests, then historical accuracy may not be a priority— although we hope this book will convince you that reasonable accuracy can be both fun and easy. If you are a living history group putting on a demonstration for the public, you have more of a responsibility to be true to the past. In any case, the most important thing is to be as honest as possible with yourselves and your guests or audience as to what you are actually doing.

Even the best living history group needs to remember that perfect accuracy is impossible. Bearing this in mind, it is important to define the degree of accuracy your group actually expects. If you expect people to meet a certain standard of authenticity, that standard needs to be clearly articulated. It is worthwhile to compile a list of "authoritative sources," people or texts one can turn to as a guide for how to prepare for the event. A source need not be perfect to be considered authoritative: it need only represent a degree of authenticity that you consider adequate for the purposes of your re-enactment. This book is in part written to provide an authoritative source of this sort.

Provide for Creature Comforts. No event can succeed without a supply of food and drink, as well as adequate seating, utensils, and the like. The food in particular can require a lot of effort, so if your organizing group is small you may want to keep it as simple as possible, choosing such dishes as will provide the greatest satisfaction for the least preparation. You will make things easier on yourselves if you prepare dishes ahead of time and serve them cold or reheated.

Define the Space. As Tudor buildings are few and far between, some effort is required to make the setting feel right. In the absence of an Elizabethan hall, an outdoor event is one possibility, especially if you can provide appropriate tentage. If the event is held indoors in a modern-looking setting, it will help to furnish the site with period household accoutrements of some sort: wall hangings will do much to disguise concrete, and much modernity can be overlooked by candlelight. It is also very important to define the physical and temporal space of the re-creation. Decide on what area is to be used and mark it off somehow, so that people know where to go when they are in the mood for the past and where to slip off for a modern break if they need one. Demarcate the beginning and end of the re-creation by some pre-arranged signal; for example, someone might welcome the guests at the official beginning and thank them at the end. A clear boundary is essential if you want to keep the modern world from spilling into the re-creation.

Arrange Entertainment. If the event is not fun, it will not succeed. This book includes a selection of easily recreated entertainments. They will not only provide enjoyment for the participants but will help them to act as Elizabethans: it is easier to play an Elizabethan game than to discuss Elizabethan politics. For the entertainments to succeed, you will need to ensure that the proper equipment is available, and it will help if the participants have some practice beforehand.

Another kind of entertainment is "scripting." If some sort of plot or plots are happening at the event—comparable perhaps to the "host a murder mystery" idea which has been a popular party theme in recent years—this will add to the interest of the occasion. For this purpose, it will help if your group has some idea beforehand of the characters who will be represented at the event.

Prepare the Participants. It is not always easy to re-create the past, and it will help if the group takes an active part in preparing people for the event. Try to ensure that beginners have guidance in assembling their outfits—sewing get-togethers are a good way of doing this. It may even be worthwhile to set up a buddy system whereby each beginner has an experienced person responsible for making sure they have everything they need.

The event will work best if there is a core of people who know what they are doing. For this reason, it is worth having a series of workshops prior to the event at which people can practice games, dances, songs, and social interaction. In addition, the day of the event is a good time to hold workshops for the benefit of out-of-town visitors.

You should also be prepared to take an active hand in arranging the social relationships between the participants' characters. Left to their own devices, people often all choose characters of the same rank (usually aristocratic), with few relationships among them. This tends to make the event both unrealistic and dull. Encourage people to come with prearranged social relationships. One possibility is service: it is relatively easy and inexpensive to portray a servant, and it can be a great deal of fun as well (there are plenty of good examples in the comedies of Shakespeare and Jonson). Other possible relationships include relatives, neighbors, and boon-companions. Again, you may find it worthwhile to organizing session to make this happen before and/or on the day.

Appendix B: Suppliers

GENERAL

Bodgeramour, Dave Hodgson, 129 Kent Rd., Mapperly, Nottingham NG3 6BS ENGLAND; (0602) 525 711. Knives, spoons, weaponry, pins, etc.

Brad Spear, 1951 Dobbs Rd. #15, St. Augustine FL 32086; (904) 797-9412. Knives, swords, powder flasks, various knickknacks.

Buzzard's Nest, William Ruppert, Jr., PO Box 146, Wrightsville PA 17368; (717) 252-2800. Leatherwork (e.g., flasks, jacks, pouches), smithwork.

Farner Foundry, Rte. 2, Box 542, Astoria OR 97103; (503) 458-6246. Cast pewter, brass, and bronzeware.

Gary Macey, 504 North Main St., Mt. Airy MD 21771; (301) 831-5173. Reproduction furniture.

Merchant Adventurers, 7341 Etiwanda Ave., Reseda CA 91335; (818) 342-3482. Stockings, cards, pipes, coins, dice, jewelry, etc.

The New England & Virginia Co., PO Box 8511, Salem MA 01971; (508) 744-7925. Books, pottery, leather goods.

Plimoth Plantation Museum Shop; (508) 746-1622 ext. 332. Reproductions and books on the seventeenth century. For address, see Appendix C: Sites.

Quartermasterie, Ian Skipper, 32 Ladbroke Rd., Enfield, Middlesex, EN1 1HX ENGLAND; (081) 367 5877. Coins, accessories.

The Stuffy Purist, Mike Tartaglia, 1 Evergreen Ave, Mays Landing NJ 08330; (609) 653-1271. Reproduction delftware, glasses, pins, etc.

Syke's Sutlering, George R. Paczolt, PO Box 363, Elton PA 15934; (814) 266-3803. Books, clothing, weaponry, etc.

Tentmasters, 4221 Livesay Rd., Sand Creek MI 49279; (517) 436-6245. Tents.
Tentsmiths, Box 496, North Conway NH 03860; (603) 447-2344. Tents.

CLOTHING AND FABRICS

Kirstie Buckland, Chippenham Gate St., Monmouth, Gwent NP5 3DH, Wales, UNITED KINGDOM; (0600) 712-158. Knitted caps.

J. L. Cooke, 3 Ronald Circle, Spencerport NY 14559; (716) 352-4730. Woolen and linen fabrics.

Hatcrafters, 20 N. Springfield Rd., Clifton Heights PA 19018; (215) 623-2620. Finished and unblocked hats.

Deborah Jarrett, 1475 Sumneytown Pike, Harleysville PA 19438; (215) 287-6939. Historical clothes.

K & K Historic Fabrics, Dennis Krowe, 2372 Rose St., Scotch Plains NJ 07076. Woolen fabrics.

Of Another Time, Louise J. Craig, PO Box 5246, St Augustine FL 32085-5246; (904) 824-4138. Elizabethan clothes.

Textile Reproductions, Box 48, West Chesterfield MA 01084; (413) 296-4437. Sewing goods, including linen thread and wool batting suitable for quilts and mattresses.

Timefarer Footwear, Gorthleck, Inverness IV1 2YS, SCOTLAND; (0456) 486 696. Elizabethan shoes.

BOOKS

Caliver Books, 816-818 London Road, Leigh-on-Sea, Essex SS9 3NH, ENGLAND; (0702) 73986. Military sources, recipe books, etc.

Falconwood Press, 193 Colonie St., Albany NY 12210-2501. Military manuals, recipe books, costuming sources, etc.

Pugliese, Patri J., 39 Capen St., Medford MA 02155; (617) 396-2870. Renaissance fencing manuals.

MUSIC

Cooperman Fife and Drum Co., PO Box 276, Centerbrook CT 06409; (203) 767-1779. Reproduction drums.

Country Dance and Song Society, 17 New South St., Northampton MA 01060; (413) 584-9913. Books and recordings relating to country dances.

The Early Music Shop, 38 Manningham Lane, Bradford, West Yorkshire BD1 1BR ENGLAND; (0274) 393-753. Period instruments (finished and kits), written music.

The Early Music Shop of New England, 59-65 Boylston St., Brookline MA 02146; (617) 277-8690. New and used instruments, written music.

ARMS AND ARMOR

Armour Class, 193A Dunbarton Rd., Clyde Bank, Glasgow G81 4XJ SCOTLAND; (0141) 951-2262.

Bailiff Forge, J. E. Denbigh, Unit 53, Colne Valley Workshops, Linthwaite, Huddersfield HD7 5QG ENGLAND; (0484) 846 973. Swords, scabbards, and hangers.

Black Rose Creations, Terri Marr, 7 Devonshire Dr., RD #22, Mays Landing NJ 08330; (609) 926-1297. Schlager-blade rapiers.

John Buck, RD 3, Box 129B, Floyd VA 24091; (703) 639-5330. Calivers and other firearms.

Rod Casteel, 106 Lynnbrook, Eugene OR 97404; (503) 688-0607. Swords and daggers.

Cimmerian Combatives Company, PO Box 150622, Nashville TN 37215-0622; (615) 644-2722. Swords and daggers.

Derek R. Cole, 35 Scotland Close, Fair Oak, Eastleigh, Hampshire SO50 7BR ENGLAND; (0703) 693-771. Armor.

Museum Replicas, Box 1840, Conyers GA 30207; 1-800-241-3664/404-922-3700. Arms and armor.

New World Arbalest, 201 West Crestland Dr., Austin TX 78752-2427; (512) 453-2628. Crossbows.

The Rifle Shoppe, Rt. 1, Box 82C, Jones OK 73049; (405) 396-2583. Matchlocks, wheellocks, snaphaunces.

J. S. Schroter Antique Arms, PO Box 10794, Costa Mesa CA 92627. Arms and armor.

Tattershall Arms, Box 1215, Flagstaff AZ 86001; (520) 774-1755. Matchlocks and parts, snaphaunces, wheellocks.

Appendix C: Contacts

Living history for this period in North America is a small but rapidly growing pursuit, and it is quite well established in England. The following are the contacts that we have been able to identify as of the time of publication.

GROUPS

The Companions Trayned Band. William Wilson, Box 1215, Flagstaff AZ 86001; (520) 774-1755. Involved in Elizabethan living history and the Spanish Period of the Southwest.

Country Dance and Song Society, 17 New South St., Northampton MA 01060; (413) 584-9913. A good place to contact to find out about country dance groups in your area.

Local Yokels, Marti Dolata, 10500 North Old Father, Tuscon AZ 85741; (602) 744-2859. Amateur Elizabethan living history group.

Men of Menendez, Robert Miller Hall, 42 Spanish St., St. Augustine FL 32084; (904) 829-9792. Recreates the activities of the Spaniards and English in Florida in Elizabeth's day.

Renaissance Military Society, Elizabeth Pidgeon, 1129 Sutter St., Vallejo CA 94590; (707) 557-2552. Active at the California Renaissance Fairs, the military society's members are involved in sixteenth-century English, Spanish, and German living history. There is a companion group in southern California: Julie Addams, 2438 Stockton, Vista CA 92084; (619) 630-6318.

Southwark Trayn'd Bands—Gardiner's Company, Jeff Morgan, 1633 Stoney Creek Dr., Charlottesville VA 22902; (804) 984-0537. This group is very active in recreating the Elizabethan period, and had a significant role in the creation of this book. There are branches in the Great Lakes area as well.

The Society for Creative Anachronism, PO Box 360743, Milpitas CA 95036-0743. Although not actually a living history organisation, the SCA remains the largest forum in North America for amateur study of the Middle Ages and Renaissance.

Tabard Inn Society, Phillip Collman, 599 Delaware Ave., Toronto, Ontario M6H 2V3 CANADA; (416) 539-0704. The TIS is a leading group in Elizabethan living history; it produced the original *Elizabethan Handbook* which formed the basis of this book.

Village of Shapwick, Steven Budge, 222 Brunswick Ave., Stratford, Ontario N5A 3M4 CANADA; (519) 271-7415. A site for amateur sixteenth- and seventeenth-century living history.

Westminster Trayn'd Bands, David Martinez, 2001 Ploverville, Austin TX 78728; (512) 990-1186. Similar to the Southwark Trayn'd Bands above.

SITES

Darnall's Chance, PO Box 730, Upper Marlboro MD 20772; (301) 952-8010. A seventeenth-century colonial site.

Elizabeth II State Historic Site, Box 155, Manteo NC 27954; (919) 473-1144. A visitor center with a reconstruction Elizabethan ship representative of the type used on Sir Walter Raleigh's expeditions to the area.

Jamestown Settlement, PO Box JF, Williamsburg VA 23187; (804) 229-1607. A reconstruction of this Jacobean settlement as it was about a decade after the death of Elizabeth, and the closest thing to an Elizabethan living history site in North America; also home to three handsome reconstructed vessels of the period.

Kentwell Hall, Long Melford, Suffolk CO10 9BA ENGLAND; (0787) 310 207. Every summer Kentwell has been the site of a month-long Tudor re-creation staffed by some 200 volunteers (a date sometime in the Tudor period is chosen each year).

Plimoth Plantation, Stuart Bolton, Carriage House, PO Box 1620, Plymouth MA 02362; (508) 746-1622. The Plantation re-creates the Plymouth colony as it is thought to have been in the 1620's; its devotion to accuracy is outstanding among living history sites.

Shakespeare's Globe, Bear Gardens, Bankside, London SE1 9ED ENGLAND. An extraordinary project to reconstruct the Globe Theater as it would have been in Shakespeare's day. The new Globe is well on its way as of 1995, and includes a museum and tours of the construction site.

St. Mary's City, Box 24, St. Mary's City MD 20686. An early seventeenth-century site, small, but featuring a handsome small oceangoing ship.

Sainte-Marie among the Hurons, PO Box 160, Midland, Ontario L4R 4K8 CANADA. Another early seventeenth-century mission.

Sainte-Marie among the Iroquois Living History Museum, Kim VanWormer, PO Box 146, Liverpool NY 13088; (315) 453-6767. Reconstruction of an early seventeenth-century French colonial mission.

JOURNALS

Call to Arms. 7 Chapmans Crescent, Buckinghamshire HP5 2QU ENGLAND; (0494) 784 271. A periodical listing of re-enactment groups and supplier, primarily in England, but also the Continent and abroad.

The Living History Registrar. Roger Emmerson, 21 Oak Road, Woolston, Southampton SO2 9BQ ENGLAND. A newsletter for sixteenth- and seventeenth-century living history enthusiasts.

The Moderne Aviso. Mary Aist, 9512 Dubarry Ave., Seabrook MD 20706; (301) 577-3457. An excellent bimonthly journal of re-enactment for the period 1560-1705.

Smoke and Fire News. PO Box 166, Grand Rapids OH 43522; (419) 832-0303. A newspaper-style publication covering all periods of re-enacting, with some information on early modern groups.

ELECTRONIC RESOURCES

By far the most efficient means of obtaining information on living history activities is the World Wide Web. The newsgroups **alt.history.living** and **soc.history.living** are a good forum in which to air any queries—the readers will be only too happy to answer. Most of the contacts listed above are in direct or indirect contact with both of these newsgroups. Other newsgroups exist for many of the specific subjects treated in this book, including textile arts, early music and dance, historical cooking, etc.

Notes

CHAPTER 2: THE ELIZABETHAN WORLD

1. On the population of England, see D. M. Palliser, *The Age of Elizabeth* (London: Longman, 1992), ch. 2. For a contemporary atlas of England, see John Speed, *The Counties of Britain* [1616] (London: Pavillion, 1988).

2. On the structure of the church see William Harrison, *Description of England* [1587] (Ithaca: Cornell University Press, 1968), Bk. 2, chs. 1-2; Palliser, ch. 11.

3. On women, see C. C. Camden, *The Elizabethan Woman* (Houston: Elsevier Press, 1952).

4. From *An Old Man's Lesson*, cited in Gamaliel Bradford, *Elizabethan Women* (Cambridge MA: Houghton Mifflin, 1936), 60.

5. On the social structure in general, see Harrison, Bk. 2, ch. 5; Sir Thomas Smith, *The State of England, A.D. 1600 [De Republica Anglorum]*, ed. F. J. Fisher. Camden Miscellany 3:52 (London: Offices of the Camden Society, 1936); Palliser, ch. 3; G. M. Trevelyan, *Illustrated English Social History* (Harmondsworth: Penguin, 1942), 243.

6. On government, see Harrison, Bk. 2, chs. 8-11; Palliser, ch. 10; Arthur Underhill, "Law," in *Shakespeare's England* (Oxford: at the Clarendon Press, 1916), 1.381-412.

7. On religious life and beliefs, see Harrison, Bk. 2, ch. 1; Michael MacDonald, "Science, Magic, and Folklore," in *William Shakespeare: His World, His Works, His Influence. Vol. 1: His World*, ed. John F. Andrews (New York: Scribner, 1985), 175-94; F. G. Emmison, *Elizabethan Life: Morals and the Church Courts* (Chelmsford: Essex County Council, 1973); Patrick Collinson, "The Church: Religion and Its Manifestations," in Andrews, 21-40; Keith Thomas, *Religion and the Decline of Magic* (New York: Scribner, 1971); Rev. Ronald Bayne, "Religion," in *Shakespeare's England*, 1.48-78. Another important source is *The Book of Common Prayer*, which

laid out the format of public religious observances [*The Prayer-Book of Queen Elizabeth 1559* (London: Griffith, 1890)].

8. On work and the economy, see Palliser, chs. 4-9; Margaret Spufford, *Contrasting Communities* (Cambridge: Cambridge University Press, 1974); George Unwin, "Commerce and Coinage," in *Shakespeare's England*, 311-45.

9. For incomes and wages, see Smith, 23; Sir John Harington, *Nugae Antiquae* (London: Vernor and Hood, 1804); Harrison, Bk. 2, ch. 5; Paul L. Hughes and James F. Larkin, *Tudor Royal Proclamations* (New Haven: Yale University Press, 1964), 3.39-41; R. H. Tawney and Eileen Power, *Tudor Economic Documents* (London: Longmans, 1924); Palliser, 118; M. St. Clare Byrne, *Elizabethan Life in Town and Country* (London: Methuen, 1950), 115; Spufford, 52.

10. For prices, see Fynes Moryson, *An Itinerary* [1617], The English Experience 387 (Amsterdam and New York: Da Capo Press, Theatrum Orbis Terrarum, 1971), III.ii.62, III.iii.151; Harrison, Bk. 3, ch. 16; Hughes and Larkin, 3.21, 39-41; James E. Thorold Rogers, *A History of Agriculture and Prices in England* (Oxford: at the Clarendon Press, 1882); *SE*, 2.136-37, 141; Palliser, 134; Marjorie Plant, *The English Book Trade* (London: G. Allen and Unwin, 1939), 220, 241; Jo McMurtry, *Understanding Shakespeare's England* (Hamden CT: Archon, 1989), 73. The daily cost of food given in this table is based on the amount of money allowed to workers for their daily food according to the official rates. The price of standard-quality bread was fixed: only the weight changed. Note that some of these were the officially decreed prices: the real prices could be rather higher, depending on the state of the economy.

CHAPTER 3: THE COURSE OF LIFE

1. On baptism and godparentage, see Fynes Moryson, *Shakespeare's Europe*, ed. Charles Hughes (London: Sherratt and Hughes, 1903), 479; Emmison, *Elizabethan Life: Morals and the Church Courts*, 139-42.

2. On churchings, see Emmison, *Elizabethan Life: Morals and the Church Courts*, 140, 159-61.

3. On childbirth, see A. Eccles, *Obstetrics and Gynaecology in Tudor and Stuart England* (Kent OH: Kent State University Press, 1982). On infant mortality, see E. A. Wrigley and R. S. Schofield, *The Population History of England 1541-1871* (Cambridge MA: Harvard University Press, 1981), 249. On the life of babies, see Byrne, *Elizabethan Life in Town and Country*, 177; Lu Pearson, *The Elizabethans at Home* (Stanford CA: Stanford University Press, 1957), 87.

4. On Elizabethan English, see Charles Barber, *Early Modern English*. The Language Library (London: André Deutsch, 1976).

5. On manners, see Byrne, *The Elizabethan Homez*, 17; F. J. Furnivall, *The Babees Book*. Early English Texts Society 32 (London: Trübner, 1868); Lacey Baldwin Smith, "'Style Is the Man': Manners, Dress, Decorum," in Andrews, 201-14.

6. On titles, see Harrison, Bk. 2, ch. 5.

7. On education generally, see Sir John Sandys, "Education," in *Shakespeare's England*, 1.224-50; E. B. Knobel et al., "The Sciences," in *Shakespeare's England*, 1.444-515; Anthony Grafton, "Education and Apprenticeship," in Andrews, 55-66.

On petty schools, see Spufford 189; Byrne, *Elizabethan Life in Town and Country*, 181 ff.

8. On literacy, see David Cressy, *Literacy and the Social Order* (Cambridge: Cambridge University Press, 1980), 175-76.

9. On writing, see Byrne, *The Elizabethan Home*, 20; Giles E. Dawson and Laetitia Kennedy-Shipton, *Elizabethan Handwriting 1500-1650* (New York: Norton, 1966); Sir Edward Thompson, "Handwriting," in *Shakespeare's England*, 1.284-310.

10. On grammar schools, see Byrne, *Elizabethan Life in Town and Country*, 182ff.

11. On universities, see Harrison, Bk. 2, ch. 3; Byrne, *Elizabethan Life in Town and Country*, 198ff.

12. On science, see Palliser, 429.

13. On the Inns of Court, see Harrison, Bk 2, ch. 3; Byrne, *Elizabethan Life in Town and Country*, 4, 6, 67; Sandys, 230, 238ff.; McMurtry, 129-136; Grafton, 56-64; S. K. Heninger, "The Literate Culture of Shakespeare's Audience," in Andrews, 170-72.

14. On growing up, see Palliser, 38.

15. On marriage, see McMurtry, 116; Emmison, *Elizabethan Life: Morals and the Church Courts*, 144-70.

16. On aging and life expectancy, see Margaret Pelling, "Medicine and Sanitation," in Andrews, 78; Joel Hurstfield and Alan G. R. Smith, *Elizabethan People: State and Society* (New York: St. Martin's Press, 1972), 48.

17. On medicine, see Pelling, 75-84; C. Webster, *Health, Medicine, and Mortality in Sixteenth-Century England* (Cambridge: Cambridge University Press, 1979); Alban H. G. Doran, "Medicine," in *Shakespeare's England*, 1.413-43.

18. On death and burial, see Moryson, *Shakespeare's Europe*, 480; Emmison, *Elizabethan Life: Morals and the Church Courts*, 170-76.

CHAPTER 4: CYCLES OF TIME

1. On the daily schedule, see Byrne, *Elizabethan Life in Town and Country*, 13, 43, 52, 80; Percy MacQuoid, "The Home," in *Shakespeare's England*, 2.134; John Dover Wilson, *Life in Shakespeare's England* (Harmondsworth: Penguin, 1949), 276-79.

2. On the weekly schedule, see Byrne, *Elizabethan Life in Town and Country*, 130.

3. On the calendar, see Harrison, Bk. 3, ch. 14.

4. On the yearly cycle, see Wilson, 11, 22; Collinson, 25. On fairs and markets, see Harrison, Bk. 2, ch. 18 and Bk. 3, ch. 15.

CHAPTER 5: THE LIVING ENVIRONMENT

1. On the home, see Harrison, Bk. 2, ch. 12; Wilson, 4; Palliser, 130; Emmison, *Elizabethan Life: Morals and the Church Courts*, 1-8; MacQuoid, "The Home," 119-52; Eric Mercer, *English Vernacular Houses* (London: Her Majesty's Stationery Office, 1975); John Schofield, ed., *The London Surveys of Ralph Treswell* (London: London Topographical Society, 1987).

2. On interiors, see Harrison, Bk. 2, ch. 12; MacQuoid, "The Home," 123-29; Victor Chinnery, *Oak Furniture. The British Tradition* (Woodbridge, Suffolk: Antique Collectors' Club, 1979); Peter Thornton, *Seventeenth-Century Interior Decoration in England, France and Holland* (New Haven: Yale University Press, 1978); S. W. Wolsey and R. W. P. Lanff, *Furniture in England: The Age of the Joiner* (New York: Praeger, 1968).

3. On heat and light, see George P. Garret, "Daily Life in Town and Country," in Andrews, 223; MacQuoid, "The Home," 122-24; Thornton, 270.

4. On the hall, see MacQuoid, "The Home," 121; F. G. Emmison, *Elizabethan Life: Home, Work and Land* (Chelmsford: Essex County Council, 1976).

5. On the chamber, see Harrison, Bk. 2, ch. 12; Thornton, 117-18, 128-29, 177; MacQuoid, "The Home," 122, 127; Emmison, *Elizabethan Life: Home, Work and Land*, 11-16.

6. On hygeine, see F. J. Furnivall, ed., *Andrew Boorde's Introduction and Dietary*, Early English Texts Society extra series 10 (London: Trübner, 1870); MacQuoid, "The Home," 142; Garret, 223-24.

7. On towns, see John Stow, *Stow's Survey of London* (London: J. M. Dent and sons; New York: E. P. Dutton and co., 1956); Byrne, *Elizabethan Life in Town and Country*, 152; Martin Holmes, *Elizabethan London* (London: Cassell, 1969); Henry B. Wheatley, "London and the Life of the Town," in *Shakespeare's England*, 2.153-81.

8. On travel, see Harrison, Bk. 3, ch. 16; Moryson, *Itinerary*, III.i.13, III.ii.61; Thomas Platter, *Thomas Platter's Travels in England 1599* (London: J. Cape, 1937), 145-46, 148-49, 154; McMurtry, 177; Byrne, *Elizabethan Life in Town and Country*, 73, 80-81; Palliser, 315; Charles Hughes, "Land Travel," in *SE*, 1.198-223; David Quinn, "Travel by Sea and Land," in Andrews, 195-200.

CHAPTER 6: CLOTHING AND ACCOUTREMENTS

1. Principal sources on Elizabethan costuming are:

Arnold, Janet, *Patterns of Fashion: The cut and construction of clothes for men and women c1560-1620* (New York: Drama Books, 1985).

Cunnington, Phyllis, and Anne Buck, *Children's Costume in England* (London: Black, 1965).

Davenport, Millia, *The Book of Costume* (New York: Crown, 1948).

Flury-Lemberg, Mechtild, *Textile Conservation and Research* (Bern: Schriften der Abegg-Stiftung, 1988).

Hunnisett, Jean, *Period Costume for Stage and Screen* (Los Angeles: Players Press, 1991).

Linthicum, M. Channing, *Costume in the Drama of Shakespeare and His Contemporaries* (Oxford: at the Clarendon Press, 1936).

Norris, Herbert, *Costume and Fashion. Vol. 3, The Tudors. Book 2: 1547-1603* (New York: Dutton, 1924).

Rutt, Richard, *A History of Hand Knitting* (Loveland CO: Interweave Press, 1987).

Stubbes, Phillip, *Phillip Stubbes's Anatomy of the Abuses in England in Shakespeare's Youth A. D. 1583*, ed. F. J. Furnivall (London: Trübner, 1879).

Trump, R. W., *Drafting & Constructing a Simple Doublet & Trunkhose of the Spanish Renaissance* (Eugene OR: Alfarhaugr Publishing Society, 1991).

Waugh, Norah, *The Cut of Men's Clothes 1600-1900* (London: Faber and Faber, 1964).

Waugh, Norah, *The Cut of Women's Clothes 1600-1930* (New York: Theater Arts, 1968).

Weavers Guild of Boston, *17th Century Knitting Patterns as adapted for Plimoth Plantation* (Boston: n. p., 1990).

Willet, C., and Phyllis Cunnington, *Handbook of English Costume in the Sixteenth Century* (London: Faber and Faber, 1954).

2. On fabrics, see Waugh, *Men's Clothes*, 36; Linthicum, 76, 94-99, 107, 120-26.

3. On colors and adornment, see Linthicum, 27, 30, 31, 86; Davenport, 228, 445, 449; Elizabeth Geddes and Moyra McNeill, *Blackwork Embroidery* (New York: Dover, 1976).

4. On shirts and smocks, see Stubbes, 53; Linthicum 189ff.; Davenport, 633-35. Janet Arnold, "Elizabethan and Jacobean Smocks and Shirts," *Waffen- und Kostümkunde* 19 (1977), 89-110, includes patterns for a shirt of circa 1585-1600 and a smock of circa 1603-15. Dorothy Burnham, *Cut My Cote* (Toronto: Royal Ontario Museum, 1973), includes a pattern for a late sixteenth-century shirt. A. M. Nylen, "Stureskjortorna," *Livrustkammaren* 4:8-9 (Journal of the Royal Armoury, Stockholm, 1948), 217-76, has detailed description, with drawings and photographs, of four Swedish shirts from 1567.

5. On breeches, see Davenport, 633; Waugh, *Men's Clothes*, 37.

6. On bodices, see Arnold, *Patterns*, 104-5, 112; Waugh, *Women's Clothes*, diagram IV and pl. 10; Linthicum, 177ff.; Davenport, 445, 551, 552; Stubbes, 77*.

7. On women's doublets, see Arnold, *Patterns*, 106; Linthicum, 199f.; Davenport, 445; Janet Arnold, "A woman's doublet of about 1585," *Waffen- und Kostümkunde* (1981), 132-42.

8. On supporting garments, see Linthicum, 179ff. and 181n.; Norah Waugh, *Corsets and Crinolines* (London: Batsford, 1954).

9. On gowns, petticoats, and kirtles, see Stubbes, 74-75; Arnold, *Patterns*, 117.

10. On Venetians and similar garments, see Waugh, *Men's Clothes*, 15, 17; Stubbes, 56.

11. On doublets and jerkins, see Percy MacQuoid, "Costume," in *Shakespeare's England*, 2.113; Linthicum, 197ff., 203f.; Stubbes, 55, 58, 73; Waugh, *Men's Clothes*, 14, 17, 18, 27.

12. On stockings, see Davenport, 633-35; MacQuoid, "Costume," 2.98; Linthicum, 240ff., 260-61; Furnivall, *Andrew Boorde's Introduction and Dietary*, 130; Stubbes, 57, 61, 76; Rutt, 69ff. Rutt, 239, gives a seventeenth-century set of instructions for knit stockings; a pattern is given in Weavers' Guild of Boston, 18-24.

13. On garters, see Linthicum, 263. For a pattern for knit garters, see Weavers' Guild of Boston, 36-37.

14. On footwear, see Linthicum, 238ff.; Stubbes, 57, 77; Davenport, 565.

15. On neckwear, see Linthicum, 155 ff., 160; Davenport, 636; Waugh, *Men's Clothes*, 25. For further information and the patterns for two surviving ruffs, see

Janet Arnold, "Three examples of late sixteenth and early seventeenth century neckwear," *Waffen- und Kostümkunde* 15 (1973), 109-24.

16. On waistcoats, see MacQuoid, "Costume," 102; Rutt, 78ff. For a pattern, see Weavers' Guild of Boston, 30-32.

17. On overgarments, see Davenport, 442; Waugh, *Men's Clothes*, 16, 28-29, 31, pl. 5; Linthicum, 196f, 203f.

18. On caps, see Davenport, 568; Rutt, 58; Kirstie Buckland, "The Monmouth Cap," *Costume* 13 (1979), 23-37.

19. On flat caps, see Stubbes, 50-51; Rutt, 59-61. See Weavers' Guild of Boston, 4-8, 15-17, for instructions for reproducing original knit flat caps as well as several other styles.

20. Patterns for several surviving hats may be found in Arnold, *Patterns*, pp. 93-94 [#24-29].

21. On coifs, see Linthicum, 223f., including a photograph of a surviving original. See also Davenport, 445.

22. On women's headgear, see Stubbes, 67, 69.

23. On buttons, see Linthicum, 278f.

24. On points see Linthicum, 282; for an example see Arnold, *Patterns*, 56 [#3].

25. On hooks and eyes, see Linthicum, 279f.; Arnold, *Patterns*, 86-87 [#21].

26. See Waugh, *Men's Clothes*, 28, for an early seventeenth-century sword belt and hanger.

27. On purses, pouches, and girdles, see Linthicum, 265. For the pouch, see Linthicum, 270; Rutt 76. See Weavers' Guild of Boston, 9-14, for some patterns.

28. On gloves and mittens, see Linthicum, 266ff.; Rutt, 69; Davenport, 564. For patterns for knit gloves and mittens, see Weavers' Guild of Boston, 25-29, 33-35.

29. On handkerchiefs, see Linthicum, 270.

30. On mirrors, see Linthicum, 273f.

31. On jewelry, see Stubbes, 70, 78; Davenport, 405-6.

32. Nylen.

33. Arnold, *Patterns*, 112-13 [#46].

34. Arnold, *Patterns*, 116-17 [#51].

35. Davenport, 633.

36. Arnold, "Elizabethan and Jacobean Smock and Shirts," 102.

37. Arnold, *Patterns*, 86-87 [#21].

38. Arnold, *Patterns*, 55-56 [#3]. For the wings and pickadills and an example of a jerkin, compare 70-71 [#9].

39. Davenport, 445.

40. Arnold, *Patterns*, 55-56 [#22].

41. For a pattern, see Weavers' Guild of Boston, 18-24.

42. This design is based on one given by Rutt, 74.

43. Linthicum, 160; Davenport, 636; Waugh, *Men's Clothes*, 25.

44. Waugh, *Men's Clothes*, 31, pl. 5.

45. For examples of various types of buttons, see Arnold, *Patterns*.

CHAPTER 7: FOOD AND DRINK

1. Principal sources on food are:

Harrison, Bk. 2, ch. 6.

Dawson, Thomas, *The Good Huswifes Jewell* [1596], ed. Susan J. Evans (Albany NY: Falconwood Press, 1988).

—*The Second Part of the Good Huswifes Jewell.* [1597], ed. Susan J. Evans (Albany NY: Falconwood Press, 1988).

The Good Huswifes Handmaide for the Kitchin, ed. Stuart Peachey (Bristol: Stuart Press, 1992).

Hess, Karen, *Martha Washington's Booke of Cookery* (New York: Columbia University Press, 1981). A manuscript collection of recipes from the seventeenth century, with copious notes: one of the best works on cookery in the early modern period.

Loram, Madge, *Dining with William Shakespeare* (New York: Atheneum, 1976).

Markham, Gervase, *The English huswife* [1615], ed. Michael R. Best (Kingston and Montréal: McGill-Queen's University Press, 1986).

Murrell, John, *A new booke of cookerie* (London: for J. Browne, 1615).

Murrell, John, *A Daily Exercise for Ladies and Gentlewomen* [1617], ed. Susan J. Evans (Albany NY: Falconwood Press, 1990).

Murrell, John, *A delightful daily exercise for Ladies and Gentlewomen* [1621], ed. Susan J. Evans (Albany NY: Falconwood Press, 1990).

Elinor Fettiplace's Receipt Book, ed. Hilary Spurling (New York: Viking, 1987).

Wilson, C. Anne, *Food and Drink in Britain* (London: Constable, 1973).

2. Dawson, *The Good Huswifes Jewell*, 1.

3. See Murrell, *A delightful daily exercise* for bread recipes; Murrell, *A Daily Exercise* for sweet breads.

4. On meats, see Harrison, Bk. 3, chs. 1-2.

5. On fish, see Harrison, Bk. 3, ch. 3.

6. On the contents of the Elizabethan garden, see Harrison, Bk. 2, ch. 20; Thomas Tusser, *Five Hundred Points of Good Husbandry*, ed. Geoffrey Grigson (Oxford: Oxford University Press, 1984).

7. Harrison, Bk. 2, ch. 6 includes a recipe for beer.

8. Hurstfield and Smith, 101.

9. On tableware, see MacQuoid, "The Home," 122-23, 132; Garret, 224; Michael R. McCarthy and Catherine M. Brooks, *Medieval Pottery in Britain AD 900-1600* (Leicester: Leicester University Press, 1988).

10. From Henry Bull, *Christian Prayers* (New York: Johnson Reprint Co., 1968), 54-55, 58.

11. On table etiquette, see Garret, 224; Byrne, *The Elizabethan Home*, 17.

12. On eating establishments, see Platter, 170; McMurtry, 216.

13. For information on making Elizabethan bread, see Hess, 118-20.

14. On roasts, see Markham, 82.

CHAPTER 8: ENTERTAINMENTS

1. Moryson, *Shakespeare's Europe*, 475-77. Principal sources on entertainments include:

Fortescue, J. W., et al., "Sports and Pastimes," in *Shakespeare's England*, 2.334-483.
Pringle, Roger, "Sports and Recreations," in Andrews, 269-80.
Strutt, Joseph, *Sports and Pastimes of the People of England* (London: Methuen, 1903).
Vale, Marcia, *The Gentleman's Recreations: Accomplishments and Pastimes of the English Gentleman, 1580-1630* (Cambridge: D. S. Brewer; Totowa, NJ: Rowman and Littlefield, 1977).

2. Principal sources for vocal music include:

Bantock, Granville and H. Orsmund Anderton, eds., *The Melvill Book of Roundels* (London: Roxburghe Club, 1916). Modern edition of a songbook of 1612, including many rollicking songs.
Chappell, William, *Popular Music of the Olden Time* (London: Chappell and co., 1859).
Greenberg, Noah, W. H. Auden and Chester Kallman, *An Elizabethan Song Book* (London and Boston: Faber and Faber, 1957). A useful collection of Elizabethan songs.
Rimbault, Edward F., *The Rounds, Catches and Canons of England. A Collection of Specimens of the Sixteenth, Seventeenth and Eighteenth Centuries, Adapted to Modern Use* (New York: DaCapo Press, 1976). Includes many catches from Ravenscroft, although many lyrics have been altered to conform to Victorian notions of propriety.
Ravenscroft, Thomas, *Pammelia, Deuteromelia*, and *Melismata* [1609, 1611], Publications of the American Folklore Society. Bibliographical and Special Series 12 (Philadelphia: American Folklore Society, 1961).

3. Stubbes, 184.
4. Randle Holme, *The Academy of Armory* [1688] (Menston: Scolar Press, 1972), 3.263-4. The final book of Holme, which the author never brought to press, was published as *The Academy of Armory* (London: Roxburghe Club, 1905).
5. Holme (1972), 3.264.
6. Principal sources for rules are:

Cotton, Charles, *The Compleat Gamester* [1674], in *Games and Gamesters of the Restoration* (London: Routledge, 1930).
Holme (1972), Bk. 3 ch. 5.
Holme (1905), Bk. 3 ch. 16.
Parlett, David, *The Oxford Guide to Card Games* (Oxford: Oxford University Press, 1990).
Willughby, Francis, *Francis Willughby's Treatise on Games*, ed. D. Cram, D. Johnston, and J. L. Singman (Leicester: Scolar Press, forthcoming [?1996]).

The outdoor games and board games are taken from Willughby, dice games from Cotton and Holme, card games from Cotton, Holme, Parlett, and Willughby.
7. Principal sources on Elizabethan dance are:

Arbeau, Thoinot, *Orchesography* [1589], trans. Mary Stewart Evans (New York: Dover, 1967).

Caroso, Fabritio, *Nobiltà di Dame* [1600], trans. Julia Sutton (Oxford: Oxford University Press, 1986).

Cunningham, James P., *Dancing in the Inns of Court* (London: Jordan and Sons, 1965).

Inglehearn, Madeleine, *Ten Dances from Sixteenth Century Italy* (Witham, Essex: Compagnie of Dansers, 1983).

Keller, Kate van Winkle, and Genevieve Shimer, *The Playford Ball* (Chicago: A Cappella Books, 1990).

Millar, John FitzHugh, *Elizabethan Country Dances* (Williamsburg VA: Thirteen Colonies Press, 1985).

Playford, John, *The English Dancing Master* [1651], ed. Margaret Dean-Smith (London: Schott, 1957).

Pugliese, P., and J. Cassaza, *Practice for Dauncinge* (Cambridge MA: n. p., 1980).

Thomas, Bernard, and Jane Gingell, *The Renaissance Dance Book* (London: London Pro Musica, 1987).

Wood, Melusine, "English Country Dancing before Playford," *Journal of the English Folk Dance and Song Society* (1937).

Bibliography

Andrews, John F., ed. 1985.*William Shakespeare: His World, His Works, His Influence. Vol. 1: His World.* New York: Scribner.

Arnold, Janet. 1977. "Elizabethan and Jacobean Smocks and Shirts." *Waffen- und Kostümkunde* 19, 89-110.

Arnold, Janet. 1985. *Patterns of Fashion: The cut and construction of clothes for men and women c1560-1620.* New York: Drama Books.

Bull, Henry. 1968. *Christian Prayers.* New York: Johnson Reprint Co.

Byrne, M. St. Clare. 1950. *Elizabethan Life in Town and Country.* London: Methuen.

Collinson, Patrick. 1985. "The Church: Religion and Its Manifestations." In Andrews, 21-40.

Davenport, Millia. 1948. *The Book of Costume.* New York: Crown.

Dawson, Thomas. 1988 [1596]. *The Good Huswifes Jewell.* Ed. Susan J. Evans. Albany, NY: Falconwood Press.

Emmison, F. G. 1973. *Elizabethan Life: Morals and the Church Courts.* Chelmsford: Essex County Council.

Emmison, F. G. 1976. *Elizabethan Life: Home, Work and Land.* Chelmsford: Essex County Council.

Furnivall, F. J., ed. 1870. *Andrew Boorde's Introduction and Dietary*, Early English Texts Society extra series 10. London: Trübner.

Garret, George. 1985. "Daily Life in City, Town, and Country." In Andrews, 215-232.

Grafton, Anthony. 1985. "Education and Apprenticeship." In Andrews, 55-66.

Harrison, William. 1968 [1587]. *Description of England.* Ithaca: Cornell University Press.

Hartley, Dorothy. 1979. *Lost Country Life.* New York: Pantheon.

Hartley, Dorothy, and Elliot, Margaret M. 1926. *Life and Work of the People of England. A pictorial record from contemporary sources. The Sixteenth Century.* New York, London: G. P. Putnam's Sons.

Heninger, S. K. 1985. "The Literate Culture of Shakespeare's Audience." In Andrews, 159-74.

Hentzner, Paul. 1881. *A Journey into England in the Year 1593,* trans. R. Bentley, ed. Horace Walpole. Edinburgh: Aungervyle Society.

Hess, Karen. 1981. *Martha Washington's Booke of Cookery.* New York: Columbia University Press.

Holme, Randle. 1972 [1688]. *The Academy of Armory.* Menston: Scolar Press.

Holme, Randle. 1905. *The Academy of Armory.* London: Roxburghe Club. [This consists of the final chapters of the *Academy,* which were not published in Holme's lifetime.]

Hughes, Paul L., and Larkin, James F. 1964. *Tudor Royal Proclamations.* New Haven: Yale University Press.

Hurstfield, Joel, and Smith, Alan G. R. 1972. *Elizabethan People: State and Society.* New York: St. Martin's Press.

Linthicum, M. Channing. 1936. *Costume in the Drama of Shakespeare and His Contemporaries.* Oxford: at the Clarendon Press.

MacQuoid, Percy. 1916. "Costume." In *Shakespeare's England,* 2.91-118.

MacQuoid, Percy. 1916. "The Home." In *Shakespeare's England,* 2.119-52.

Markham, Gervase. 1986 [1615]. *The English huswife.* Ed. Michael R. Best. Kingston and Montréal: McGill-Queen's University Press.

McMurtry, Jo. 1989. *Understanding Shakespeare's England. A Companion for the American Reader.* Hamden, CT: Archon.

Moryson, Fynes. 1971 [1617]. *An Itinerary.* The English Experience 387. Amsterdam and New York: Da Capo Press, Theatrum Orbis Terrarum.

Moryson, Fynes. 1903. *Shakespeare's Europe.* Ed. Charles Hughes. London: Sherratt and Hughes. [This consists of the final chapters of the *Itinerary,* which were not published in Moryson's lifetime.]

Murrell, John. 1990 [1617]. *A Daily Exercise for Ladies and Gentlewomen.* Ed. Susan J. Evans. Albany, NY: Falconwood Press.

Murrell, John. 1990 [1621]. *A delightful daily exercise for Ladies and Gentlewomen.* Ed. Susan J. Evans. Albany, NY: Falconwood Press.

Nylen, A. M. 1948. "Stureskjortorna." *Livrustkammaren* 4:8-9, 217-76.

Palliser, D. M. 1992. *The Age of Elizabeth.* London and New York: Longman.

Pelling, Margaret. 1985. "Medicine and Sanitation." In Andrews, 75-84.

Platter, Thomas. 1937. *Thomas Platter's Travels in England 1599,* trans. Clare Williams. London: J. Cape.

Rutt, Richard. 1987. *A History of Hand Knitting.* Loveland, CO: Interweave Press.

Sandys, Sir John. 1916. "Education." In *Shakespeare's England,* 1.224-50

Shakespeare's England. An Account of the Life and Manners of his Age. 2 vols. 1916. Oxford: at the Clarendon Press.

Smith, Sir Thomas. 1936.*The State of England, A.D. 1600 [De Republica Anglorum],* ed. F. J. Fisher. Camden Miscellany 3:52. London: Offices of the Camden Society.

Spufford, Margaret. 1974. *Contrasting Communities: English villagers in the sixteenth and seventeenth centuries.* Cambridge: Cambridge University Press.

Stubbes, Phillip. 1879. *Phillip Stubbes's Anatomy of the Abuses in England in Shakespeare's Youth A. D. 1583.* Ed. F. J. Furnivall. London: Trübner.

Thornton, Peter. 1978. *Seventeenth-Century Interior Decoration in England, France and Holland.* New Haven: Yale University Press.

Trevelyan, G. M. 1942. *Illustrated English Social History.* Harmondsworth: Penguin.

Tusser, Thomas. 1984. *Five Hundred Points of Good Husbandry,* ed. Geoffrey Grigson. Oxford: Oxford University Press.

Waugh, Norah. 1964.*The Cut of Men's Clothes 1600-1900.* London: Faber and Faber.

Waugh, Norah. 1968. *The Cut of Women's Clothes 1600-1930.* New York: Theater Arts.

Weaver's Guild of Boston. 1990. *17th Century Knitting Patterns as adapted for Plimoth Plantation.* Boston: n. p.

Wilson, John Dover. 1949. *Life in Shakespeare's England.* Harmondsworth: Penguin.

NOVELS

A fair number of novels have been set in Elizabethan England—below are some of the more recent ones.

Burgess, Anthony. 1993. *A Dead Man in Deptford.* London: Hutchinson.

Cowell, Stephanie. 1993. *Nicholas Cooke.* New York: Norton.

Finney, Patricia. 1991. *Firedrake's Eye.* London: St Martin's Press.

Garrett, George. 1971. *Death of the Fox* Garden City, NY: Doubleday.

—. 1983.*The Succession. A Novel of Elizabeth and James.* Garden City, NY: Doubleday.

Scott, Melissa, and Barnett, Lisa A. 1988. *The Armor of Light.* New York: Baen.

Tourney, Leonard. 1980. *The Players' Boy is Dead.* New York: Harper-Row.

—. 1982. *Low Treason.* New York: Dutton.

—. 1984. *Familiar Spirits.* New York: St. Martin's Press.

—. 1986.*The Bartholomew Fair Murders.* New York: St. Martin's Press.

—. 1988.*Old Saxon Blood.* New York: St. Martin's Press.

—. 1991.*Knaves Templar.* New York: St. Martin's Press.

—. 1992.*Witness of Bones.* New York: St. Martin's Press.

FURTHER READING

There are quite a number of very good sources for information on Elizabethan daily life. Those which relate to particular topics covered in this book have been included in the footnotes, but a few general sources are worth particular note.

Two very useful anthologies of articles on various aspects of life in this period are *Shakespeare's England. An Account of the Life and Manners of his Age* (Oxford: at the Clarendon Press, 1916), and *William Shakespeare: His World, His Works, His Influence. Vol. 1: His World,* ed. John F. Andrews (New York: Scribner, 1985). For an overview of Elizbethan society, a particularly good introduction is D. M. Palliser's, *The Age of Elizabeth* (London and New York: Longman, 1992). A good introductory narrative of Elizabethan history is J. E. Neale, *Queen Elizabeth I* (London: Cape, 1954); a readable account of the Armada is Garret Mattingly, *The Armada* (Boston: Houghton Mifflin, 1959).

Two vivid modern interpretations of daily life, although they deal with colonial life in the 1620s, are Kate Waters' *Sarah Morton's Day. A Day in the Life of a Pilgrim Girl* (New York: Scholastic, 1989) and *Samuel Eaton's Day. A Day in the Life of a Pilgrim Boy* (New York: Scholastic, 1993). Geared towards younger readers, they are nonetheless interesting and enjoyable at any level, and richly illustrated with photographs taken at the Plimoth Plantation living history site.

Many useful primary sources have been published in modern editions. Probably the best single description of Elizabethan society and life by a contemporary is William Harrison's *Description of England*, dating to 1587 (Ithaca: Cornell University Press, 1968). An intimate glimpse into daily life is provided by contemporary dialogues from language-instruction manuals, edited in M. St. Clare Byrne, *The Elizabethan Home* (London: Cobden-Sanderson, 1930). For pursuit of specific topics in a wide variety of fields, including social structure, games, music, technology, agriculture, and many more, Randle Holme's *Academy of Armory* is an indispensable source, even though it dates to the late seventeenth century. Most of the book was published in Holme's lifetime, and has been reprinted in facsimile (Menston: Scolar Press, 1972); a few remaining manuscript chapters were published centuries after Holmes' death (London: Roxburghe Club, 1905).

The plays of Ben Jonson, especially *Bartholomew Fair*, provide a literary image of the Elizabethan world. Although Jonson's heyday was slightly after Elizabeth's reign, his works offer a lively picture of people in this period as they imagined themselves.

RECORDINGS

1588. Music from the Time of the Spanish Armada. The York Waits (Saydisc).

A Reasonable Facsimile. About as close as you can get. Street and Popular Music of the Renaissance. (Available from Second from the Bottom Records, PO Box 294, Rochester MI 48308-0294.)

Country Capers. Music from John Playford's The English Dancing Master. The New York Renaissance Band (Arabesque).

"How the World Wags." Social Music for a 17th Century Englishman. The City Waites (Hyperion).

In the Streets and Theatres of London. Elizabethan Ballads and Theatre Music. The Musicians of Swanne Alley (Virgin Classics).

"New Fashions." Cries and Ballads of London. Circa 1500 and Redbyrd (CRD Records).

O for a Muse of Foyre.. A basic introduction to the pronunciation of early seventeenth-century English. (Available from Caliver Books; see Appendix B: Suppliers.)

Penny Merriment. English Songs from the Time of the Pilgrims. (Available from Plimoth Plantation; see Appendix B: Suppliers.)

The Tale of Ale. (Free Reed Records). Historical songs relating to ale, including several from the Elizabethan period.

There were three Ravens. The Consort of Musicke (Virgin Classics).

Watkins Ale. Music of the English Renaissance. The Baltimore Consort (Dorian Recordings).

FILMS

A Man for All Seasons (Burbank CA: RCA/Columbia Home Video, 1983). Set during the lifetime of Elizabeth's father, Henry VIII: the clothing is quite different, but many aspects of society are similar. The film is not a bad representation of some of the personalities and events that shaped the Elizabethan world. On a similar line is *The Six Wives of Henry VIII*, the admirable British television series on this same period.

Blackadder II (Los Angeles: Fox Video, 1989). When you are ready for a refreshing break from serious history, you may want to sit back with this witty comedy series set in Elizabethan England.

Elizabeth R. This remarkable BBC television series follows the reign of Elizabeth with unique faithfulness. Sets and costumes are quite accurate, and much of the script is taken from original sources. Soon to be released on video: phone 1-800-778-7007 for ordering information.

Henry V. A film version of the Shakespeare play starring Lawrence Olivier. The first act and part of the second are an evocation of the play as it might have been performed in an Elizabethan theater: the image is somewhat dated but still worthwhile.

ILLUSTRATION SOURCES

Ashdown, Emily Jessie. 1910. *British Costume*. London: T. C. and E. C. Jack.

Castle, Egerton. 1892. *Schools and Masters of Fence*. London: Bell.

Clinch, George. 1910. *English Costume*. Chicago and London: Methuen and Co.

Furnivall, F. J. 1877. *Harrison's Description of England in Shakspere's Youth*. London: Trübner.

—. 1879. *Phillip Stubbes' Anatomy of Abuses*. London: Trübner.

Gay, Victor. 1887. *Glossaire Archéologique*. Paris: Librairie de la Société Bibliographique.

Gentleman, Francis. 1804. *Prolegomena to the Dramatick Writings of Will. Shakspere* London: John Cawthorn.

Hatcher, Orie Latham. 1916. *A Book for Shakespeare Plays and Pageants*. New York: E. P. Dutton.

Hindley, Charles, ed. 1837-74. *The Roxburghe Ballads*. London: Reeves and Turner.

Hymns Ancient and Modern. 1909. London: William Clowes and Sons.

Holinshed, Raphael. 1577. *The Chronicles of England, Scotlande and Irelande*. London: I. Hunne.

Norris, Herbert. 1924. *Costume and Fashion. Vol. 3. The Tudors. Book 2: 1547-1603*.

Ruding, Rogers. 1840. *Annals of the Coinage of Great Britain.* London: J. Hearne.

Scott, Walter. 1809. *A Collection of Tracts on the Most Interesting and Entertaining Subjects.* London: T. Cadell and W. Davies.

Shakespeare's England. An Account of the Life and Manners of his Age. 2 vols. 1916. Oxford: at the Clarendon Press.

Illustrations by Victoria Hadfield, David Hoornstra, and Jeffrey Singman were produced expressly for this volume.

Index

Page numbers in *italics* indicate illustrations.

About the Author

JEFFREY L. SINGMAN is an editor at the *Middle English Dictionary* project at the University of Michigan. He is a practitioner of Elizabethan living history as a founding member of the University Medieval and Renaissance Association (Tabard Inn Society) of Toronto and the Trayn'd Bandes of London, an international living history organization. Singman has published and lectured on games literature and game theory, medieval languages and literatures, and the Robin Hood legend.

17, $^{12}/_{11}$ 24c 9/17 5/19
√ $^{10}/_{12}$
18, $^{12}/_{13}$
√ $^{10}/_{14}$
√8/15